INTERNATIONALER DESIGNPREIS
BADEN-WÜRTTEMBERG
UND MIA SEEGER PREIS 2020

BADEN-WÜRTTEMBERG
INTERNATIONAL DESIGN AWARD
AND MIA SEEGER PRIZE 2020

↗
DESIGN CENTER
BADEN-WÜRTTEMBERG

avedition

FOCUS OPEN 2020

INHALT CONTENTS

INHALT

VORWORTE	4–11
Design: ein starker Wirtschaftsfaktor → Dr. Nicole Hoffmeister-Kraut MdL	4
Zukunftsweisendes Design – auch in pandemischen Zeiten → Wolfgang Reimer und Christiane Nicolaus	6
Let's Focus	12

DIE JURY	
Bettina Baacke	40
Holm Gießler	84
Meike Harde	188
Tina Kammer	126
Reinhard Renner	156
Luciana Silvares	214

AUSGEZEICHNETE PRODUKTE	16–227
1	Investitionsgüter, Werkzeuge	16
2	Healthcare	42
3	Bad, Wellness	52
4	Küche, Haushalt, Tischkultur	62
5	Interior	86
6	Lifestyle, Accessoires	110
7	Licht	128
9	Freizeit, Sport, Spiel	140
10	Gebäudetechnik	158
11	Public Design, Urban Design	168
12	Mobility	190
13	Service Design	198
14	Materials & Surfaces	216

MIA SEEGER PREIS 2020	228

APPENDIX A–Z	246–256
Adressen	247
Namensregister	250
Das Design Center: → Alle Formate und Services	254
Impressum	256

CONTENTS

FOREWORDS	4–11
Design: a strong economic factor → Dr. Nicole Hoffmeister-Kraut MdL	5
Forward-looking design – even in pandemic times → Wolfgang Reimer and Christiane Nicolaus	9
Let's Focus	12

THE JURY	
Bettina Baacke	40
Holm Gießler	84
Meike Harde	188
Tina Kammer	126
Reinhard Renner	156
Luciana Silvares	214

THE AWARD-WINNING PRODUCTS	16–227
1	Capital goods, tools	16
2	Healthcare	42
3	Bathroom, wellness	52
4	Kitchen, household, table	62
5	Interiors	86
6	Lifestyle, accessories	110
7	Lighting	128
9	Leisure, sports, play	140
10	Building technology	158
11	Public design, urban design	168
12	Mobility	190
13	Service design	198
14	Materials & surfaces	216

MIA SEEGER PRIZE 2020	228

APPENDIX A–Z	246–256
Addresses	247
Index of names	250
The Design Center: → all formats and services	254
Publishing details	256

DESIGN: EIN STARKER WIRTSCHAFTSFAKTOR

DR. NICOLE HOFFMEISTER-KRAUT MDL

Sehr geehrte Damen und Herren,
liebe Preisträgerinnen und Preisträger,

das Jahr 2020 wird uns mit all den besonderen Herausforderungen, die die Corona-Pandemie mit sich bringt, noch lange in Erinnerung bleiben. Und leider ist noch nicht absehbar, wie lange uns diese Krise, die alle Bereiche des gesellschaftlichen Lebens und alle Wirtschaftsbranchen betrifft, weiter beschäftigen wird. Besonders stark waren die Unternehmen der Kultur- und Kreativwirtschaft mit ihrem hohen Anteil an Solo-Selbstständigen von den Auswirkungen der Pandemie betroffen. Die Landesregierung hat gemeinsam mit der Bundesregierung alles dafür getan, um mit branchenübergreifend angelegten Unterstützungsprogrammen einen Beitrag zum Erhalt der Unternehmen und damit der Arbeitsplätze in unserem Land zu leisten.

Ende 2018 waren in den 6.750 Unternehmen der baden-württembergischen Designwirtschaft rund 21.000 Kernerwerbstätige beschäftigt. Diese erwirtschafteten einen Umsatz von 2,7 Milliarden Euro. Eine Studie, die im Jahr 2018 im Auftrag des Wirtschaftsministeriums erstellt wurde, zeigte, dass Designer*innen auch in vielen anderen Unternehmen weit über die Kernbranche hinaus tätig sind. Allein in Baden-Württemberg hatten Ende 2016 rund 171.000 Erwerbstätige in Designunternehmen insgesamt ein Umsatzvolumen von ca. 22,3 Milliarden Euro erwirtschaftet. Fest steht: Die Designwirtschaft ist eine der stärksten Branchen der Kreativwirtschaft in Baden-Württemberg.

Die bei Focus Open 2020 ausgezeichneten Arbeiten offenbaren auch in diesem Jahr das komplexe und beachtliche Wissen, das bei der Produktentwicklung erforderlich ist. Außerdem wird klar, dass Designleistung ein sehr breites Spektrum an unterschiedlichsten Kompetenzen erfordert. Alle hier dargestellten Unternehmen und Designbüros belegen, dass Design, im Sinne aller in diesem Buch aufgeführten Kriterien, ein maßgeblicher Innovationstreiber, ein wichtiges Differenzierungsmerkmal und damit ein starker Wirtschaftsfaktor für unser Land ist.

Je gesättigter die Märkte, desto stärker beeinflusst die Gestaltung die Kaufentscheidung. Der erste Eindruck ist dabei entscheidend, denn wir befassen uns zuerst mit den Produkten, von denen wir uns angezogen fühlen, denen wir spontan zutrauen, dass sie unsere Ansprüche erfüllen. Dass Designkompetenz jedoch weit über die Gestaltung des Erscheinungsbildes hinaus auch maßgeblichen Einfluss auf Anwendung, Funktion und Umgang mit Ressourcen hat, belegen auch die diesjährigen Preisträgerinnen und Preisträger wieder in beeindruckender Weise.

Somit spielt Design auch bei Kundenbindung und Markenstärkung eine Schlüsselrolle, denn wir vertrauen in Marken, deren Produkte sich in der Anwendung bewähren, die verlässlich sind und die uns das Leben erleichtern. Die Wirkung von Designleistung ist umso stärker, je früher sie in die Produktentwicklung eingebunden wird. Die Preisträger-Interviews in diesem Buch bestätigen dies einmal mehr und sind sicherlich ein guter Leitfaden für Unternehmen, die zukünftig stärker auf Designkompetenz setzen möchten.

Viele Hersteller und Designbüros haben sich um die Auszeichnung Focus Open 2020 beworben. Mit Blick auf die momentan schwierigen Rahmenbedingungen ist es umso erfreulicher, dass der Staatspreis für Design auch in diesem Jahr wieder auf solch großes Interesse bei den Unternehmen gestoßen ist.

Als Baustein der Wirtschafts- und Designförderung des Landes ist der Internationale Designpreis Baden-Württemberg Focus Open etwas ganz Besonderes. Seine nichtkommerzielle Ausrichtung verschafft ihm in der Landschaft deutscher internationaler Designwettbewerbe einen hohen Stellenwert. Durch seine staatliche Verankerung sind die Kosten für die Teilnehmenden moderat - auch Newcomer und kleinste Unternehmen können es sich leisten, teilzunehmen und sich mit ihren innovativen Produkten auf internationaler Ebene zu messen. Das Spektrum der Gewinner reicht daher wieder vom kleinsten Unternehmen bis hin zum industriellen Schwergewicht, vom Newcomer bis zum seit Jahrzehnten etablierten Hersteller.

Der Benefit für die Preisträgerinnen und Preisträger ist groß - sie gewinnen die Rückmeldung von unabhängigen Expertinnen und Experten und hohe öffentliche Wahrnehmung über die zahlreichen Kommunikationsplattformen des Design Center Baden-Württemberg.

Dieser Nutzen wird insbesondere bei der Markenkommunikation positiv spürbar: Die Label »Focus Meta«, »Focus Gold«, »Focus Silver«, »Focus Special Mention« sind Gütesiegel und wertvolle Instrumente innerhalb des Markenauftritts.

Die erneut sehr hochkarätig besetzte Jury, der ich für ihre Arbeit meinen herzlichen Dank ausspreche, konnte eine große Zahl an Auszeichnungen vergeben. Erstmals wurde 2020 der Sonderpreis »Focus Meta« für beispielhafte Lösungen für übergreifende und besonders aktuelle Themen verliehen. 13 Produkte wurden in diesem Jahr mit der Auszeichnung »Focus Gold« für zukunftsweisende und herausragende Leistungen belohnt, 16 Mal wurde der »Focus Silver« für außergewöhnliche Qualität vergeben und 26 Produkten verlieh die Jury die Auszeichnung »Focus Special Mention« für ein Designlevel, das über das etablierte Niveau hinausgeht.

Allen Preisträgerinnen und Preisträgern gratuliere ich im Namen der Landesregierung von Baden-Württemberg für diese hohen Auszeichnungen ganz herzlich!

Mit dem vom Design Center Baden-Württemberg herausgegebenen Jahrbuch zu Focus Open 2020 haben Sie, liebe Leserinnen und Leser, die Möglichkeit, sich selbst von der sehr hohen Qualität der für diesen Wettbewerb eingereichten Produkte zu überzeugen.

DR. NICOLE HOFFMEISTER-KRAUT MDL
Ministerin für Wirtschaft, Arbeit und Wohnungsbau des Landes Baden-Württemberg

DESIGN: A STRONG ECONOMIC FACTOR

DR. NICOLE HOFFMEISTER-KRAUT MDL

Dear Reader,
dear prize winners,

In view of all the special challenges facing us due to the corona pandemic, 2020 is definitely a year we'll remember for a long time to come. And unfortunately, it's still impossible to foresee how long we will have to deal with this crisis, which is impacting all areas of society and all sectors of the economy. With their high share of one-person businesses, the cultural and creative industries were hit particularly hard by the effects of the pandemic. Together with the federal government, the state government of Baden-Württemberg has done everything it can to help safeguard companies and thus also jobs in our state by initiating cross-sector assistance programmes.

At the end of 2018, the 6,750 companies that make up Baden-Württemberg's design sector had a core workforce of approx. 21,000 people. Together they generated revenue of 2.7 billion euros. A study commissioned by the Ministry of Economic Affairs in 2018 showed that designers also work in many other companies well outside the core industry. At the end of 2016, the approx. 171,000 people working in design companies had generated total revenue of approx. 22.3 billion euros in Baden-Württemberg alone. One thing is certain: the design industry is one of the creative economy's strongest sectors in Baden-Württemberg.

This year too, the works honoured with a Focus Open 2020 award reveal the complex and considerable knowledge that is essential for successful product development. It is also apparent that design calls for a very broad and diverse spectrum of skills. All the companies and design firms presented on these pages prove that design, in the sense of all the criteria cited in this book, is a significant innovation driver, an important differentiating feature and thus also a strong economic factor for our state.

The more saturated markets become, the stronger the influence design has on the purchase decision. The first impression is crucial, because the products we consider first are those that we feel attracted to, those that we spontaneously trust to meet our requirements. But as impressively demonstrated by the award-winners again this year, design expertise goes far beyond appearances; it also has a major impact on how a product is used, on its function and the resources needed to produce it.

Design therefore also plays a key role in strengthening both customer loyalty and the brand, because the brands we trust are those whose products prove themselves in practice, are reliable and make our lives easier. The earlier design is involved in the product development process, the stronger its impact. That is confirmed once again by the interviews with award-winners featured in this book, which will certainly provide useful guidance for companies wanting to increase their reliance on design expertise in future.

Many manufacturers and design firms competed for the Focus Open 2020 awards. In view of the difficult circumstances right now, it's all the more gratifying that the state award for design met with such great interest from companies again this year.

The Baden-Württemberg International Design Award Focus Open is a truly special part of the state's efforts to promote economic development and design. The non-commercial orientation of Focus Open is responsible for its high standing among Germany's international design competitions. The fact that it is a state-run competition ensures moderate entry fees – even newcomers and the smallest of companies can afford to enter their innovative products and compete at international level. As a result, the winners once again range from small businesses to industrial heavyweights, from newcomers all the way to manufacturers who have been established players for decades.

The benefits for award-winners are considerable – besides feedback from the independent experts on the jury, they can also look forward to a publicity boost from the Design Center Baden-Württemberg's numerous communication platforms. This latter benefit has a particularly positive impact on brand communications: the Focus Gold, Focus Silver and Focus Special Mention labels are a mark of quality and a valuable branding tool.

Once again, we were fortunate to have a top-calibre jury lineup and the judges deserve a heartfelt thank you for their work. They presented a large number of awards, including the Focus Meta – a special prize for exemplary solutions to overarching and topical issues that was awarded for the very first time in 2020. This year the Focus Gold was awarded to 13 products for forward-looking and outstanding achievements, the Focus Silver was presented 16 times for exceptional quality and the jury honoured 26 products with the Focus Special Mention for design that surpasses the established standard.

On behalf of the state government of Baden-Württemberg, I would like to extend my warmest congratulations to all the winners on receiving these high accolades!

Published by the Design Center Baden-Württemberg, this Focus Open 2020 yearbook will give readers the opportunity to convince themselves of the extremely high quality of the products entered for the competition.

DR. NICOLE HOFFMEISTER-KRAUT MDL
State Minister of Economic Affairs, Labour and Housing

FOCUS OPEN 2020

ZUKUNFTSWEISENDES DESIGN – AUCH IN PANDEMISCHEN ZEITEN

DESIGN SCHAFFT MEHRWERT, DESIGN SCHAFFT WETTBEWERBSVORSPRUNG

Noch nie war professionelles Design so wichtig und selbstverständlich wie heute. Focus Open, der Staatspreis des Landes Baden-Württemberg, zeigt, was in Sachen Gestaltung, Innovation und Nachhaltigkeit State of the Art ist – jährlich und transparent. Auch 2020 belohnte der Focus Open die Innovations- und Designqualität neuer Produkte, Services und Konzepte.

Unternehmen und professionelle Designer aus aller Welt waren erneut aufgerufen, ihre aktuellen und innovativen Produkte beim Focus Open 2020 – Internationaler Designpreis Baden-Württemberg einzureichen. Nicht nur etablierte Designagenturen und Unternehmen, sondern auch Start-ups und Newcomer*innen waren eingeladen, mit ihren innovativen Projekten teilzunehmen. Schließlich zielt der Wettbewerb auch darauf ab, die jährlichen Preisträger*innen bei der Vermarktung ihrer Innovationen zu fördern. Und das ist für Newcomer*innen ein ganz besonders wertvoller Benefit.

CORONA KONNTE DEN FOCUS OPEN 2020 NICHT AUSBREMSEN

Dass Sie dieses Jahrbuch heute in Händen halten, ist alles andere als selbstverständlich! Lange Zeit war nicht sicher, ob wir die Preisträger*innen des Focus Open 2020 in bewährter Weise würden ermitteln können.

Ein kurzer Rückblick: Die beiden Jurytage waren eigentlich für April geplant – eigentlich … Ab Ende Februar veränderte die Corona-Pandemie jedoch alles. An eine Anlieferung der angemeldeten Produkte und Designlösungen im April war nicht mehr zu denken, die Nachrichten überschlugen sich täglich. Also entwickelten wir zahlreiche Szenarien, um eine Jurierung vor Ort mit Originalprodukten durchführen zu können. Aber in diesen Tagen hatten Entscheidungen eine Halbwertzeit von einer Nacht – am nächsten Tag waren sie bereits überholt.

DESIGNAUSZEICHNUNGEN IN CORONA-ZEITEN

Ein Gedanke hat uns immer wieder beschäftigt: Welchen Stellenwert haben Designauszeichnungen in Corona-Zeiten, welche Relevanz hat die Durchführung eines Designpreises vor dem Hintergrund der dramatischen Entwicklungen? Liegt der Fokus der Unternehmen und der Designcommunity in solchen Ausnahmesituationen nicht an anderer Stelle? Werden die Ergebnisse überhaupt wahrgenommen?

Es waren unnötige Zweifel. Als wir die Verschiebung der Jurierung von April auf Juli kommunizierten, erhielten wir von den Einreicher*innen durchweg positive Rückmeldungen – gekoppelt mit dem Appell, auf jeden Fall am Focus Open 2020 festzuhalten. Denn, so der Tenor, gerade in Zeiten negativer Meldungen und wirtschaftlicher Schwierigkeiten sei der Bedarf an positiven Nachrichten groß. Eine Auszeichnung, so stellten wir fest, hilft gerade kleinen Unternehmen und Designagenturen, auch in Ausnahmezeiten sichtbar zu bleiben.

BEWERTUNG ANALOG VS. ONLINE

Die Jurierung ganz zu streichen, stand allerdings auch nie zur Debatte. Im Gegenteil, es war uns zu jedem Zeitpunkt wichtig, den Focus Open 2020 am Laufen zu halten.

Ein Aussetzen hätte weitreichende Folgen nach sich gezogen: Ohne Jurierung keine Preisträger*innen – ohne Preisträger*innen kein Jahrbuch, keine Preisverleihung, keine Ausstellungen in Ludwigsburg, Stuttgart und Karlsruhe 2021, keine Berichterstattung und keine Präsentationen vorbildlicher Designlösungen im Rahmen des Focus Open 2020!

Nicht zu vergessen: Viele externe Partner*innen sind am Focus Open beteiligt! Verlässliche Partner*innen, die teils seit vielen Jahren hochkarätige Arbeit für uns leisten und deren Expertisen wir sehr schätzen. Die meisten von ihnen sind selbstständig und wurden von der Corona-Pandemie zum Teil hart getroffen. Auch für sie war es wichtig, dass wir unseren Designpreis möglichst ohne Einschränkungen durchführen.

Wir haben uns daher riesig gefreut, dass nach einer Durststrecke wieder alle mit an Bord waren und bedanken uns an dieser Stelle sehr herzlich für die außergewöhnlichen Partnerschaften und die großartige Arbeit!

Im äußersten Notfall hätten wir eine reine Online-Jurierung initiiert, beispielsweise per Video-Chat. Aber wäre auf diesem Wege wirklich eine ausreichende und seriöse Bewertung möglich gewesen? Kann man ein Produkt, ohne es in Händen zu halten, im wahrsten Sinne des Wortes derart begreifen, dass man es auch guten Gewissens fair bewerten kann? Wir hatten Zweifel – gerade besonders innovative Lösungen, die noch nicht gelernt sind, wären vermutlich nicht umfassend zu bewerten gewesen. Auch deshalb sind wir froh, dass wir den virtuellen Weg nicht gehen mussten. Dank der Terminverschiebung von April auf Juli konnte die Jurierung, zwar mit reichlich Verspätung, aber in bewährter Weise stattfinden.

VERSCHOBENER TERMIN – VERÄNDERTE KONSTELLATION

An dieser Stelle gilt unser großes Dankeschön auch den Juror*innen des diesjährigen Focus Open, die ein riesiges Maß an Flexibilität gezeigt haben.

Denn die eigentlich geplante Zusammensetzung der Jury war nicht mehr realisierbar: Joa Herrenknecht konnte nicht ohne Quarantäne aus Kanada einreisen, für Roland de Fries aus New York war eine Reise schlicht undenkbar. Beide haben ihr Mandat auf 2021 verschoben. Kurz entschlossen haben Meike Harde und Luciana Silvares die beiden Lücken gefüllt. Bettina Baacke, Tina Kammer, Holm Gießler und Reinhard Renner waren trotz der terminlichen Neuaufstellung weiter dabei. Diese Solidarität mit unserem Preis hat uns die Arbeit sehr erleichtert.

WOLFGANG REIMER
Präsident Regierungspräsidium Stuttgart

CHRISTIANE NICOLAUS
Direktorin Design Center Baden-Württemberg

KATEGORIEN

1 INVESTITIONSGÜTER, WERKZEUGE
2 HEALTHCARE
3 BAD, WELLNESS
4 KÜCHE, HAUSHALT, TISCHKULTUR
5 INTERIOR
6 LIFESTYLE, ACCESSOIRES
7 LICHT
9 FREIZEIT, SPORT, SPIEL
10 GEBÄUDETECHNIK

11 PUBLIC DESIGN, URBAN DESIGN
12 MOBILITY
13 SERVICE DESIGN
14 MATERIALS & SURFACES

KRITERIEN

✓ GESTALTUNGSQUALITÄT
✓ FUNKTIONALITÄT
✓ INNOVATIONSHÖHE
✓ ERGONOMIE
✓ INTERFACE DESIGN / CONNECTIVITY
✓ USABILITY
✓ NACHHALTIGKEIT

✓ ÄSTHETIK
✓ BRANDING
✓ ENTWICKLUNGSSPRUNG
✓ USER JOURNEY
✓ DIGITALE INTELLIGENZ
✓ SINNHAFTIGKEIT
✓ ANGEMESSENHEIT
✓ AUTHENTIZITÄT

FOCUS OPEN 2020

56 PREISTRÄGER
13 GOLD-AWARDS
16 SILVER-AWARDS

26 SPECIAL MENTIONS
1 META
SOCIAL DESIGN

DIE JURY

✓ BETTINA BAACKE
✓ HOLM GIESSLER
✓ MEIKE HARDE

✓ TINA KAMMER
✓ REINHARD RENNER
✓ LUCIANA SILVARES

In dieser zentralen Phase des Awards konnten wir die besonderen Qualitäten des Focus Open wieder ausspielen: Jedes Jahr werden neue Jurymitglieder berufen. Die Juror*innen verpflichteten sich im Vorfeld, keine eigenen Arbeiten einzureichen. Falls ein Produkt über einen Kunden doch den Weg bis zur Jurierung gefunden hätte, wäre es von der Bewertung ausgeschlossen worden. Es gab, wie beim Focus Open üblich, keine Vorauswahl der eingereichten Produkte anhand von Bildmaterial – jede Designlösung wurde der Jury vorgelegt. Nur in begründeten Ausnahmefällen wurde auf das Originalprodukt verzichtet. Und auch beim Focus Open 2020 war die Jury wieder völlig unabhängig in ihren Entscheidungen. Als Veranstalter haben wir weder Stimmrecht noch Einfluss auf die Bewertungen – eine Vorgabe an die Jury, wie viele Auszeichnungen zu vergeben sind, gibt es ebenfalls nicht.

Über zwei Tage hinweg wurden alle Produkte genauestens begutachtet, untersucht und kritisch hinterfragt. So ergaben sich in der Auseinandersetzung mit den einzelnen Einreichungen auch in diesem Jahr wieder lebhafte, interessante und konstruktive Diskussionen. Impressionen dazu finden Sie in diesem Jahrbuch.

An dieser Stelle nochmals ein ganz herzliches Dankeschön an unsere diesjährigen Jurorinnen und Juroren für ihre kompetente, sorgfältige und fokussierte Arbeit!

FOCUS META – EINE NEUE AUSZEICHNUNG

Die Qualität der Einreichungen war in diesem Jahr hoch – eine besondere Herausforderung für die Jury, die Besten herauszufiltern.

Verliehen wird der Focus Open bekanntlich in drei Stufen. Zukunftsweisende und herausragende Lösungen werden auf das Podest »Focus Gold« gehoben. Der »Focus Silver« prämiert außergewöhnliche Qualität, und ein Designlevel, das über das etablierte Niveau hinausweist, erhält den »Focus Special Mention«.

Erstmals in diesem Jahr wurde auch der »Focus Meta« vergeben, eine neue Auszeichnung im Sinne eines Sonderpreises, der beispielhafte Lösungen für übergreifende und aktuelle Themen belohnt – 2020 für Social Design.

WIR ZEIGEN HINTERGRÜNDE

Auch in diesem Jahr haben wir wieder hinter die Kulissen geschaut. Die mit »Focus Meta« und »Focus Gold« ausgezeichneten Preisträger*innen haben uns in Interviews mehr über die Produktkonzeption, über die Realisierung und die Designrelevanz berichtet. Denn Design lässt sich nicht auf das formale Ergebnis verkürzen, sondern entfaltet bereits bei der Entwicklung eines Produktes oder Services seine Wirkkraft. Und zwar auch in Branchen, die nicht unmittelbar mit Design in Verbindung gebracht werden, in KMUs genauso wie in Großunternehmen. Mit den Interviews leuchten wir die Hintergründe aus, die erfolgreiches Design ermöglichen. Diesem Ansatz folgt übrigens auch unsere Reihe Erfolgsgeschichten, die Sie auf unserer Website finden und die Kooperationen zwischen baden-württembergischen Unternehmen und Designagenturen präsentieren.

HERZLICHEN GLÜCKWUNSCH

Allen hier im Jahrbuch dargestellten Produkten wurde ein ganz besonderer Wert beigemessen – sie wurden prämiert mit dem Focus Open 2020 im Rahmen des Internationalen Designpreis Baden-Württemberg, einem Designpreis, der hohe Maßstäbe setzt!

Auszeichnungen wie diese sind starke Gütesiegel. In ihrer Außenwirkung verkörpern sie die Wertvorstellung der preisgekrönten Unternehmen und tragen zur Markenstärkung bei. In der Innenwirkung steigern sie den Wert der Kooperation zwischen Auftraggeber*innen und Designer*innen, egal ob intern oder extern.

Auf den nächsten Seiten sehen Sie Ergebnisse von Partnerschaften, die zum Teil seit vielen Jahren erfolgreich bestehen und die durch Auszeichnungen wie diese bestätigt und gefestigt werden.

Wir beglückwünschen die diesjährigen Preisträger*innen zu ihren hervorragenden Leistungen, wünschen ihnen für ihre innovativen Produkt- und Konzeptlösungen viel Erfolg und weiterhin wertvolle und erfolgreiche Kooperationen!

Unser Dank gilt darüber hinaus allen Teilnehmer*innen für ihre Einsendungen und die Bereitschaft, sich trotz schwieriger Zeiten im internationalen Vergleich zu präsentieren.

FOCUS OPEN 2020

FORWARD-LOOKING DESIGN – EVEN IN PANDEMIC TIMES

DESIGN ADDS VALUE AND GIVES COMPANIES A COMPETITIVE EDGE

Never before has professional design been so important and so much a matter of course as it is today. The Baden-Württemberg state award Focus Open provides an annual and transparent round-up of what's state of the art when it comes to design, innovation and sustainability. And in 2020, Focus Open once again rewarded new products, services and concepts for their innovativeness and design quality.

This year too, companies and professional designers from all over the world were called on to enter their newest and most innovative products for the Baden-Württemberg International Design Award: Focus Open 2020. Besides established design agencies and companies, startups and newcomers were also invited to submit their innovative projects. After all, one of the competition's aims is to provide its annual winners with marketing support for their innovations – and that's a particularly valuable benefit for newcomers.

CORONA COULDN'T STOP FOCUS OPEN 2020

The fact that you're holding this yearbook in your hands today is anything but self-evident! For a long time it was by no means certain that we'd be able to select the winners of Focus Open 2020 in the tried-and-tested way.

A quick flashback: the jury was scheduled to meet for two days in April – actually ... But from late February on, the corona pandemic changed everything. It was unthinkable for the products and design solutions that had been entered for the competition to be delivered in April as originally planned – things were happening so fast that it was almost impossible to keep up with the news pouring in on a daily basis. So we developed numerous scenarios that would enable the judging to take place on site and on the basis of the physical products. But during those difficult weeks, decisions had a life expectancy of one night – they were obsolete the next day.

DESIGN AWARDS IN CORONA TIMES

One thought was constantly on our minds: what significance do design awards have in corona times, how relevant is it to hold a design competition against the backdrop of such dramatic developments? In such exceptional circumstances, aren't companies and the design community focusing on other things? Will anybody even take notice of the results?

We needn't have worried. When we announced that we were postponing the judging from April to July, the feedback we received from entrants was positive across the board – and accompanied by an appeal not to give up on Focus Open 2020 whatever happened. The general tenor: good news fulfils an important need – especially in times of bad news and economic difficulties. We realised that an award – especially in the case of small companies and design agencies – helps the winners remain visible even in exceptional times such as these.

THE JUDGING: ANALOGUE VS. ONLINE

One thing, however, was never up for debate: cancelling the judging entirely was out of the question. On the contrary: at every juncture, we were convinced it was important to keep Focus Open 2020 going.

Calling it off would have had far-reaching consequences: no judging would have meant no award-winners – and no award-winners would have meant no yearbook, no award ceremony, no exhibitions in Ludwigsburg, Stuttgart and Karlsruhe in 2021, no coverage and no presentation of exemplary design solutions under the Focus Open 2020 label!

And then there are all the external partners who are involved with Focus Open – reliable partners, some of whom have been doing top-class work for us for many years and whose expertise we greatly appreciate. Most of them are self-employed, and some were hit very hard by the corona pandemic. For them too, it was important that we should go ahead and hold our design awards with as few limitations as possible.

So we were delighted when, after a lean period, everybody was back on board again – a big thank you for all the excellent partnerships and fantastic work!

If the worst had come to the worst, we would have initiated a purely online judging process, for instance via video chat. But would that really have permitted an adequate and serious assessment of the entries? Without holding a product in your hands, can you really get a good enough »feel« for it that you can be confident of evaluating it fairly? We had our doubts – a comprehensive assessment would probably have been difficult, especially in the case of particularly innovative and out-of-the-ordinary solutions. That's another reason why we're glad we didn't have to take the virtual route. Postponing the date from April to July meant that the judging could take place – much later than normal, admittedly, but at least in the normal way.

POSTPONED DATE – DIFFERENT LINEUP

At this point we'd also like to say a heartfelt thank you to the jurors of this year's Focus Open, who showed a huge degree of flexibility.

The lineup we'd originally planned was no longer feasible: Joa Herrenknecht couldn't have travelled to Germany from Canada without going into quarantine, and for Roland de Fries from New York the journey was quite simply unthinkable. Both will take up their seat on the jury in 2021 instead. Without hesitation, Meike Harde and Luciana Silvares agreed to step in and fill the two vacancies. And Bettina Baacke, Tina Kammer, Holm Gießler and Reinhard Renner still kindly took part despite the new timing. Their solidarity with our award made our work a great deal easier.

WOLFGANG REIMER
President District Government
Stuttgart

CHRISTIANE NICOLAUS
Head of Design Center
Baden-Württemberg

CATEGORIES

1 CAPITAL GOODS, TOOLS
2 HEALTHCARE
3 BATHROOM, WELLNESS
4 KITCHEN, HOUSEHOLD, TABLE
5 INTERIORS
6 LIFESTYLE, ACCESSORIES
7 LIGHTING
9 LEISURE, SPORTS, PLAY
10 BUILDING TECHNOLOGY

11 PUBLIC DESIGN, URBAN DESIGN
12 MOBILITY
13 SERVICE DESIGN
14 MATERIALS & SURFACES

CRITERIA

✓ DESIGN QUALITY
✓ FUNCTIONALITY
✓ INNOVATIVENESS
✓ ERGONOMICS
✓ INTERFACE DESIGN / CONNECTIVITY
✓ USABILITY
✓ SUSTAINABILITY

✓ AESTHETICS
✓ BRANDING
✓ STEP CHANGE IN DEVELOPMENT
✓ USER JOURNEY
✓ DIGITAL INTELLIGENCE
✓ MEANINGFULNESS
✓ APPROPRIATENESS
✓ AUTHENTICITY

FOCUS OPEN 2020

56 PRIZE WINNERS
13 GOLD AWARDS
16 SILVER AWARDS

26 SPECIAL MENTIONS
1 META
SOCIAL DESIGN

THE JURY

✓ BETTINA BAACKE
✓ HOLM GIESSLER
✓ MEIKE HARDE

✓ TINA KAMMER
✓ REINHARD RENNER
✓ LUCIANA SILVARES

In this key phase of the awards, the special qualities of Focus Open made themselves felt once again: new jurors are appointed every year; the jury members agreed in advance not to submit any of their own work; and if, despite this rule, a product had made its way before the judges via a client, it would have been excluded. As is always the case with Focus Open, there was no pre-selection of entries on the basis of photographs – every design solution was presented to the jury. Only in exceptional and justified cases did the jury make its assessment without the product being physically present. And as every year, the Focus Open 2020 jury was totally independent in its decision-making. As the organisers, we have no vote and no influence on the judging – nor do we tell the jury how many awards are to be presented.

In the course of two days, all the products were examined, inspected and evaluated. This year too, the jury's consideration of the individual entries resulted in some lively, interesting and constructive discussions, impressions of which have been captured in this yearbook.

We'd like to take this opportunity to say another big thank you to this year's jurors for their capable, conscientious and focused work!

FOCUS META – A NEW AWARD

The quality of this year's entries was so high that filtering out the very best of them was a particularly challenging task for the jury.

In the past, there have always been three tiers on the Focus Open winners' podium. Forward-looking and outstanding solutions that make the top tier receive the Focus Gold. The Focus Silver is presented for exceptional quality and the Focus Special Mention for design that surpasses the established level.

In addition, a new category of award made its debut this year: the Focus Meta, a special prize presented for exemplary solutions that address overarching topical issues – in 2020, the subject was social design.

WE TELL THE BACKGROUND STORY

This year too, we took a look behind the scenes and interviewed the winners of the Focus Meta and Focus Gold awards. Besides telling us more about the product concept and its implementation, they also shared their thoughts on the relevance of design. Because the role design plays can't be reduced to the final result, to the outward form alone; it has an impact right from the start, as soon as the development of a product or service gets underway. That holds true even in sectors that aren't directly associated with design, in SMEs and major companies alike. The interviews aim to shed light on the background stories that make successful design possible in the first place – the same approach taken by the Success Stories series on our website, in which we showcase collaborations between Baden-Württemberg companies and design agencies.

CONGRATULATIONS!

All the products presented in this yearbook have been attributed with very special merit: they have been awarded the Focus Open 2020 – the Baden-Württemberg International Design Award, an accolade that sets high standards!

Awards like this are powerful quality labels. In terms of their external impact, they embody the values of the prize-winning companies and help strengthen their brands. Internally, they increase the value of the cooperation between client and designer, regardless of whether the design is created in-house or by an external studio.

On the following pages we present the results of successful partnerships, some of which have been in place for many years – and all of which are validated and strengthened by awards such as these.

We congratulate this year's prize winners on their excellent achievements. We hope they continue to benefit from worthwhile and productive collaborations and wish them every success with their innovative products and concepts!

We'd also like to thank all those who took part for their entries and their willingness to compete at international level despite the difficult times that have confronted us this year.

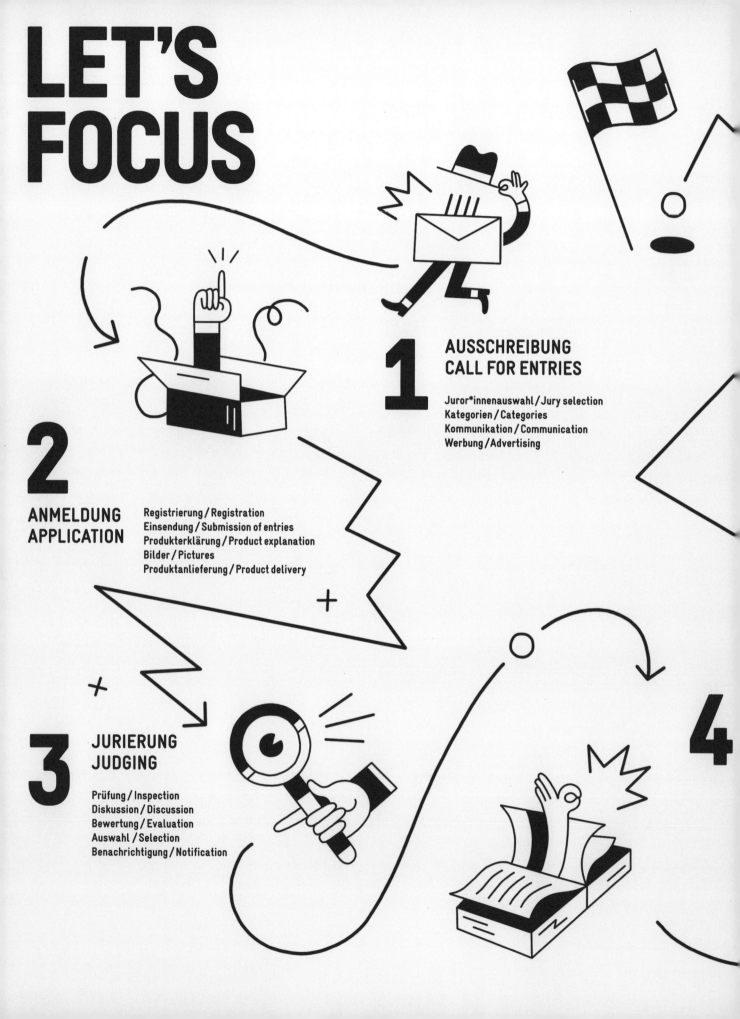

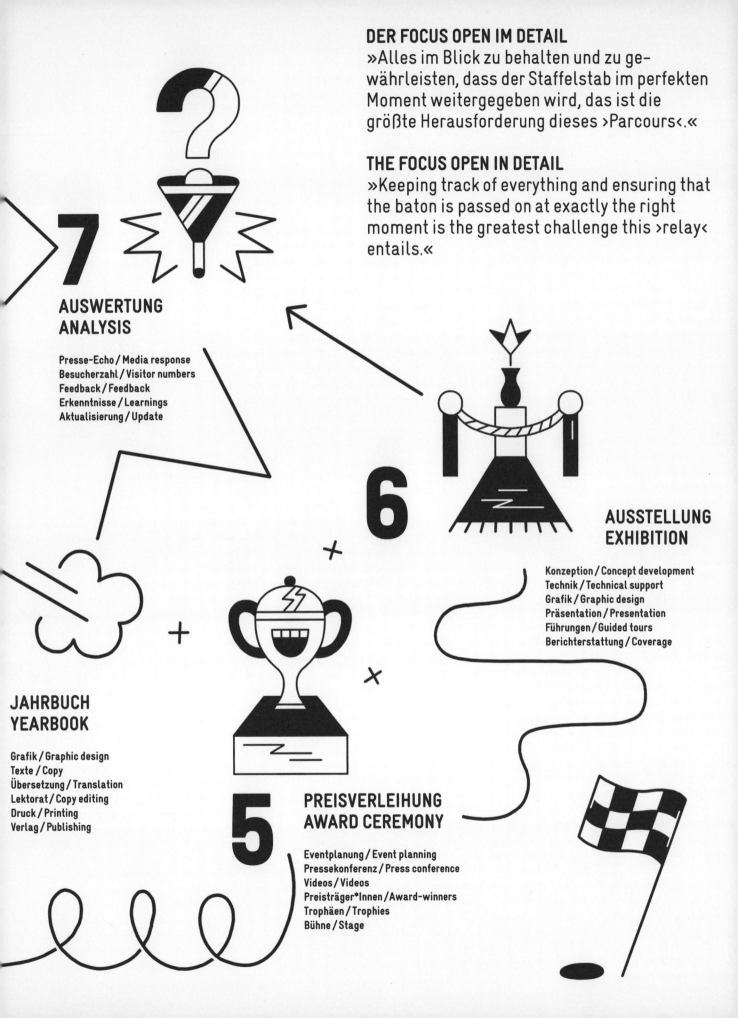

S/P	BETTINA BAACKE
40	Cognito Design und Engineering GbR, Karlsruhe
S/P	REINHARD RENNER
156	Teams Design GmbH, Esslingen
S/P	TINA KAMMER
126	InteriorPark., Stuttgart
S/P	HOLM GIESSLER
84	Erco GmbH, Lüdenscheid
S/P	LUCIANA SILVARES
214	Mazda Motor Europe GmbH, Oberursel
S/P	MEIKE HARDE
188	Studio Meike Harde, Köln / Cologne

→ von links / from left

1 → SEITE / PAGE
   18–23

2 → SEITE / PAGE
   24, 32

3 → SEITE / PAGE
   25, 33

4 → SEITE / PAGE
   26, 34

5 → SEITE / PAGE
   27, 35

6 → SEITE / PAGE
   28, 36

7 → SEITE / PAGE
   29, 37

8 → SEITE / PAGE
   30, 38

INVESTITIONSGÜTER, WERKZEUGE
CAPITAL GOODS, TOOLS

GOLD:
1 **6425**
   Andreas Maier GmbH & Co. KG
   Fellbach

SILVER:
2 **SWINGMASTER 500**
   Fill GmbH
   Gurten
   Österreich / Austria

3 **HORST 900**
   Fruitcore Robotics GmbH
   Konstanz / Constance

SPECIAL MENTION:
4 **POWER-FAST II**
   Fischerwerke GmbH & Co. KG
   Waldachtal

5 **PRO**
   Sprimag Spritzmaschinenbau
   GmbH & Co. KG
   Kirchheim/Teck

6 **SPEEDE II ELECTRIC**
   Wiha Werkzeuge GmbH
   Schonach

7 **S1**
   Diana Electronic-Systeme GmbH
   Schwaikheim

8 **GECKO 200**
   Ribler GmbH
   Stuttgart

Funktionalität und Design ergänzen sich ideal – das beweisen ganz klar Maschinen oder Tools für den professionellen Nutzer. Industriedesign widmet sich heute selbst speziellsten Arbeitsgeräten, strukturiert Bedienabläufe, optimiert die Ergonomie, treibt Innovationen voran und verbessert im Idealfall sogar die ökologische Bilanz. Nicht zu vergessen: Das Design differenziert die Produkte am Markt und stärkt die Marke – auch bei kleinsten Produkten.

Functionality and design can complement each other in ideal fashion – as is vividly demonstrated by machines or tools for professional users. Nowadays industrial design applies itself to even the most specialised equipment, structures operating procedures, optimises ergonomics, drives innovations and, at its best, even improves the ecological footprint. Last but by no means least, design also ensures differentiation on the market and strengthens the brand – no matter how small the products are.

GOLD　　　　6425　　　　MODULARER SCHRAUBBOCK
　　　　　　　　　　　　　MODULAR SCREW JACK

6425

MODULARER
SCHRAUBBOC

INVESTITIONSGÜTER, WERKZEUGE
CAPITAL GOODS, TOOLS

18
19

FOCUS GOLD

K

MODULARER SCHRAUBBOCK
MODULAR SCREW JACK

GOLD — 6425

JURY STATEMENT

Obwohl es sich hier um ein rein technisches Produkt handelt, das zudem enorm robust und belastbar sein muss, haben die Entwickler die Idee der Modularität formal sehr gut gelöst. Die seriöse Gestaltung vermittelt hohe Präzision, Flexibilität und ein einfaches Handling.

Although this is a purely technical product that has to be extremely robust and resilient, the developers have come up with a very good solution for translating the modularity idea into concrete form. The sober design conveys a high degree of precision, flexibility and straightforward handling.

HERSTELLER / MANUFACTURER
Andreas Maier GmbH & Co. KG
Fellbach

DESIGN
Inhouse

VERTRIEB / DISTRIBUTOR
Andreas Maier GmbH & Co. KG
Fellbach

→ SEITE / PAGE
18–20, 22–23

Ein Schraubbock dient vor allem in der metallverarbeitenden Industrie dazu, meist sehr massereiche Werkstücke sicher, exakt und montagegerecht zu fixieren. Das hier ausgezeichnete Modell passt sich dank seiner modularen Konzeption rasch an unterschiedliche Teilegeometrien an. So erlauben die Stütz- und Richtspannelemente des Systems durch entsprechende Kombination eine maximale Bauhöhe von 162 Zentimetern bei einer Tragfähigkeit von sechs Tonnen. Sowohl für den vertikalen wie horizontalen Aufbau nutzbar, lässt sich der Schraubbock sogar unter Last verstellen. Die einzelnen Kopf-, Zwischen- und Fußelemente werden werkzeugarm mittels des Verbindungsrings kraftschlüssig kombiniert, wobei der Ring zusätzlich vor Verschmutzung schützt. Die Modularität sorgt für mehr Flexibilität bei der Nutzung und reduziert die Menge spezieller Spann- und Stützelemente.

Especially in the metalworking industry, screw jacks are used to hold mostly very heavy workpieces precisely in place ready for assembly. Thanks to its modular design, this award-winning model can be rapidly adapted to different part geometries. The corresponding combination of the system's various head and clamping elements permits a maximum height of 162 centimetres and a load of up to six tonnes. Suitable for both vertical and horizontal setups, the screw jack can even be adjusted under load. The individual head, spacer and base elements are plugged together and connected with rings, which also provide protection from soiling. The modular design ensures greater flexibility of use and reduces the amount of special clamping and head elements required.

DOMENICO FARINA   **DESIGNER,
ANDREAS MAIER GMBH & CO. KG**

»Wir betrachten das Design nicht als optionale Zusatzdisziplin, sondern als feste Komponente der Produktentwicklung.«

»Rather than seeing design as an optional extra discipline, we consider it an integral part of the product development.«

DOMENICO FARINA

DESIGNER, ANDREAS MAIER GMBH & CO. KG

→ **Ein Schraubbock ist nicht gerade ein typisches Designprodukt – was hat Sie veranlasst, die Gestaltung miteinzubeziehen?**
Design für Industrieprodukte hat sich aus meiner Sicht noch nicht flächendeckend in der Branche etabliert, meist steht allein die Funktionaliät im Vordergrund. Bei AMF ist das Produktdesign ein fester Bestandteil der Entwicklung bei allen Neuprodukten. Der Blickwinkel weitet sich dadurch: Neben der Funktionalität rücken Faktoren wie Produktgrafik, Wertigkeit, Ästhetik und Markenkonformität weiter in den Vordergrund. Der Wiedererkennungswert unserer Produkte wird größer, das stärkt unsere Marke und wir grenzen uns besser vom Wettbewerb ab.

Mit welchen Vorgaben begannen Sie Ihre Arbeit?
Die Idee für das Produkt stammt aus der hausinternen Fertigung, also aus der Praxis. In Zusammenarbeit mit dem Vertrieb, dem Produktmanagement und der Technik analysierten wir zunächst das Wettbewerbsumfeld und befragten Anwender. Dadurch entstanden Vorgaben, die im intensiven Austausch zwischen Entwicklung und Design bearbeitet wurden. Dabei ging es dann auch um Materialwahl, Oberfläche, Design-Features, Bedienerfreundlichkeit und das gesamte Erscheinungsbild.

Sie haben das Design intern entwickelt – warum nicht mit einem externen Designbüro?
AMF ist ein Traditionsunternehmen mit inzwischen 130-jähriger Geschichte. Um das breite Produktsortiment zu überblicken, braucht es Jahre. Wir binden das Design bereits im frühen Entwicklungsstadium ein. Auf diese Weise ist die interne Designabteilung stets auf dem aktuellen Stand und ständiger Ansprechpartner für die Entwicklung und das Produktmanagement.

Design wird oft als Kostenfaktor gesehen – welchen Anteil hatte das Design an den gesamten Entwicklungskosten?
Wir betrachten das Design nicht als optionale Zusatzdisziplin, sondern als feste Komponente der Produktentwicklung. Von den ersten Besprechungen und Skizzen der Idee bis hin zur Serienreife begleitet das Design den Entwicklungsprozess. Durch eine andere Perspektive, durch Gestaltungskompetenz und spezielle Fähigkeiten der kommunikativen Visualisierung spart das Design vielleicht sogar Kosten ein, da das Produkt besser verstanden wird und Entscheidungen unter Umständen schneller getroffen werden können.

Das 1890 als Andreas Maier Fellbach (AMF) gegründete Unternehmen ist heute ein Komplettanbieter in der Spanntechnik und gehört weltweit zu den Marktführern. AMF entwickelt Projektanfertigungen und Speziallösungen für Kund*innen sowie Standardlösungen, die sich am Markt durchsetzen. Mit mehr als 5.000 Produkten sowie zahlreichen Patenten gehören die Schwaben zu den Innovativsten ihrer Branche.

www.amf.de

→ **A screw jack isn't exactly a typical design product – what made you include design in the development process?**
In my view, design for industrial products hasn't established itself throughout the sector yet, for the most part the focus is solely on functionality. At AMF, on the other hand, product design is an integral part of development for all new products. That broadens your perspective: in addition to functionality, factors like product graphics, perceived value, aesthetics and brand fit are given greater emphasis. That increases recognition of our products, which strengthens our brand and enables us to set ourselves apart from our competitors better.

What guidelines did you have when you started your work?
The idea for the product originates from our in-house production, i.e. from real-life practice. Working with sales, product management and engineering, we started off by analysing the competitive environment and consulting users. That resulted in specifications that were then worked up in an intense exchange between development and design, and covered things like the choice of materials, surfaces, design features, usability and the overall corporate design.

You developed the design internally – why not with an external design firm?
AMF is an old-established company with a history that goes back 130 years. It takes years to get an overview of the broad product range. We involve design at an early stage of the development process. That way, the internal design department is always bang up to date and serves as the permanent point of contact for development and product management.

Design is often seen as a cost factor – what share of the total development costs can be attributed to the design?
Rather than seeing design as an optional extra discipline, we consider it an integral part of the product development. Design accompanies the development process all the way, from the first meetings and sketches of the idea right up to the production-ready stage. By adding a different perspective and contributing its expertise and special skills in communicative visualisation, design can even save costs because the product is understood better and decisions can be made earlier under certain circumstances.

Founded in 1890 under the name Andreas Maier Fellbach (AMF), today the company is a one-stop supplier for clamping technology and a global market leader in its field. AMF develops project-based and customised solutions, as well as standard products that enjoy widespread success on the market. With more than 5,000 products and numerous patents, the Baden-Württemberg company is one of the most innovative in its field.

www.amf.de

SILVER   SWINGMASTER 500   CORPORATE PRODUCT DESIGN
                           CORPORATE PRODUCT DESIGN
         → SEITE / PAGE
         32

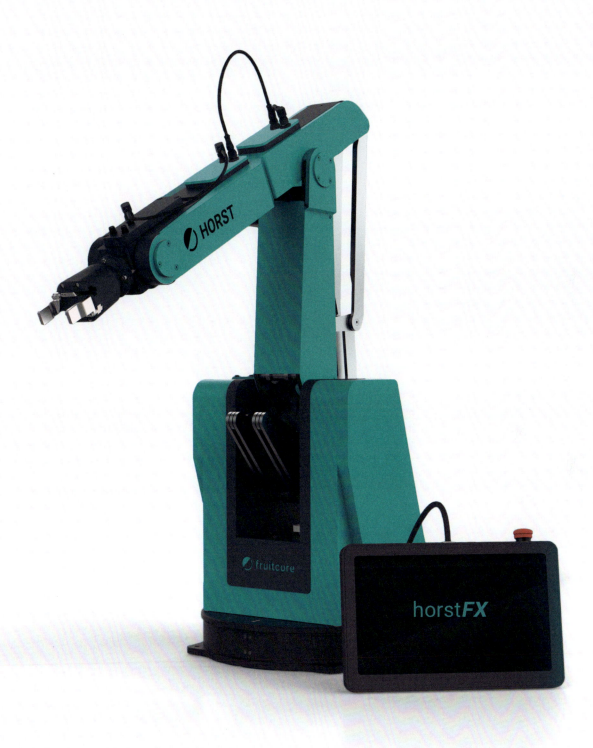

SPECIAL MENTION   POWER-FAST II   SPANPLATTENSCHRAUBE
                                    CHIPBOARD SCREW
                   → SEITE / PAGE
                   34

SPECIAL MENTION · PRO → SEITE / PAGE 35 · LACKVERSORGUNGSSYSTEM / PAINT SUPPLY SYSTEM

| SPECIAL MENTION | SPEEDE II ELECTRIC
→ SEITE / PAGE
36 | ELEKTRISCHER SCHRAUBENDREHER
ELECTRIC SCREWDRIVER |

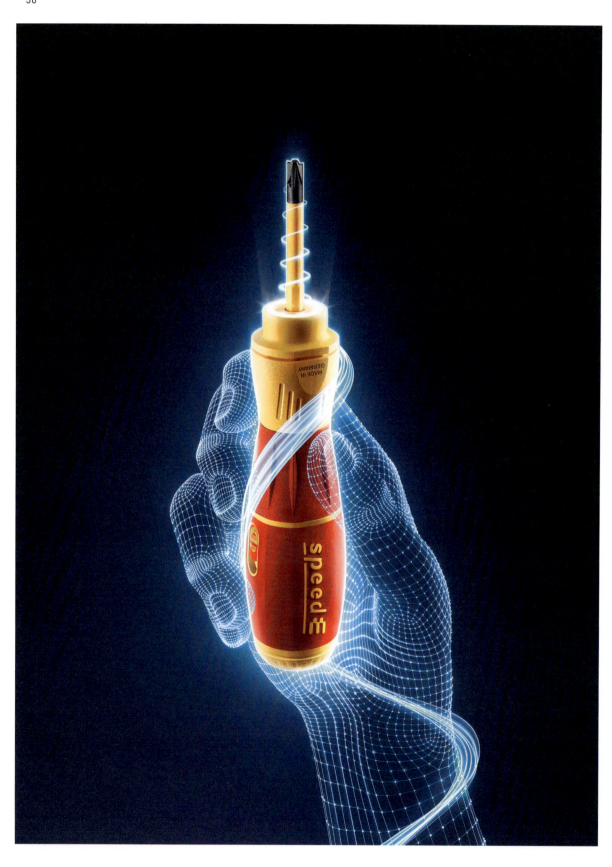

SPECIAL MENTION — S1 — SIGNALSÄULE / SIGNAL TOWER

→ SEITE / PAGE 37

SPECIAL MENTION GECKO 200 KLEBEBINDEMASCHINE
→ SEITE / PAGE 38 ADHESIVE BINDING MACHINE

SILVER

SWINGMASTER 500
CORPORATE PRODUCT DESIGN
CORPORATE PRODUCT DESIGN

JURY STATEMENT

Ein sehr gelungenes und durchdachtes Gesamtkonzept mit sachlichem Grundtenor. Tatsächlich gelingt es elegant, konsistente Designelemente in alle Maschinen zu integrieren und die Marke trotz des zurückhaltend verwendeten Firmenlogos erkennbar zu machen.

A very successful and well thought-through overall concept with an objective basic tenor. It manages to integrate elegant, consistent design elements into all the machinery and makes the brand recognisable despite its understated use of the company's logo.

HERSTELLER / MANUFACTURER
Fill GmbH
Gurten
Österreich / Austria

DESIGN
Formquadrat GmbH
Linz
Österreich / Austria

VERTRIEB / DISTRIBUTOR
Fill GmbH
Gurten
Österreich / Austria

→ SEITE / PAGE
24

Wer Maschinen und Anlagen mit unterschiedlichsten Funktionalitäten im Portfolio versammelt, steht vor der Herausforderung, diesen ein einheitliches Erscheinungsbild zu verleihen.

Das Portfolio des Anlagenbauers besteht aus unterschiedlichsten Spezialmaschinen, die funktionsbedingt ein heterogenes Gesamtbild ergeben. Das Corporate Product Design hat die Aufgabe, ein konsistenteres Bild zu erzeugen und die Markenwerte über die Produktgestaltung zu transportieren. Das Konzept zielt auf klare Marktpositionierung, Differenzierung und Wiedererkennung. Dafür definiert das Corporate Product Design Gestaltungsrichtlinien für die verschiedenen Produkte. Beispielhaft zeigt dies Swingmaster 500, eine Anlage, die Gussteile nach dem Schwingprinzip automatisch entkernt – oder der Grind Performer R, dessen Roboter Guss- und Schmiedeteile in rauen Gießerei-Umgebungen entgratet und schleift.

A portfolio full of machinery and plant with a wide range of different functions presents the manufacturer with the challenge of developing a consistent corporate design.

The plant manufacturer's portfolio consists of a wide range of specialised machinery; the functions involved result in a highly diverse overall picture. The job of the corporate product design is to create a more consistent look that communicates the brand values. The concept aims to ensure a clear market positioning, differentiation and recognition by defining unifying design guidelines for the various products. This is exemplified by the Swingmaster 500, a machine that automatically decores castings based on the swing principle, or by the Grind Performer R, whose robot deburrs and grinds castings and forgings in harsh foundry environments.

SILVER — HORST 900 — INDUSTRIEROBOTER / INDUSTRIAL ROBOT

JURY STATEMENT

Eine ehrliche Sache, dieser Roboter. Die Kinematik ist nachvollziehbar und fließt in das Design ein. Die flächige Formensprache bedeutet geringe Werkzeugkosten und signalisiert, dass es sich um ein funktions- und kostenoptimiertes Tool handelt. Und die Namensgebung macht den Roboter kumpeltauglich.

An honest thing, this robot. The kinematics are comprehensible and influence the design. Its planar vocabulary means low tooling costs and signals that the mechanical assistant has been optimised for maximum functionality and value for money. Last but not least, the robot's name identifies it as a buddy rather than a rival.

HERSTELLER / MANUFACTURER
Fruitcore Robotics GmbH
Konstanz / Constance

DESIGN
Inhouse
Christoph Keller

VERTRIEB / DISTRIBUTOR
Fruitcore Robotics GmbH
Konstanz / Constance

→ SEITE / PAGE
25

Industrieroboter sollen auch für kleine und mittlere Unternehmen nutzbar werden – noch aber stehen Kosten und komplizierte Handhabung dieser Vision entgegen. Mit Horst soll sich das ändern, denn der sechsachsige Roboter ist so konstruiert, dass er weitgehend ohne teure Sensorik auskommt und ein einfaches Antriebssystem auf Basis so genannter Viergelenkketten nutzt. Dieses Prinzip prägt auch das bewusst technisch-funktional gehaltene Design des fünf Kilogramm handhabenden Roboters, der sich so von anderen, organischer anmutenden Wettbewerbern differenziert. Das Verkleidungskonzept und die außen liegenden Kabel erlauben eine schnelle Zugänglichkeit bei Wartungen.

It ought to be feasible for small and medium-sized companies to use industrial robots too – but for the time being, the costs and complicated handling involved still stand in the way of this vision. Horst is intended to change that, because the six-axis robot is engineered in such a way that it largely dispenses with expensive sensor technology and uses a simple drive system based on what's known as four-bar linkages. The same principle governs the design, which has a deliberately technical, functional character that sets it apart from its organic-looking competitors.
The robot can handle a payload of up to five kilograms. The housing concept and exterior cables ensure rapid maintenance access.

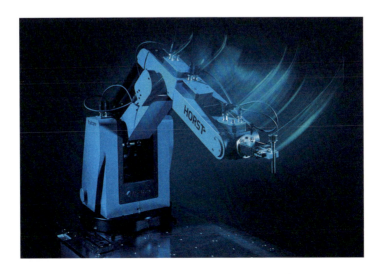

SPECIAL MENTION **POWER-FAST II** **SPANPLATTENSCHRAUBE**
CHIPBOARD SCREW

JURY STATEMENT

Dass selbst bei rein technisch erscheinenden Produkten die designzentrierte Entwicklung neue Qualitäten entstehen lässt, zeigt diese Spanplattenschraube. Gegenüber vergleichbaren Typen bietet sie wesentliche Verbesserungen für den/die Nutzer*in – und zeigt diese auch.

The chipboard screw demonstrates that design-centric development can result in new qualities, even in the case of products that seem purely technical. As compared to similar types of screw, it delivers key improvements for the user – and visualises them as well.

HERSTELLER / MANUFACTURER
Fischerwerke GmbH & Co. KG
Waldachtal

DESIGN
Inhouse

VERTRIEB / DISTRIBUTOR
Fischerwerke GmbH & Co. KG
Waldachtal

→ **SEITE / PAGE**
26

Die neue Hochleistungs-Schraube ist das Ergebnis eines interdisziplinären Entwicklungsprozesses. Beteiligt waren Holz- und Maschinenbau-Ingenieure sowie der Produzent. Für Holz-Holz-, Holz-Metall- und Kunststoffdübel-Verbindungen konzipiert, wurden alle Features der unterschiedlichen Schnittbereiche so aufeinander abgestimmt, dass der Profianwender eine maximale Gesamtleistung bekommt. Die Spitze ist für den Vorschnitt optimiert, der Kopf mit seiner Doppelkegelform senkt sich selbstständig ein. Trotz unterschiedlicher Längen, Durchmesser und Antriebsarten ist das Designprinzip durchgehend identisch, die Schraube mit ihren professionellen Features sofort erkennbar.

The new high-performance screw is the result of an interdisciplinary development process that involved mechanical and wood construction engineers as well as the producer. Designed for wood-wood, wood-metal and in-plug connections, all the features of the different areas were harmonised to ensure maximum overall performance for professional users. The tip is optimised for a quick bite and the head countersinks itself thanks to its double cone geometry. Despite the different lengths, diameters and screw head types, the design principle is identical throughout the entire series of professional fixings, making the screw immediately recognisable.

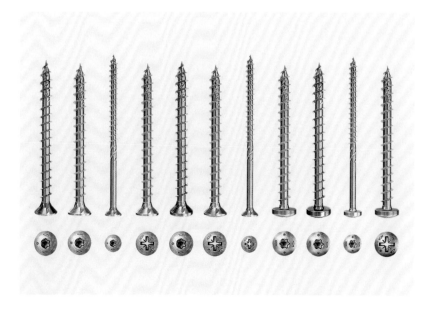

SPECIAL MENTION PRO LACKVERSORGUNGSSYSTEM / PAINT SUPPLY SYSTEM

JURY STATEMENT

Ein rein technisches Produkt, das eine zentrale Rolle innerhalb des industriellen Lackierprozesses einnimmt. Jetzt wurde es entsprechend dieser Bedeutung neu gestaltet, seine Formensprache ist sachlich und der Anwendung angemessen. Anwender*innen profitieren von den glatten und damit leichter zu reinigenden Flächen, von der seriellen Verkettbarkeit sowie vom deutlich verbesserten Handling der schweren Fässer.

A purely technical product that plays a key role in the industrial coating process. It has now been redesigned to reflect its importance and speaks an objective language in keeping with the area of application. Users benefit from the smooth, easy-to-clean surfaces, from the possibility of linking multiple units into a series and from the significantly improved handling of the heavy barrels.

Industrielle Lackieranlagen mit kontinuierlichem Durchsatz benötigen eine ebenso kontinuierliche Versorgung mit Beschichtungsmaterial, das meist in Fass-Gebinden angeliefert wird. Die neu konzipierte Versorgungseinheit sorgt für stetiges Rühren des Materials, für dessen richtige Dosierung und ist zudem mit mehreren Fassgrößen kompatibel. Gegenüber dem Vorgänger wurde die Anordnung der Bedienelemente ergonomisch optimiert und klarer strukturiert. Ein spezielles Fasswagen-Konzept erlaubt, die Gebinde sehr einfach und schnell zuzuführen. Außerdem lassen sich die Versorgungseinheiten problemlos nebeneinander stellen und optional mit einer schützenden Einhausung versehen.

Industrial paint shops with continuous throughput also need a continuous supply of the coating material, which normally comes in barrels. The newly designed supply unit, which is compatible with several barrel sizes, ensures that the material is stirred constantly and dosed correctly. As compared to the previous model, the control elements have been arranged more ergonomically and structured more clearly. A special barrel dolly concept makes the container very quick and easy to transport. In addition, the supply units can be placed next to one another and enclosed in an optional protective housing if required.

HERSTELLER / MANUFACTURER
Sprimag Spritzmaschinenbau
GmbH & Co. KG
Kirchheim/Teck

DESIGN
Braake Design
Stuttgart

VERTRIEB / DISTRIBUTOR
Sprimag Spritzmaschinenbau
GmbH & Co. KG
Kirchheim/Teck

→ SEITE / PAGE
27

SPECIAL MENTION

SPEEDE II ELECTRIC
ELEKTRISCHER SCHRAUBENDREHER
ELECTRIC SCREWDRIVER

JURY STATEMENT

Der Schraubendreher lässt sich sehr gut handhaben, trotz des integrierten Motors liegt er ergonomisch in der Hand. Gut gelöst wurde die Aktivierung des Rechts-/Linkslaufes durch den Drehring. Weil kompakt, eignet sich der Schraubendreher auch für beengte Situationen. Erwähnenswert ist auch das zugehörige, robuste Ladegerät.

The screwdriver is very easy to handle and ergonomically designed to sit comfortably in the hand. The ring switch is a good solution for activating right or left rotation. Because it's so compact, the screwdriver is also suitable for use in cramped conditions. The robust accompanying charger also deserves special mention.

Der elektrische Schraubendreher ist für die professionelle Elektro-Installation gedacht, damit diese schneller und materialschonender verlaufen kann. Per Schiebeschalter lässt sich das maximale Drehmoment des Schraubers von 0,4 Nm auf 1,0 Nm wechseln – die farblich codierte Schalterposition findet ihre Entsprechung in den ebenso gekennzeichneten Bit-Einsätzen. Den Antrieb selbst aktiviert man direkt bei der Nutzung über einen Ringschalter im vorderen Griffbereich. Ein LED-Ring sorgt für die Ausleuchtung des Arbeitsfelds, etwa in dunklen Schaltkästen.

The electric screwdriver is intended for professional electricians and aims to help them work faster and prevent damage to materials. A sliding switch is used to set maximum torque at 0.4 or 1.0 newton metres – the colour-coding of the two switch positions correlates with that of the bits. The driving action itself is turned on and off via a ring switch at the front end of the handle. An LED ring can be used to illuminate the work area, for instance in dark electrical enclosures.

HERSTELLER / MANUFACTURER
Wiha Werkzeuge GmbH
Schonach

DESIGN
Inhouse

VERTRIEB / DISTRIBUTOR
Wiha Werkzeuge GmbH
Schonach

→ SEITE / PAGE
28

SPECIAL MENTION S1 SIGNALSÄULE / SIGNAL TOWER

JURY STATEMENT

Mit dieser Signalsäule wird es möglich, auch komplexe Zustände eigenständig arbeitender Maschinen mittels eindeutiger Lichtanzeigen anzuzeigen. Formal ist die Integration zweier Lichtsäulen gut gelungen, der Bereich dazwischen bietet Platz für das Label des Anlagenbauers.

This tower makes it possible to indicate the status of independently functioning machines by means of unambiguous light signals, even in complex situations. The integration of two columns of signals is resolved by a convincing design that provides space for the plant manufacturer's label between them.

HERSTELLER / MANUFACTURER
Diana Electronic-Systeme GmbH
Schwaikheim

DESIGN
Inhouse
Martin Weller

VERTRIEB / DISTRIBUTOR
Diana Electronic-Systeme GmbH
Schwaikheim

→ SEITE / PAGE
29

Die Zeiten, da Maschinen lediglich roten oder grünen Status anzeigen mussten, sind längst vorbei. Die Prozesse sind komplexer geworden – und damit auch die Anforderungen an die Signalsäulen. So leuchtet die S1 nicht nur in unterschiedlichsten, klar differenzierbaren Farben, sie beherrscht auch Wechsel-, Lauf- und Pulslicht, kann blinken und Blitzlichter produzieren. Die 50 LED-Segmente hinter den zylindrischen Diffusoren sind einzeln ansteuerbar. Mit ihren beiden Lichtsäulen vereint die S1 zwei unabhängige Anzeigen in einem Bauteil, das auch magnetisch an der zugehörigen Maschine platzierbar ist.

The days when machinery only had to display red or green status are long gone. Processes have become more complex – and the requirements signal towers have to meet along with them. That's why the S1 doesn't just glow in all sorts of different, clearly distinguishable colours, it can also emit alternating, running and pulsating light, as well as blinking and flashing signals. The 50 LED segments behind the cylindrical diffusers can be controlled individually. With its two light columns, the S1 combines two independent displays in a single component, which can be mounted on the corresponding machine by means of a magnetic base if required.

SPECIAL MENTION GECKO 200 KLEBEBINDEMASCHINE
ADHESIVE BINDING MACHINE

JURY STATEMENT

Individuelle Bücher liegen im Trend, vor allem eigene Fotobücher. Die Anlage ermöglicht es, diese nun nachhaltiger und schneller produzieren zu können – und das bei besserer sowie langlebigerer Bindung. Der Innovationsgrad des Verfahrens ist hoch, das Design nimmt sich dagegen zurück, bleibt fast neutral.

Self-published books are very much on trend – especially personalised photo albums. Besides permitting faster and more sustainable production, the system also ensures a better and more durable binding. The highly innovative process is paired with an unobtrusive, almost neutral design.

HERSTELLER / MANUFACTURER
Ribler GmbH
Stuttgart

DESIGN
Bunse05
Hagen

VERTRIEB / DISTRIBUTOR
Ribler GmbH
Stuttgart

→ SEITE / PAGE
30

Die Maschine erstellt Hardcover-Bücher mit LayFlat-Bindung erstmals in nur einem automatisierten Arbeitsgang. Durch Freilegung und Vorbehandlung der Zellulosefasern an den Klebekanten reduziert sich die notwendige Klebermenge dabei um bis zu 80 Prozent. Der eigens entwickelte Kleber ist wasserbasiert und erfordert keinen eigenen Trocknungsprozess. So fällt der Energiebedarf laut Hersteller um bis zu 99 Prozent geringer aus als bei bisherigen Verfahren. Die Maschine, gedacht für die Book-on-Demand-Produktion, kann vernetzt und aus der Ferne gewartet werden.

Die transparente Front macht alle Prozessschritte jederzeit einsehbar. Der Zugang zu den Werkzeugen ist mit einem Griff möglich und die Arbeitshöhe ergonomisch ausgelegt.

The machine is the first to produce hardcover books with a lay-flat binding in just one automated step. Exposing and pretreating the cellulose fibres on the spinal edges reduces the amount of adhesive required by up to 80 percent. The specially developed adhesive is water-based and does not require a separate drying process. According to the manufacturer, that reduces the amount of energy required by up to 99 percent as compared to previous practices. The machine, which is intended for book-on-demand production, can be connected to the internet and maintained remotely.

Thanks to the transparent front, every step in the process can be monitored at any time. The tools can be accessed in one easy move and are positioned at an ergonomic height.

BETTINA BAACKE   **COGNITO DESIGN UND ENGINEERING GBR, KARLSRUHE**

»Design ist ein Kostenfaktor, aber einer, der sich auszahlt. Denn Designer*innen bringen neue Lösungsansätze ein, was das Engineering alleine so nicht könnte. Dabei geht es um Ergonomie, Haptik und Usability, aber auch um die Emotionalität. Schließlich ist der emotionale Mehrwert der Differenzierungsfaktor schlechthin und kaufentscheidend.«

»Design is a cost factor, but it's an investment that pays off. That's because designers contribute new solution strategies in a way that engineering couldn't on its own. It's about things like ergonomics, tactile qualities and usability, but also about emotionality. At the end of the day, the added emotional value is the ultimate differentiating factor and plays a crucial role in the purchase decision.«

Bettina Baacke führt seit 2013 gemeinsam mit Gründer Prof. Jürgen Goos die Geschäfte der Cognito Design und Engineering GbR, die sich primär der interdisziplinären Gestaltung von langlebigen Investitionsgütern widmet.

In ihrem ersten Beruf ist Bettina Baacke Schreinerin und Betriebsassistentin des Handwerks. Sie studierte Industriedesign an der Hochschule Pforzheim, wo sie seit 2011 im Fachbereich Gestaltung als Dozentin für CAD tätig ist.

Bettina Baacke has been running Cognito Design und Engineering GbR together with its founder Prof. Jürgen Goos since 2013. The firm's main focus is on the interdisciplinary design of durable capital goods.

Bettina Baacke started her professional life as a carpenter and assistant works manager. She studied industrial design at Pforzheim University of Applied Sciences, where she has been lecturing on CAD in the School of Design since 2011.

www.cognito.de   www.cognito.de

1 → SEITE / PAGE
44–49

2 → SEITE / PAGE
50–51

HEALTHCARE
HEALTHCARE

GOLD:
1 **MARLED X**
Gebrüder Martin GmbH & Co. KG
Tuttlingen

SPECIAL MENTION:
2 **MYECC PUPIL**
HomeBrace Germany UG
Urbach

Wer medizinische Geräte gestaltet, bewegt sich in einem besonders sensiblen Bereich und übernimmt große soziale Verantwortung für Patient*innen wie auch für das medizinische Personal. Neben Produkten für die klinische Akutversorgung verlangen auch barriereabbauende Geräte und Hilfsmittel für Personen mit eingeschränkten Möglichkeiten oder chronischen Problemen ausgefeilte Gestaltungskonzepte.

Designers of medical equipment operate in a particularly sensitive area and have a high level of social responsibility towards patients and medical staff alike. That calls for sophisticated design concepts – not just for products for acute clinical care, but for devices, aids and appliances that tackle the barriers faced by people with certain impairments or chronic problems too.

GOLD   MARLED X   OPERATIONSLEUCHTE
                      OPERATING LIGHT

MARLED X

OPERATIONS
LEUCHTE

HEALTHCARE
HEALTHCARE

44
45

FOCUS GOLD

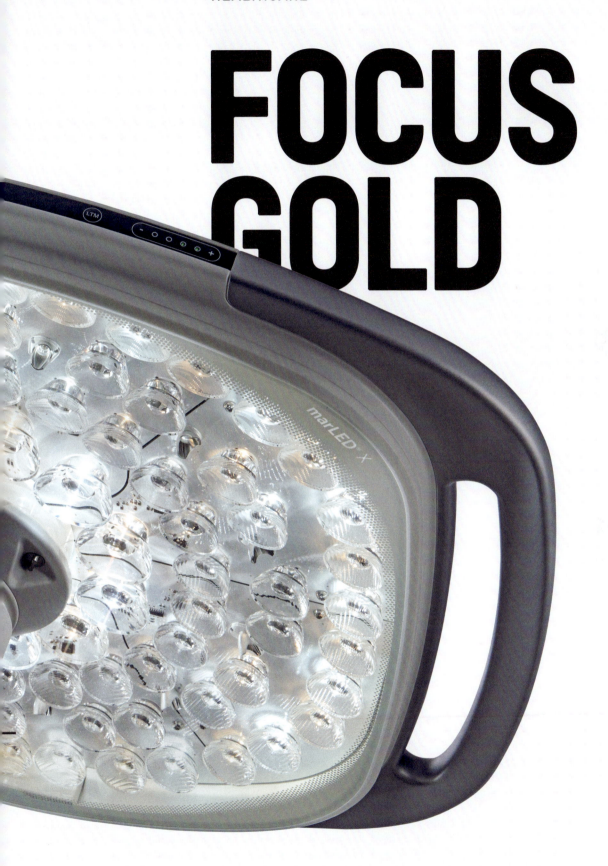

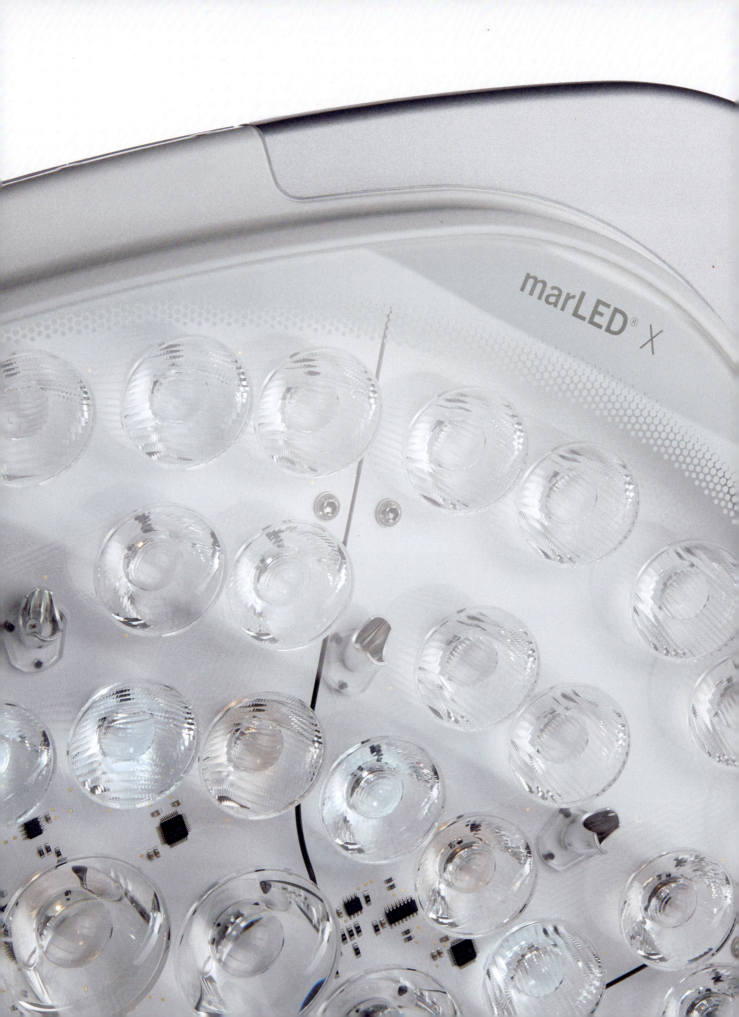

GOLD — MARLED X — OPERATIONSLEUCHTE / OPERATING LIGHT

JURY STATEMENT

Trotz ihrer Größe bleibt die Leuchte filigran in der Anmutung, die vielen Lichtoptionen sind erst dank des sauber gestalteten Interface wirklich nutzbar. Ein hervorragendes Beispiel für das Zusammenspiel von technischer Innovation und nutzerzentriertem Designkonzept.

Despite its considerable size, the light nevertheless makes a filigree impression. It offers a great many lighting options, made genuinely accessible by the impeccable design of the interface. A superb example of the synergy that can be achieved when technical innovation is combined with a user-centric design concept.

HERSTELLER / MANUFACTURER
Gebrüder Martin GmbH & Co. KG
Tuttlingen

DESIGN
UP Designstudio GmbH & Co. KG
Stuttgart

VERTRIEB / DISTRIBUTOR
Gebrüder Martin GmbH & Co. KG
Tuttlingen

→ SEITE / PAGE
44–46, 48–49

Die Arbeit im OP verlangt Präzision und höchste Konzentration. Dass die Ausleuchtung des Operationsfeldes dabei eine wesentliche Rolle spielt, versteht sich von selbst. Die prämierte OP-Leuchte basiert auf 96 einzeln ansteuerbaren LEDs – Lichtstärke und Lichtfarbe passen sich so an die jeweilige Situation und Gewebeart an. Direkt aufrufbare Lichtfeld-Geometrien vermeiden Schatten oder Blendwirkungen, die Bedienung erfolgt dabei entweder direkt am Gehäuse der Leuchte oder mittels eines zusätzlichen Steuergeräts, dessen Interaktions- und Interface-Konzept integraler Bestandteil der Designentwicklung war. Denn erst das Bedienkonzept ermöglicht die Nutzung der vielen Einstelloptionen der Leuchte und das Aufrufen kompletter, auf spezifische Operationsarten angepasste Lichtszenarien.

Mit ihrer geschlossenen Oberfläche entspricht die Leuchte den hohen hygienischen Anforderungen des klinischen Betriebs, ihre flache Bauweise reduziert zudem den Einfluss auf Luftströmungen im OP-Saal.

Working in an operating theatre calls for precision and complete concentration – and it goes without saying that the illumination of the operating area plays an essential role in that. The award-winning operating light is based on 96 LEDs that can be actuated individually, allowing the intensity and colour temperature to be adapted to the respective situation and tissue type. Directly accessible light field geometries prevent shadows or glare and there are two options for controlling the functions: either via a panel on the housing itself or by means of a separate, optional control unit whose interaction and interface concept was an integral part of the design development. That was essential, because it's the UI concept that enables the user to access the many setting options, as well as complete lighting scenarios tailored to specific types of operation.

Thanks to its closed surface, the light complies with the strict hygiene requirements of clinical settings, while the flat design reduces its impact on air currents in the operating theatre.

SVEN ZEHNDER DIRECTOR PRODUCT MANAGEMENT,
GEBRÜDER MARTIN GMBH & CO. KG

»Unser Design ist davon geprägt, Lösungen zu entwickeln, die Anwender*innen begeistern und sich auszahlen.«

»Our design is shaped by the desire to develop solutions that wow users and are worth the investment.«

SVEN ZEHNDER

DIRECTOR OF PRODUCT MANAGEMENT, GEBRÜDER MARTIN GMBH & CO. KG

→ **Eine OP-Leuchte ist ein komplexes Produkt – wann und wie wurde das Design einbezogen?**
Wir haben das Designbüro schon während der Konzeptphase eingebunden. In enger Zusammenarbeit wurden die Do's and Dont's besprochen, Mitbewerber analysiert und Bauräume abgestimmt. Diese Entscheidungen bilden den Rahmen für den Rest eines Projekts und wirken sich direkt auf die Kosten, Erfolge und potenzielle Probleme aus. Schließlich näherten wir uns iterativ der finalen Lösung an – bei der OP-Leuchte mussten wir nur marginale Änderungen im weiteren Verlauf der Entwicklung umsetzen.

Je multifunktionaler ein Produkt ist, desto wichtiger sind eindeutige Bedienkonzepte. Wie entwickelt man ein solches Konzept?
Das Produktmanagement hat bereits im Lastenheft die Anforderung aufgestellt, dass sämtliche Funktionen einfach und individuell angepasst werden können. Dies garantiert maximale Flexibilität während der Entwicklung, aber auch in der Zukunft in der laufenden Serie. So stand sehr frühzeitig fest, dass die Lösung nur mit einem Touch-Panel-Interface realisiert werden kann. Bei der Entwicklung des Konzepts waren die Teammitglieder sowie das Designbüro involviert: Wir haben die Anforderungen aufgestellt, die sich aus den Funktionen, Markt- und Wettbewerbsanalysen ergeben haben. Darauf basierend erarbeitete das Designbüro unterschiedliche Konzepte, welche das Projektteam dann aus Sicht des Anwenders diskutierte und bewertete. Mittels eines internen Usability-Tests haben wir das favorisierte Konzept auf Anwenderfreundlichkeit und intuitive Bedienung geprüft. Per Click-Dummy wurden während der gesamten Entwicklung die Menüs und Effekte visualisiert sowie Vor- und Nachteile evaluiert.

Welche Rolle spielt das Design, wenn es um die Beschaffung von Medizinprodukten durch Kliniken geht?
Dies ist je nach Land sehr unterschiedlich. Generell bin ich der Meinung, dass das Design eine sehr große Rolle spielt. Investiert ein Krankenhaus in einen Neubau, in neuestes und modernstes Equipment, dann legt man natürlich auch Wert auf ein ansprechendes und funktionales Design. Viele der Anwender*- und Entscheider*innen befassen sich auch im privaten Bereich mit gut gestalteten Produkten – warum sollten die Arbeitsplätze ihrer Mitarbeiter*innen weniger attraktiv sein?

Was zeichnet die Designsprache von Gebr. Martin aus?
Unser Design ist davon geprägt, Lösungen zu entwickeln, die Anwender*innen begeistern und sich auszahlen. Übersichtliches, funktionales und innovatives Design verleiht unseren Produkten einen Wert, der höher ist als der Preis, den sie kosten.

In Tuttlingen verortet, gehört Gebrüder Martin zur KLS Martin Group. Unter dieser international aktiven Dachmarke versammeln sich verschiedene Unternehmen, die für die Chirurgie Instrumente, Implantatsysteme, Lasergeräte und komplette OP-Lösungen entwickeln.

www.klsmartin.com

→ **An operating light is a complex product – when and how did you factor design into the equation?**
We bring design firms on board early on, during the concept stage. We work closely with them to clarify the do's and don'ts, analyse competitors and agree on the design spaces. These decisions provide the framework for the rest of a project and have a direct impact on costs, success and potential problems. Then we approach the final solution in an iterative process – in the case of the operating light, we only had to implement marginal changes as the development progressed.

The more multifunctional a product is, the more important unambiguous UI concepts are. How do you develop a concept like that?
Product management had already specified in the product requirements document that all the functions had to be easily and individually adaptable. That guarantees maximum flexibility during development, but also in the future when production is already underway. As a result, it was obvious at a very early stage that a touch panel interface was the only way to implement the solution. Both the team members and the design firm were involved with the development of the concept: we formulated the requirements that resulted from the functions and from our market and competitor analysis. The design firm used that as the basis for working up different concepts that the project team then discussed and evaluated from the user's perspective. After that, we used an internal usability test to check the favoured concept for user-friendliness and intuitiveness. During the entire development process, click dummies were used to visualise the menus and effects and evaluate the pros and cons.

What role does design play in clinics' procurement of medical products?
That varies a lot from one country to another. In general, I believe the design plays a very important role. If a hospital is investing in a new building and looking for the newest, state-of-the-art equipment, it will obviously attach great importance to an appealing and functional design. A lot of the users and decision-makers surround themselves with well-designed products in their private lives too – why should work environments be any less attractive?

What makes Gebrüder Martin's design language stand out?
Our design is shaped by the desire to develop solutions that wow users and are worth the investment. Clearly structured, functional and innovative design gives our products a value that's higher than the price customers pay for them.

Based in Tuttlingen, Gebrüder Martin is part of the KLS Martin Group, an internationally operating umbrella brand for various companies that develop surgical instruments, implant systems and laser devices, as well as complete operating room solutions.

www.klsmartin.com

SPECIAL MENTION | MYECC PUPIL → SEITE / PAGE 51 | AUGENSTEUERUNG FÜR ROLLSTÜHLE
EYE TRACKING-BASED CONTROL SYSTEM FOR WHEELCHAIRS

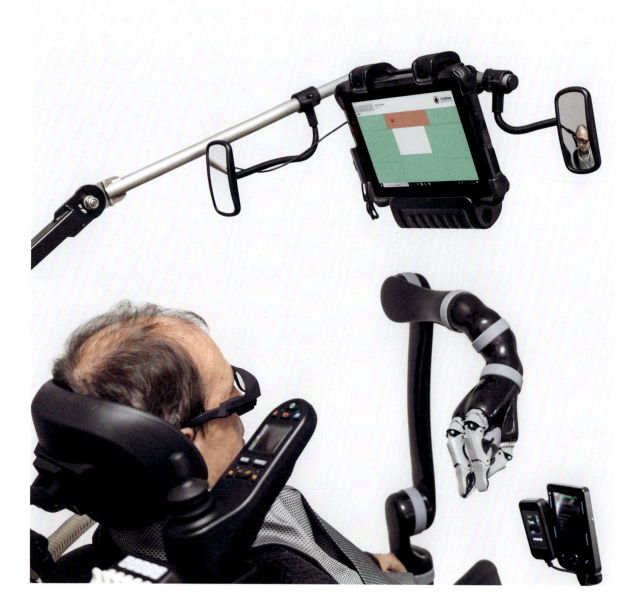

SPECIAL MENTION — MYECC PUPIL

AUGENSTEUERUNG FÜR ROLLSTÜHLE
EYE TRACKING-BASED CONTROL SYSTEM FOR WHEELCHAIRS

JURY STATEMENT

Das sichtbare Kernstück dieses innovativen Systems ist zweifellos die Brille – sie integriert geschickt technische Komponenten und Sonnenschutz, trägt kaum auf und wirkt kaum stigmatisierend. Zudem nutzt das Design die individualisierenden Möglichkeiten der additiven Fertigung optimal aus.

There's no question that the headset is the visible centrepiece of this innovative system – it cleverly integrates the technical components and solar protection, doesn't look bulky and doesn't stigmatise the wearer. What's more, the design makes optimal use of the customisation possibilities provided by additive manufacturing.

HERSTELLER / MANUFACTURER
HomeBrace Germany UG
Urbach

DESIGN
DQBD GmbH
Schorndorf

VERTRIEB / DISTRIBUTOR
HomeBrace Germany UG
Urbach

→ SEITE / PAGE
50

Es ist eine seltene Krankheit, aber oft eine mit gravierendem Verlauf: Menschen, die an amyotropher Lateralsklerose leiden, können ihre Muskelfunktionen komplett verlieren und in der Folge bewegungsunfähig werden. Stephen Hawking oder Jörg Immendorff litten unter ALS – bei voller geistiger Präsenz. Spezielle Elektrorollstühle können diesen Menschen ein Stück Selbstbestimmung zurückbringen, allerdings wollen diese auch gesteuert werden. Dafür sorgen Systeme, die Augenbewegungen in Fahrbefehle umsetzen. MyEcc Pupil besteht aus einer Brille mit integriertem Sensor, der alle Augenbewegungen erfasst und an eine Auswertungs-Software weiterleitet. So lässt sich neben dem Rollstuhl auch ein unterstützender Roboterarm aktiv steuern.

Dank der Produktion im 3D-Verfahren integriert die leichte und robuste Brille Sensor, Kabel und Buchse, außerdem lässt sie sich bestens individuell anpassen. Ein weiteres Plus: Die Brille nutzt phototrope Gläser und ist so optimiert, dass das System erstmals auch bei Sonneneinstrahlung funktioniert.

It's a rare disease, but one that often has a severe impact: people with amyotrophic lateral sclerosis can suffer a complete loss of muscle function, resulting in paralysis. Stephen Hawking and German artist Jörg Immendorff both suffered from ALS – without it affecting their intellectual abilities. While special electric wheelchairs can restore some degree of self-determination, they have to be controlled somehow. Systems that translate eye movements into motion commands provide a solution. MyEcc Pupil consists of a headset with an integrated sensor that tracks all eye movements and sends the data to an analysis software. In addition to the wheelchair, the user can actively control a robotic arm in the same way.

Thanks to the additive production process, the light and robust headset integrates the sensor, cable and port and can be customised for a perfect fit. Another benefit is that the headset uses phototropic lenses and has been optimised so that the system is the first of its kind to work in bright sunlight.

1 → SEITE / PAGE
54–59

2 → SEITE / PAGE
60–61

BAD, WELLNESS
BATHROOM, WELLNESS

GOLD:
1 **ICON 3D**
Grohe AG
Düsseldorf

SPECIAL MENTION:
2 **BLACK LINE**
Grohe AG
Düsseldorf

Schon lange sind die Zeiten vorbei, als das Badezimmer ein unkomfortabler Raum für die Körperreinigung war. Heute ist das Bad ein emotional und sinnlich aufgeladenes Wellness-Refugium, das höchsten Anforderungen nach Individualität, Ästhetik und Atmosphäre gerecht wird. Entsprechend präsentiert sich die Welt der Armaturen in einer formal, funktional und werkstofflich extrem ausdifferenzierten Vielfalt.

The days when the bathroom was an uncomfortable space reserved for personal hygiene are well and truly over. Today the bathroom is an emotionally appealing and sensuous wellness retreat that meets the very highest standards in terms of individuality, aesthetics and atmosphere. Accordingly, fittings are available in an extremely wide variety of forms, functions and materials.

GOLD · ICON 3D · BADARMATUREN BATHROOM TAPS

ICON 3D

BAD— ARMATUREN

BAD, WELLNESS
BATHROOM, WELLNESS

FOCUS GOLD

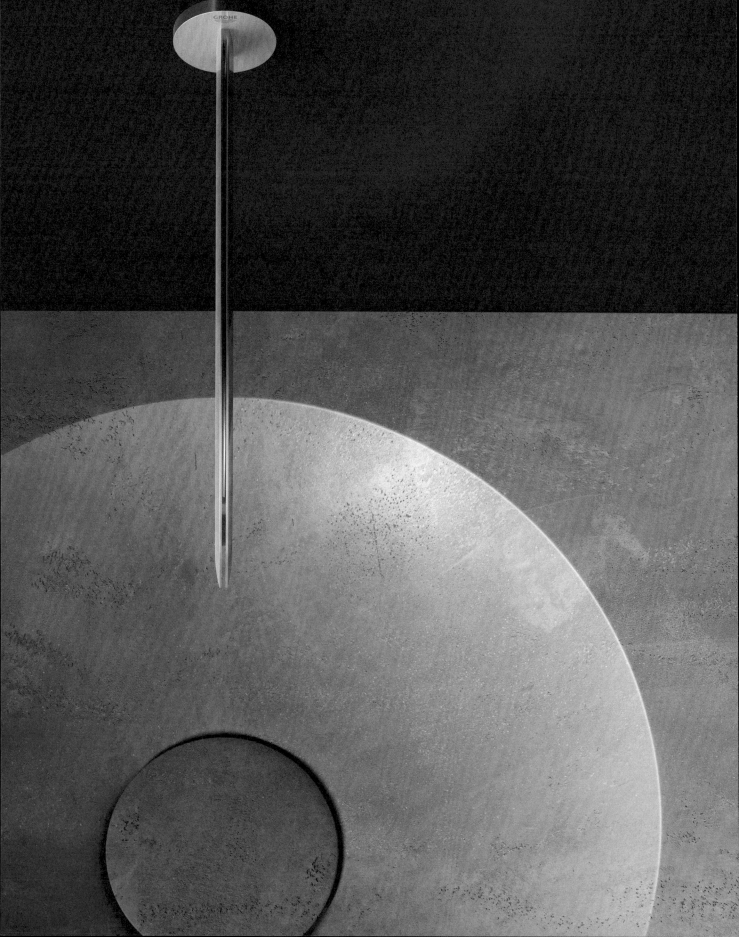

GOLD ICON 3D BADARMATUREN / BATHROOM TAPS

JURY STATEMENT

Ein mutiges, visionäres Design! Als Studien bewertet, geben die Armaturen eine Ahnung des Potenzials, das in der industriellen Nutzung von 3D-Fertigungsverfahren steckt. Besonders interessant: Der eher technische Gesamtlook erhält durch die fast geheimnisvolle Wasserführung eine spielerische Note.

A bold, visionary design! Taken as studies, the taps give an idea of the potential inherent in the industrial usage of 3D manufacturing processes. The almost mysterious route taken by the water is particularly interesting and adds a playful touch to the otherwise rather technical overall look.

HERSTELLER / MANUFACTURER
Grohe AG
Düsseldorf

DESIGN
Inhouse

VERTRIEB / DISTRIBUTOR
Grohe Deutschland Vertriebs GmbH
Porta Westfalica

→ SEITE / PAGE
54–56, 58–59

Additive Fertigungsverfahren ermöglichen Konstruktionsweisen, die mit konventionellen Technologien nicht machbar wären – zum Beispiel besonders komplex geformte Produkte oder gewichts- und belastungsoptimierte Teile. Daneben bietet sich auch die Chance zur Individualisierung von Produkten sowie zur Realisierung neuartiger Formen. Letzteren Ansatz verfolgt die Grohe AG mit ihren beiden Badarmaturen, die im Laserschmelz-Verfahren aus einem eigens entwickelten Metallpulver entstehen. Jede Armatur besteht aus 4700 Schichten zu je 0,06 Millimetern, nach der Entnahme aus dem Pulverbett wird mit einer CNC-Fräsmaschine nachgearbeitet und schließlich manuell geschliffen sowie gebürstet. Formal unterscheiden sich die beiden Armaturen stark – der facettierten und kantigen Allure Brilliant steht die schlanke und einen eleganten Bogen beschreibende Atrio zur Seite. Verbindendes Element ist bei beiden eine sehr filigrane Struktur und die samtige Oberfläche. Bedient werden beide Armaturen über zwei im gleichen Verfahren hergestellte Drehknöpfe. Produziert werden die Armaturen als Unikate in exklusiven, geringen Stückzahlen.

Additive manufacturing processes permit designs that wouldn't be feasible with conventional technologies – products with particularly complex forms, for example, or weight- and load-optimised components. It also provides the possibility of customising products and implementing unprecedented forms. Grohe AG takes the latter approach with these two bathroom tap lines, which are made from a specially developed metal powder using a laser fusion process. Each tap consists of 4,700 layers with an individual thickness of 0.06 millimetres; after being removed from the powder bed, it is reworked by a CNC milling machine before being manually ground and brushed. In terms of form, the two tap collections differ considerably – Allure Brilliant is faceted and angular, whereas the slender Atrio line describes an elegant arc. The connecting element between the two is a very filigree structure paired with a velvety surface. Both mixers are operated by means of two handles, which are manufactured using the same process. Produced in small, exclusive editions, every single tap is unique.

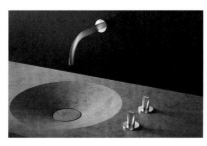

PATRICK SPECK VICE PRESIDENT LIXIL GLOBAL DESIGN AND
CONSUMER EXPERIENCE EMENA

»Durch die Reduktion des Designs auf ein absolutes Minimum und die Betonung der puren Essenz der Formen sparen wir während des Herstellungsprozesses wertvolle Ressourcen.«

»By reducing the design to an absolute minimum and emphasising the pure essence of the forms, we save valuable resources during the manufacturing process.«

PATRICK SPECK
VICE PRESIDENT, LIXIL GLOBAL DESIGN AND CONSUMER EXPERIENCE EMENA

→ **Additive Manufacturing bietet revolutionäre Möglichkeiten – was macht das Verfahren für Grohe interessant?**

Unsere Armaturen Atrio Icon 3D und Allure Brilliant Icon 3D sind Beispiele dafür, wie wir Technologie und Materialität sinnvoll einsetzen. Die Komponenten werden aus Metall im Pulverbett-Laserschmelzverfahren hergestellt. Durch die Reduktion des Designs auf ein absolutes Minimum und die Betonung der puren Essenz der Formen sparen wir während des Herstellungsprozesses wertvolle Ressourcen. So konnten wir im Vergleich zur Messingausführung bei der Allure Brilliant eine Gewichtsreduktion von 55 Prozent erreichen.

Werden additive Verfahren bald die traditionelle Gussproduktion ersetzen?

Es gibt viele Vorteile, die sich aus der Nutzung des sich noch entwickelnden 3D-Metalldrucks ergeben, etwa der effizientere Einsatz von Materialien. Auf diese Weise können additive Verfahren herkömmliche Herstellungstechnologien sinnvoll unterstützen. Sie werden diese aber in naher Zukunft nicht vollständig ersetzen.

Wie schreitet die Digitalisierung des Badezimmers und seiner Armaturen voran?

Die Entwicklung unserer Produktlösungen basiert immer auf den tatsächlichen Bedürfnissen unserer Konsumenten. Dabei sollte der Einsatz von Technik nie um ihrer selbst willen geschehen, sondern dem Nutzer einen konkreten Mehrwert bieten. Unsere sensorgestützten Badtechnologien ermöglichen es hygieneorientierten Nutzer*innen, sich berührungslos im Badezimmer zu

bewegen. Darüber hinaus unterstützen intelligente Technologien und wassersparende Produkte dabei, bedarfsorientierte Badezimmererlebnisse zu kreieren und wertvolle Ressourcen zu schonen.

Was treibt die Entwicklung neuer Armaturen bei Grohe an – die formale oder die funktionale Seite?

Bevor wir uns mit der Form eines Produkts beschäftigen, tauchen wir in das ein, was wir als Presearch-Prozess bezeichnen. Dabei versetzen wir uns in die Lage des Konsumenten und gestalten anhand unserer erworbenen Erkenntnisse als Fundament relevante und nutzerfreundliche Produkte. Schließlich soll die Form der Produkte die Funktion beschreiben und unterstützen.

Unsere klar definierten Designwerte und die charakteristischen Designelemente helfen uns dabei, eine unverkennbare Designsprache mit unseren Produkten zu verfolgen, die die visuelle und emotionale Identität unserer Marke widerspiegelt.

Als führende Marke für ganzheitliche Badlösungen und Küchenarmaturen setzt die Firma Grohe mit Hauptsitz in Düsseldorf seit vielen Jahren auf die Markenwerte Technologie, Qualität, Design und Nachhaltigkeit. Grohe beschäftigt derzeit mehr als 6.500 Mitarbeiter*innen, davon rund 2.460 in Deutschland. Seit 2014 ist Grohe Teil des Markenportfolios von Lixil, einem japanischen Hersteller von Wassertechnologien und Gebäudeausstattungen.

www.grohe.de

→ **Additive manufacturing opens up revolutionary possibilities – what makes the process interesting for Grohe?**

Our Atrio Icon 3D and Allure Brilliant Icon 3D taps are prime examples of how we make meaningful use of both technology and materials. The components are made out of metal in a process known as laser powder bed fusion. By reducing the design to an absolute minimum and emphasising the pure essence of the forms, we save valuable resources during the manufacturing process. That enabled us to achieve a weight reduction of 55 percent as compared to the brass version of Allure Brilliant.

Will additive processes replace traditional casting-based production in the foreseeable future?

3D metal printing is still evolving, but there are a lot of benefits to using it, like a more efficient use of materials. That's one way in which additive processes can provide meaningful support for conventional manufacturing technologies. But they won't completely replace those methods in the near future.

How is the digitalisation of the bathroom and its fittings progressing?

The development of our product solutions is always based on the actual needs of our consumers. At the same time, making use of technology should never be an end in itself – it has to deliver a concrete added value for the user. Our sensor-based bathroom technologies turn the bathroom into a touchless environment for

hygiene-oriented users. What's more, intelligent technologies and water-saving products help to create needs-based bathroom experiences and conserve valuable resources.

What drives the development of new fittings at Grohe – form or function?

Before we start addressing the form of a product, we immerse ourselves in what we call the presearch process. That involves putting ourselves in the consumer's position and using the lessons we learn as the basis for designing relevant and user-friendly products. Ultimately, the form of the products ought to describe and support their function. Our clearly defined design values and characteristic design elements help us to ensure our products speak an unmistakable design language that reflects the visual and emotional identity of our brand.

Grohe is a leading brand for complete bathroom solutions and kitchen fittings. The Düsseldorf-based company has been committed to the brand values technology, quality, design and sustainability for many years. Grohe currently employs a workforce of more than 6,500 people, approx. 2,460 of them in Germany. Since 2014, Grohe has been part of the brand portfolio belonging to Lixil, a Japanese manufacturer of water technologies and building equipment.

www.grohe.de

SPECIAL MENTION

BLACK LINE
→ SEITE / PAGE
61

**ARMATUREN-KOLLEKTION
FITTINGS COLLECTION**

SPECIAL MENTION — BLACK LINE — ARMATUREN-KOLLEKTION / FITTINGS COLLECTION

JURY STATEMENT

Die schwarze Beschichtung verleiht den Armaturen mit ihren Rändelknöpfen und -tasten eine hohe Prägnanz und unterstreicht den grafischen Gesamtcharakter. Die Oberfläche ist von ähnlicher Perfektion wie die klassische Verchromung.

The black coating adds a striking touch to the fittings, which feature textured knobs and buttons, and underscores the graphicness of their overall character. The perfection of the surfaces is comparable to that of the classic chrome finish.

HERSTELLER / MANUFACTURER
Grohe AG
Düsseldorf

DESIGN
Inhouse

VERTRIEB / DISTRIBUTOR
Grohe Deutschland Vertriebs GmbH
Porta Westfalica

→ SEITE / PAGE
60

Badarmaturen, Thermostate und Kopfbrausen in sattem Tiefschwarz? Es war nur eine Frage der Zeit, bis die angesagte Trendfarbe den Sprung in die heutigen Wellness-Landschaften der Badezimmer schafft. Mit der Black Line erweitert der Hersteller die Farboptionen seiner Armaturen-Kollektionen, die mit innovativer Technik und durchdachten Designs den gehobenen Ansprüchen eines anspruchsvollen Publikums Rechnung tragen. Schwarz soll im Bad kraftvolle Akzente setzen, im Zusammenspiel mit hellen Materialien mutige Kontraste entfalten und einen Hauch von Provokation versprühen.

Bathroom taps, thermostats and overhead showers in deep black? It was only a matter of time until the on-trend colour made its way into the wellness sanctuaries of contemporary bathrooms. With Black Line, the manufacturer is expanding the colour options for its fittings collections, which meet the demanding standards of a sophisticated clientele with innovative technology and meticulous designs. In the bathroom, black can add high-impact accents, create bold contrasts with light-coloured materials and conjure up a hint of provocation.

1 → SEITE / PAGE 64–69
2 → SEITE / PAGE 70, 74
3 → SEITE / PAGE 71, 75

4 → SEITE / PAGE 72, 76
5 → SEITE / PAGE 73, 77
6 → SEITE / PAGE 78–83

KÜCHE, HAUSHALT, TISCHKULTUR
KITCHEN, HOUSEHOLD, TABLE

GOLD:
1 **TRIFLEX HX1**
Miele & Cie. KG
Gütersloh

SILVER:
2 **SK59**
Mono GmbH
Mettmann

3 **FROMAĜO**
Robert Herder GmbH und Co. KG
Solingen

4 **SMART CONTROL KITCHEN**
Grohe AG
Düsseldorf

5 **KAYA**
Maomi
Mannheim

META SOCIAL DESIGN:
6 **W1 CLASSIC GUIDELINE**
Miele & Cie. KG
Gütersloh

Kaum ein Wohnbereich ist so perfektioniert, funktional durchdacht und ästhetisch auf so hohem Niveau wie die Küche. Clevere Details, die das Kochen erleichtern, sind ebenso gefragt wie neue Oberflächen oder neue Materialien. Technologische Neuerungen wiederum erleichtern die Arbeit im Haushalt auf überraschende Weise – auch für Menschen mit eingeschränkten Wahrnehmungen.

There are few areas of the home that exhibit such perfectionism, such well thought-through functionality and such high aesthetic standards as the kitchen. Clever details that make cooking easier are just as much in demand as new finishes or new materials, while technological innovations come up with surprising ways to take the effort out of household chores – even for people with sensory impairments.

GOLD TRIFLEX HX1 HANDSTAUBSAUGER
HANDSTICK VACUUM CLEANER

TRIFLEX HX1

HANDSTAUB SAUGER

KÜCHE, HAUSHALT, TISCHKULTUR
KITCHEN, HOUSEHOLD, TABLE

64
65

FOCUS GOLD

GOLD TRIFLEX HX1 HANDSTAUBSAUGER / HANDSTICK VACUUM CLEANER

JURY STATEMENT

Verglichen mit anderen Handstaubsaugern zeigt dieses Modell eine betont zurückhaltende und zudem eigenständige Formensprache. Dank seiner Umbauoptionen und Multifunktionalität lässt sich der Sauger für unterschiedlichste Szenarien nutzen. Er ersetzt so zusätzliche Geräte und bremst den wuchernden Maschinenpark im Haushalt.

Compared to other handstick vacuum cleaners, this model speaks an emphatically understated and very original design language. Thanks to its configuration options and multifunctionality, the cleaner can be used for a wide range of different scenarios. As a result, it can help downsize the rapidly growing fleet of household helpers by making additional appliances superfluous.

HERSTELLER / MANUFACTURER
Miele & Cie. KG
Gütersloh

DESIGN
Miele Designcenter
Gütersloh

VERTRIEB / DISTRIBUTOR
Miele & Cie. KG
Gütersloh

→ SEITE / PAGE
64–66, 68–69

Seine modulare Konzeption nach dem 3-in-1-System macht den kabellosen Handstaubsauger zu einem flexibel einsetzbaren Reinigungstool. Das Herzstück, die PowerUnit, besteht aus Motoreinheit, Akku und Staubbox. Im Solobetrieb entfernt sie Krümel und Flusen, auch im Auto. Oberhalb des Saugrohrs montiert, verhilft sie zu einer komfortablen Reinigung unter Möbeln und sogar an der Decke. Wird die PowerUnit unterhalb des Saugrohrs angebracht, verschiebt sich der Schwerpunkt und macht ein ermüdungsfreies Saugen auch großer Flächen möglich. Zudem verhindert diese Einstellung lästiges Umkippen – der Sauger steht von selbst. Der leistungsstarke Lithium-Ionen-Akku gestattet je nach gewählter Leistungsstufe eine Laufzeit von 15 bis zu 60 Minuten.

Based on a 3-in-1 system, the modular design of the cordless handstick makes it a highly flexible cleaning tool. The PowerUnit, consisting of the motor, rechargeable battery and dust box, is the core element of the appliance. Used on its own, it's ideal for removing crumbs and fluff, including in the car. Mounted above the suction tube, it provides a convenient solution for cleaning under furniture and even vacuuming the ceiling. If the PowerUnit is fitted below the suction tube, the centre of gravity changes so that even large areas can be cleaned effortlessly and without fatigue. In addition, this configuration prevents the appliance from tipping over – the vacuum cleaner stands upright by itself. Depending on the power setting, the high-performance lithium ion battery provides a runtime of between 15 and 60 minutes.

ANDREAS ENSLIN   LEITUNG DESIGN,
                    MIELE & CIE. KG

»Ein Produkt wie der Triflex wäre gar nicht möglich, würden Designer und Ingenieure nicht Hand in Hand arbeiten.«

»A product like the Triflex simply wouldn't be possible if designers and engineers didn't work hand in hand.«

ANDREAS ENSLIN

HEAD OF DESIGN, MIELE & CIE. KG

→ **Was zeichnet den Triflex HX1 gegenüber anderen Handstaubsaugern aus?**
Die Art und Weise der Handhabung: Durch einfaches Umstecken passt er sich drei unterschiedlichen Anwendungssituationen an. Daher kommt auch der Name Triflex. Die Idee war, drei modulare Applikationen in einem Gerät zu vereinen, wobei die Geometrie des Gehäuses die größte Herausforderung war.

Eine demnächst in Kraft tretende EU-Richtlinie sieht vor, dass Haushalts-Großgeräte künftig einfacher reparierbar sein sollen. Sollte dies nicht auch für Kleingeräte gelten?
Einfache Reparierbarkeit ist eine Grundanforderung und sollte für alle Geräte gelten. Natürlich wäre es am besten, wenn ein Gerät möglichst lange hält. Aber geht ein Bauteil einmal kaputt, sollte es repariert oder ausgetauscht werden können. Hier zeigen sich dann auch die Unterschiede zwischen den Herstellern – allein die Verfügbarkeit von Ersatzteilen kann da zum Wettbewerbsvorteil werden. Ebenso sollte sich ein Akku, der ja im Wesentlichen die Lebensdauer bestimmt, austauschen lassen. Bei Miele-Geräten ist das möglich und wir bieten, ganz im Sinne der Nachhaltigkeit, bis zu 15 Jahre lang Ersatzteile für unsere Produkte an – meist sogar länger.

Lassen sich Auswirkungen der Corona-Pandemie auf das Haushaltsgeräte-Segment ablesen?
Wir erleben derzeit, dass sich mehr Menschen für ihre Hausgeräte interessieren. Es wird mehr zuhause gekocht und viel ausprobiert. Unsere Produkte sind nach wie vor gefragt, vielleicht auch, weil mehr Menschen Zeit zuhause verbringen und sich fragen, ob das eine oder andere nicht auch leichter und besser geht.

Miele gestaltet seine Produkte intern. Warum?
Es geht um die Wahrnehmung der Marke: Ich kenne keinen Markenhersteller, der es langfristig geschafft hätte, ohne internes Design ein klares Markenbild zu entwickeln und zu pflegen. Da steckt viel von unserer DNA drin – Miele ist mehr als nur gute Produkte. Diese Gene werden sichtbar, wenn alle ein gemeinsames Ziel haben und zusammenarbeiten. Das macht eine Marke und ein Unternehmen stark.

Ein Produkt wie der Triflex wäre gar nicht möglich, wenn Designer und Ingenieure nicht Hand in Hand arbeiten würden. Die Ideen werden von den Designern bereits sehr früh in 3D-CAD-Programmen modelliert, um sich Klarheit über die Bauräume und – speziell hier – über die trickreiche Geometrie des Umsteckens zu verschaffen. Die Ingenieure sind sich wiederum bewusst, dass nicht alles, was technisch funktioniert, auch für spätere Anwender*innen verständlich und geeignet ist.

> Von einer 1899 nahe Gütersloh gegründeten Zentrifugierfabrik mit elf Mitarbeitern hat sich die Miele & Cie. KG bis heute zu einem weltweit agierenden Premiumanbieter für Haushaltsgeräte entwickelt. Die Miele-Gruppe beschäftigt weltweit etwa 20.500 Menschen, davon etwa 11.000 in Deutschland.
>
> **www.miele.de**

→ **What stands out about the Triflex HX1 as compared to other handstick vacuum cleaners?**
The handling: it can be adapted to three different usage situations simply by reconfiguring the parts. That's where the name Triflex comes from too. The idea was to combine three modular applications in a single appliance; in the end, it was the geometry of the housing that posed the biggest challenge.

An EU directive that's about to come into force stipulates that, in future, large household appliances have to be easier to repair. Shouldn't the same apply to small appliances as well?
Ease of repair is a basic requirement that should be met by any appliance. Obviously the best thing would be for an appliance to last as long as possible. But if a part does happen to break, it should be possible to repair or replace it. This is where the differences between manufacturers become apparent – just the availability of spare parts can be enough to give you a competitive advantage. And a rechargeable battery, which essentially determines the product's life span, should also be replaceable. That's possible with Miele appliances, and in the interests of sustainability we offer spare parts for our products for up to 15 years – in most cases even longer.

Is the corona pandemic having any noticeable impact on the household appliance segment?
We're seeing that more people are showing an interest in their household appliances. They're cooking at home more and trying things out. Our products are still very much in demand, perhaps because more people are spending time at home and wondering if there's not an easier and better way to do certain things.

Miele designs its products internally. Why?
It's all about brand perception: I don't know any brand-name manufacturer that's been able to develop and manage a clear brand image long term without internal design. There's a lot of our DNA in our design – there's more to Miele than just good products. When everybody has a common goal and works together, that genetic makeup becomes visible. That's what makes a brand and a company strong.

A product like the Triflex simply wouldn't be possible if designers and engineers didn't work hand in hand. The designers model the ideas in 3D CAD programs at a very early stage so as to get a clear picture of the design spaces and – especially in this case – the tricky geometry involved due to the reconfigurable parts. On the other hand, the engineers are very much aware that just because something works at a technical level doesn't necessarily mean it will be clear and suitable for future users.

> Founded near Gütersloh as a centrifuge factory with 11 employees in 1899, Miele & Cie. KG has evolved into a globally active supplier of premium household appliances. The Miele Group employs approx. 20,500 people all over the world, around 11,000 of them in Germany.
>
> **www.miele.de**

SILVER SK59 KOCHMESSERSERIE
              KITCHEN KNIFE SERIES
        → SEITE / PAGE
          74

SILVER — SMART CONTROL KITCHEN → SEITE / PAGE 76 — KÜCHENARMATUR KITCHEN TAP

SILVER KAYA PORZELLANSERIE 72
 → SEITE / PAGE PORCELAIN SERIES 73
 77

SILVER SK59 KOCHMESSERSERIE / KITCHEN KNIFE SERIES

> **JURY STATEMENT**
>
> Es überrascht, wie gut die Messer trotz ihrer ungewöhnlichen Griffform in der Hand liegen. Auch die Klinge folgt diesem neuen formalen Ansatz, der Knicke und Kanten statt organischer Linien zelebriert. Nebenbei benötigen die durchbrochenen Griffe weniger Kunststoff-Material.
>
> It's surprising how well the knives sit in the hand despite their unusually shaped handles. The blade takes the same new approach, celebrating kinks and edges rather than organic lines. In addition, the voids in the handles mean less plastic is required.

HERSTELLER / MANUFACTURER
Mono GmbH
Mettmann

DESIGN
Wahrmann Design
Gido Wahrmann
Sprockhövel

VERTRIEB / DISTRIBUTOR
Mono GmbH
Mettmann

→ SEITE / PAGE
70

In der Form unerwartet, in der Handhabung sofort vertraut – das ist der Ansatzpunkt für die Konzeption der dreiteiligen High-End-Messerserie. Die Form von Klinge und Griff wird dabei zusammenhängend aus rostfreiem Hochleistungs-Chromstahl ausgeschnitten und anschließend gehärtet. Es folgt der Schliff, zudem werden die Klingen nach traditioneller Art des Solinger Feinschleifens gepließtet. Dieses aufwendige, mit rotierenden Lederscheiben arbeitende Verfahren verbessert nochmals die Schneidqualität, Schnitthaltigkeit und Rostbeständigkeit der Klinge. Das anschließende Ummanteln der Griffe mit glasfaserverstärktem Polyamid im Spritzgussverfahren sorgt für eine angenehme Haptik und setzt einen bewusst dunklen Kontrast zur silberfarbigen Schneide.

An unexpected shape, an immediate sense of familiarity as soon as they're put to use – that was the starting point for the concept behind this three-piece series of high-end knives. The blade and handle are cut out of high-performance stainless chromium steel in one piece and then tempered. The blades are then ground and finished using the traditional Solingen fine-grinding technique known as »Pliessten«, an elaborate process based on rotating leather wheels that enhances the cutting quality, edge-retention and corrosion-resistance of the knives. An injection moulding process is then used to coat the handles with glass fibre reinforced polyamide, ensuring a pleasant feel and creating a deliberate contrast with the silver blades.

SILVER

FROMAĜO

MESSERSERIE
KNIFE RANGE

JURY STATEMENT

Die Messerreihe überzeugt ästhetisch, funktional und natürlich durch ihre hochwertige Verarbeitung. Mit ihren etwas längeren Holzgriffen ermöglichen die Messer unterschiedliche Greifoptionen – was individuellen Nutzungsvorlieben entgegenkommt.

The knife range is compelling – not just because of its aesthetic and functional qualities but due to the top-quality workmanship as well. The wooden handles are slightly longer than usual, which permits different gripping options and accommodates users' individual preferences.

HERSTELLER / MANUFACTURER
Robert Herder GmbH und Co. KG
Solingen

DESIGN
Inhouse
Tim Wieland

VERTRIEB / DISTRIBUTOR
Robert Herder GmbH und Co. KG
Solingen

→ SEITE / PAGE
71

Käse ist nicht gleich Käse – das gilt sowohl für seinen Geschmack als auch für die Konsistenz, die von cremig-weich über elastisch-fest bis hin zu bröckelig-hart variiert. Mit dem Ziel, professionelle Arbeitswerkzeuge zum Zerteilen und Servieren unterschiedlichster Käsesorten zu konzipieren, wurde in Zusammenarbeit mit der Frômagerie Guillaume diese vierteilige Messerserie entwickelt.

Zwei spezielle Messer – eines für Weichkäse, eines für Ziegenkäse – ergänzen das breitere Universalkäsemesser. Ein darauf abgestimmtes Brotmesser komplettiert die Serie. Alle Klingen bestehen aus rostfreiem Chrom-Molybdän-Vanadium-Stahl und sind von Hand bearbeitet. Die eingeschliffenen Wellen sowie die gewölbte Schneide beim Ziegenkäsemesser sorgen für ein müheloses Zerteilen. Hoch angesetzte Griffe aus heimischem Pflaumenholz ermöglichen eine große Handfreiheit beim Schneiden.

No two cheeses are the same – not just in terms of taste but consistency too, which can range from soft and creamy or firm and springy all the way to hard and crumbly. This four-piece knife range was developed in collaboration with Fromagerie Guillaume with the aim of designing professional tools for cutting and serving all sorts of different cheeses.

The universal cheese knife, which has a wider blade, is complemented by two special-purpose knives – one for soft cheese, one for goat's cheese. A matching bread knife completes the collection. All the blades are made of stainless chromium-molybdenum-vanadium steel and handcrafted. The ground serrations and convex cutting edge of the goat's cheese knife ensure effortless cutting. The handles are made of plum wood and attached at a high position to ensure plenty of space for the hand.

SILVER

SMART CONTROL KITCHEN
KÜCHENARMATUR / KITCHEN TAP

JURY STATEMENT

Die Armatur überzeugt durch das neuartige Bedienkonzept, das ausgesprochen anwendungsoptimiert gedacht ist. Die eigene formale Sprache unterstreicht diese besondere Funktionsintegration.

The tap's unprecedented control concept is compelling and intended for optimal usability. The distinctive design language underscores the exceptional integration of the functions.

HERSTELLER / MANUFACTURER
Grohe AG
Düsseldorf

DESIGN
Inhouse

VERTRIEB / DISTRIBUTOR
Grohe Deutschland Vertriebs GmbH
Porta Westfalica

→ SEITE / PAGE
72

Küchen zählen heutzutage als gleichberechtigte Lebensbereiche zu einem individuellen Lifestyle. Dort, wo man arbeitet, sich aber auch trifft, mag man es gern unkompliziert und praktisch. Hier setzt die neu gedachte, hebellose Armatur an. Bedienen lässt sie sich per Knopfdruck – das funktioniert auch mit Handgelenk oder Ellbogen, wenn man gerade keine Hand frei hat. Eine Drehbewegung am Knopf regelt die gewünschte Wassermenge von sparsam bis kräftig. Die Temperatur lässt sich über ein Ventil am formal reduzierten, kegelförmig zulaufenden Armaturenkörper einstellen. Die herausziehbare Brause erweitert den Aktionsradius an der Spüle, integrierte Magnethalterungen gewährleisten eine reibungslose Rückführung der Brause.

Nowadays kitchens are just as much part of an individual lifestyle as any other area of the home. And in places where people not only work but congregate, they like things to be straightforward and practical. That's precisely where this newly conceived, lever-less tap comes in. It's turned on and off by pushing a button – which you can do with your wrist or elbow if you don't have a hand free. Turning the button regulates the flow, adjusting the amount of water from economical to powerful as required. The temperature is adjusted by means of a valve on the understated conical body of the tap. The pullout spray increases the tap's reach when working at the sink, while integrated magnetic holders ensure it glides back into place easily after use.

SILVER — KAYA — PORZELLANSERIE / PORCELAIN SERIES

JURY STATEMENT

Reduziert, schlicht, unaufgeregt – in ihrer Vereinfachung wirkt die Serie fast schon japanisch. Das gilt insbesondere für die matt-samtigen Oberflächenvarianten mit ihrer haptisch einfühlsamen Anmutung. Und mit dem Schwerpunkt auf kleine Formate setzt die Serie einen erfrischenden Gegenpol zu den aktuell beliebten großen Gedecken.

Understated, unpretentious, self-possessed – its simplicity gives the series an almost Japanese-like quality. That's particularly true of the variants with a velvety matt finish, which have a very tactile, sensitive appeal. And with its focus on small formats, the series provides a refreshing alternative to the large tableware that's currently in vogue.

HERSTELLER / MANUFACTURER
Maomi
Mannheim

DESIGN
Inhouse

VERTRIEB / DISTRIBUTOR
Maomi
Mannheim

→ SEITE / PAGE
73

Jedes Stück ist ein Unikat: Die Porzellanserie kombiniert zeitlos-edle Ästhetik mit einer hochwertigen, einzeln und von Hand aufgetragenen Glasur. Zwei matte Pastellfarbtöne sowie glänzendes Weiß bestimmen das Erscheinungsbild der Serie, die fünf Tellergrößen, drei Schalenvarianten und zwei verschiedene Tassen umfasst. Das macht ein individuelles Kombinieren der Elemente auf dem Tisch möglich – ob im Einsatz als Espresso-Gedeck, Frühstücksgeschirr oder als komplettes Essservice.

Produziert wird die Serie bei einem Partnerunternehmen in Vietnam, das Teil einer internationalen Entwicklungskooperative ist und sich für sozial und ökologisch nachhaltige Produktionsbedingungen einsetzt.

Every piece is unique: the porcelain series combines a timeless, graceful aesthetic with a top-quality glaze that is applied to the individual pieces by hand. The series is available in two matt pastel shades and glossy white and includes plates in five sizes, three bowls and two different cups. That permits a wide range of individual combinations – the tableware can be used as an espresso or breakfast set as well as a complete dinner service.

The series is made in Vietnam by a partner company that is part of an international development cooperative and committed to socially and ecologically sustainable production conditions.

META
SOCIAL DESIGN

W1 CLASSIC
GUIDELINE

WASCHMASCHINE
WASHING MACHINE

W1 CLASSIC GUIDELINE

WASCH— MASCHINE

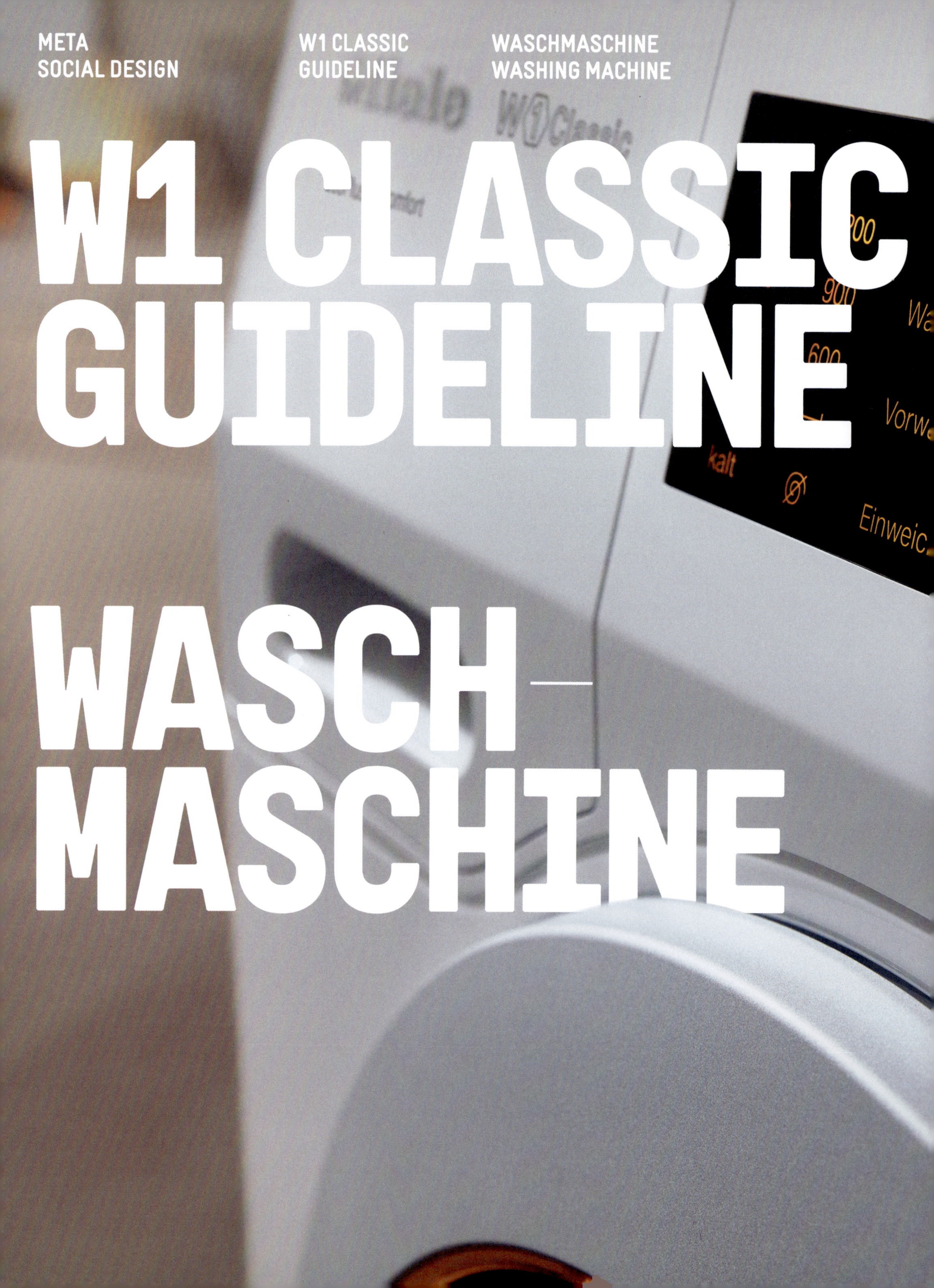

KÜCHE, HAUSHALT, TISCHKULTUR
KITCHEN, HOUSEHOLD, TABLE

META
SOCIAL
DESIGN

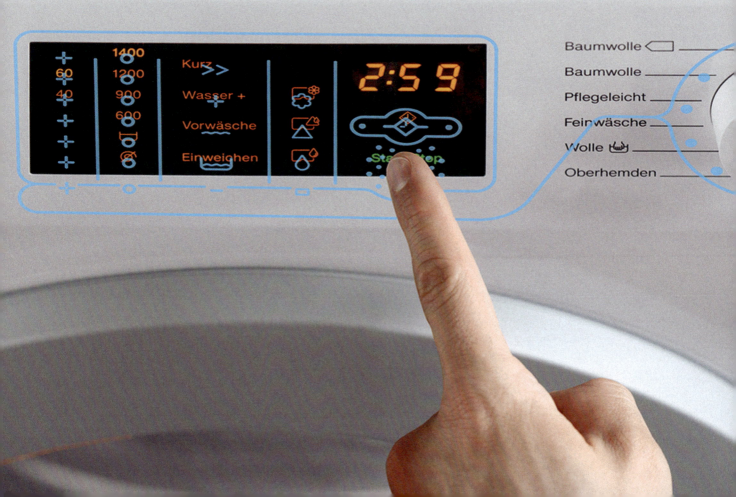

META
SOCIAL DESIGN

W1 CLASSIC
GUIDELINE

WASCHMASCHINE
WASHING MACHINE

JURY STATEMENT

Ein sehr lobenswertes Konzept, das die Selbstständigkeit von sehbeeinträchtigten und blinden Menschen im Alltag deutlich verbessern kann. Besonders interessant: Die Lösung ist vergleichsweise einfach umsetzbar, die Barrierefreiheit erfordert nur wenige Änderungen am Grundmodell. So wird die Waschmaschine durch die Einbeziehung der Nutzergruppe ein Alltagsgerät und für alle nutzbar – und zum Vorbild für ein pragmatisches Universaldesign.

A very commendable concept that can make a considerable difference to visually impaired and blind people's everyday lives by improving their independence. It's particularly interesting to note that the solution is relatively simple to implement: it only takes a few changes to the basic model to ensure accessibility. The inclusion of this user group turns the washing machine into an everyday appliance that can be used by anybody – and a prime example of pragmatic universal design.

HERSTELLER / MANUFACTURER
Miele & Cie. KG
Gütersloh

DESIGN
Miele Designcenter
Gütersloh

VERTRIEB / DISTRIBUTOR
Miele & Cie. KG
Gütersloh

→ SEITE / PAGE
78–80, 82–83

Für und mit sehbehinderten sowie blinden Menschen wurde das Bedienkonzept GuideLine entwickelt, das die vorhandene Bedienoberfläche mit haptischen Zusatzelementen und akustischen Signalen ergänzt. Die Verknüpfungen mit den Waschfunktionen erklärt eine eigens erstellte Audio-Gebrauchsanweisung im Daisy-Format. Bei Aktivierung per Drehschalter ertönt ein spezifischer Einschaltklang, um den taktil gekennzeichneten Drehknopf herum befinden sich tastbare Rasterpunkte für die Zuordnung zu den Waschprogrammen. Von dort leitet eine erhabene Führungslinie zum Touchfeld mit seinen Detaileinstellungen. Auch diesen sind eindeutige haptische Icons sowie hörbare Signale zugeordnet, jeder Ton steht dabei für eine bestimmte Einstellung. Das GuideLine-Konzept ist additiv gedacht, setzt also auf vorhandenen, langlebigen Maschinenmodellen auf.

The GuideLine UI concept was developed for and with partially sighted and blind people and supplements the existing user interface with additional tactile elements and acoustic signals. A specially produced audio instruction manual in Daisy format explains the correlations with the washing functions. A specific »on« sound is emitted when the machine is activated by turning the dial, which is located by means of a tactile identifier and surrounded by raised dots for identifying the washing programmes. A raised line guides the user's hand from the dial to the touch panel, which is used to select detailed settings. They too have been labelled with clear tactile icons and allocated audible signals, with each individual sound representing a specific setting. The GuideLine concept takes an additive approach and is based on the manufacturer's existing, long-lasting washing machine models.

FOCUS OPEN META
Mit diesem neuen Preis wird erstmals in diesem Jahr ein Produkt ausgezeichnet, das beispielhafte Lösungsansätze für ein übergeordnetes und aktuelles gestalterisches, technisches oder gesellschaftliches Thema aufzeigt. Die Jury verleiht diese Auszeichnung unabhängig von den Produktkategorien – und sie wählt auch das konkrete Thema des Focus Open Meta.

FOCUS OPEN META
Awarded for the first time this year, this new prize honours a product that features exemplary solution strategies for addressing the design-related, technical or societal challenges relating to a current and overarching issue. The jury presents this award independently of the product categories. It also selects the specific topic of the Focus Open Meta.

ANDREAS ENSLIN   LEITUNG DESIGN, MIELE & CIE. KG

»Wir wollten eine einfache Bedienung im Sinne des Universal Design ermöglichen, die allen Nutzer*innen zugute kommt.«

»We wanted to ensure ease of use in the sense of universal design that all users will benefit from.«

ANDREAS ENSLIN — HEAD OF DESIGN, MIELE & CIE. KG

→ **Was hat den Ausschlag zur Entwicklung des barrierefreien Interfaces gegeben?**

Universal Design ist schon lange ein Thema bei Miele. Wir boten in der Vergangenheit zum Beispiel für einen Teil unserer Geräte Braille-Folien auf Anfrage kostenfrei an. Bei den neuen Waschmaschinen und Trocknern sollte nun ein Touch-Interface zum Einsatz kommen, also haben wir überlegt, wie man Menschen mit Sehbehinderung die eigenständige Nutzung der Maschinen besser ermöglichen kann. Immerhin gibt es alleine in der Bundesrepublik über 660.000 Menschen mit Sehbehinderung.

Wie groß war die Herausforderung, das visuelle Interface auf eine akustische und taktile Ebene zu bringen?

Wir haben gelernt, dass unsere ersten Lösungsideen nur eingeschränkt funktioniert haben. Eine Braille-Folie etwa muss eben auch gelesen, das heißt ertastet werden können. Die meisten Blinden sind aber oft erst im Alter erblindet. Diese Menschen lernen Braille oft gar nicht mehr richtig oder haben durch mangelnde Empfindlichkeit ihrer Fingerkuppen Probleme, die Braille-Punkte zu spüren. Auch eine Spracheinund -ausgabe umzusetzen, ist gar nicht so leicht.

Zudem wollten wir ja eine einfache Bedienung im Sinne des Universal Design ermöglichen, die allen Nutzer*innen zugute kommt. Das hat dazu geführt, weiterhin eine preiswerte und einfach anzubringende Folie als Adapter zu verwenden. Wir schalten dann auf eine Softwarevariante um, die das Verhalten der Steuerung ändert: Es gibt hier zusätzliche Gerätetöne und einen Touch-Doppelklick, damit beim Darüberstreichen oder einer einfachen Berührung nicht unbeabsichtigt eine Funktion ausgelöst wird.

In welcher Form haben Sie die Nutzergruppe in die Entwicklung involviert?

Eine Mitarbeiterin unseres Unternehmens, Susanne Wegener-Dreckmann, war Regionalvorsitzende des Deutschen Blindenbundes in Nordrhein-Westfalen. Leider ist sie inzwischen verstorben. Die Zusammenarbeit mit ihr hat uns sehr geholfen, die Bedürfnisse von Blinden und Sehbehinderten zu verstehen, das Thema voranzutreiben und die vorliegende Lösung zu entwickeln. Es ist wie immer: Ohne Menschen, die sich einsetzen, geht es nicht.

Welche Bedeutung hat die barrierefreie Nutzung von Hausgeräten für Miele? Wird es weitere Geräte geben?

Ja, das ist unser Anspruch. Damit ist nicht nur Menschen mit Einschränkungen geholfen, denn der Effekt auf die Qualität einer Bedienung ist wesentlich größer. Eine solche Steuerung wird von fast allen Nutzer*innen leicht verstanden. Sie findet sich heute in der einen oder anderen Variante bei gut der Hälfte unserer Waschmaschinen wieder und ist sehr beliebt. Übrigens gibt es auch Lösungen für Hörgeschädigte, die wir zusammen mit einem führenden Hersteller innovativer Hörsysteme entwickelt haben. Ich glaube, dass wir so auch einen wesentlichen gesellschaftlichen Beitrag leisten.

> Von einer 1899 nahe Gütersloh gegründeten Zentrifugierfabrik mit elf Mitarbeitern hat sich die Miele & Cie. KG bis heute zu einem weltweit agierenden Premiumanbieter für Haushaltsgeräte entwickelt. Die Miele-Gruppe beschäftigt weltweit etwa 20.500 Menschen, davon etwa 11.000 in Deutschland.
>
> **www.miele.de**

→ **What was the decisive factor for the development of the barrier-free interface?**

Miele has been interested in universal design for a long time. In the past, for instance, Braille overlays were available for some of our appliances free of charge on request. The new washing machines and dryers were to have a touch interface, so we thought about how we can make it easier for the visually impaired to use the appliances independently. After all, there are more than 660,000 people with visual impairments in Germany alone.

How challenging was it to reproduce the visual interface at acoustic and tactile level?

We learned that our first ideas for a solution only worked to a limited extent. Take a Braille overlay, for instance: it still has to be read, i.e. deciphered by touch. But in most cases, blind people are quite old when they lose their sight. They often don't learn Braille properly any more or don't have the necessary sensitivity in their fingertips to feel the Braille dots. And voice input and output isn't all that easy to implement.

We also wanted to ensure ease of use in the sense of universal design that all users will benefit from. That resulted in us continuing to use an inexpensive, easy-to-apply overlay as an adapter. Then we switch to a software version that changes the behaviour of the controls: the appliance makes additional sounds and you have to double-click on the function so that you don't activate anything by mistake simply by running your hand over the controls or touching them.

How did you involve the user group in the appliance's development?

One of our employees, Susanne Wegener-Dreckmann, was regional chairwoman of the German Association for the Blind in North Rhine-Westphalia. Sadly, she's since passed away. Working with her really helped us to understand the needs of the blind and visually impaired, keep pushing forward and develop the present solution. It's the same as always: you don't get anywhere without the efforts of committed people.

How important is the barrier-free usability of household appliances to Miele? Will there be more such appliances?

Yes, that's our goal. It's not just a help for people with limitations: the impact on the quality of an appliance's usability is much bigger than that. Almost all users find controls like this easy to understand. A good half of our washing machines have some form of touch interface nowadays – it's a very popular feature. And by the way: there are solutions for people with impaired hearing too, developed in collaboration with a leading manufacturer of innovative hearing systems. I believe we're making an important contribution to society in that way too.

> Founded near Gütersloh as a centrifuge factory with 11 employees in 1899, Miele & Cie. KG has evolved into a globally active supplier of premium household appliances. The Miele Group employs approx. 20,500 people all over the world, around 11,000 of them in Germany.
>
> **www.miele.de**

HOLM GIESSLER **ERCO GMBH, LÜDENSCHEID**

»Zugegeben, sich über das Design zu differenzieren, wird aufwendiger. Aber je früher Designer*innen bei der Entwicklung eines Produktes dabei sind, desto mehr können sie innovative Impulse setzen. Dazu gehören neben formalen Fragen der Gestaltung auch komplexere Themen wie Nachhaltigkeit, Kreislauffähigkeit und neue Fertigungsmethoden.«

»It's certainly true that differentiating yourself through design means going to more effort. But the earlier designers are involved in a product's development, the more they're able to provide innovative input and ideas. Besides questions of form, that includes more complex issues like sustainability, circularity and new production methods as well.«

In Dresden geboren, studierte Holm Gießler Industrial Design an der Universität Duisburg-Essen mit Auslandsaufenthalt an der HDK im schwedischen Göteborg. Zunächst als Freelancer bei Scherf Design in Köln beschäftigt, arbeitete Holm ab 2007 bei Flöz Design in Essen, 2013 wechselte er zu Erco nach Lüdenscheid. Dort ist er als Inhouse Designer für die Entwicklung neuer LED-basierter Leuchtensysteme zuständig.

www.erco.com

Born in Dresden, Holm Gießler studied industrial design at the University of Duisburg-Essen, with a period abroad at the HDK (Academy of Design and Crafts) in Gothenburg, Sweden. After initially working as a freelancer for Scherf Design in Cologne, he went to work for Flöz Design in Essen in 2007. In 2013 he joined Erco in Lüdenscheid, where he is an in-house designer responsible for the development of new LED-based luminaire systems.

www.erco.com

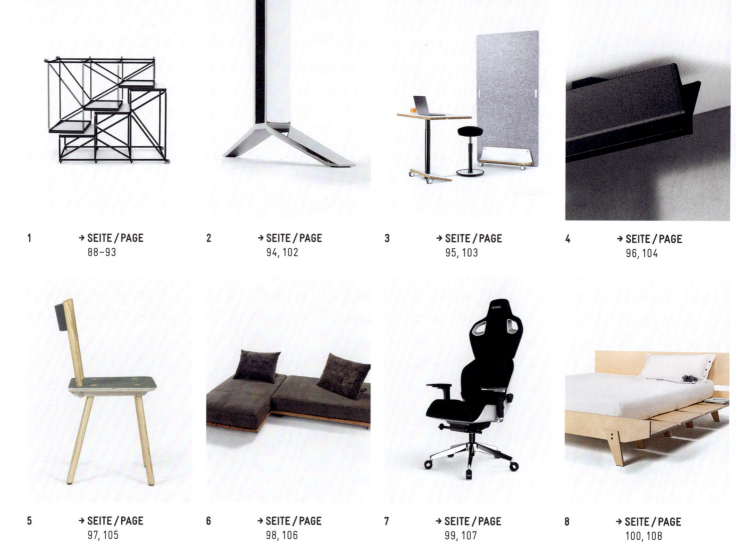

| 1 | → SEITE / PAGE 88–93 | 2 | → SEITE / PAGE 94, 102 | 3 | → SEITE / PAGE 95, 103 | 4 | → SEITE / PAGE 96, 104 |

| 5 | → SEITE / PAGE 97, 105 | 6 | → SEITE / PAGE 98, 106 | 7 | → SEITE / PAGE 99, 107 | 8 | → SEITE / PAGE 100, 108 |

INTERIOR
INTERIORS

GOLD:
1 **SITUP**
System 180 GmbH
Berlin

SILVER:
2 **MASTERLIFT 5**
Inwerk GmbH
Meerbusch

3 **POP-UP OFFICE**
Ongo GmbH
Stuttgart

4 **WINGS**
Zimmer + Rohde GmbH
Oberursel

SPECIAL MENTION:
5 **TÜBINGER STUHL 2.0**
Pozsgai Möbelschreinerei
Heitersheim

6 **TAO**
Bullfrog Marketing Design GmbH
Michelau

7 **EXO**
Recaro Gaming GmbH & Co. KG
Stuttgart

8 **FRANK & FREI**
Stadtnomaden GmbH
Riedhausen

Ein Stuhl, ein Tisch, ein Bett und ein Regal – was braucht man mehr?
Und doch ist das Universum der Möbel immens weit, wandelt sich stetig,
erneuert sich und spielt mit Volumina, Materialien, Oberflächen,
Farben. Möbeldesign ist eine der populärsten Gestaltungsdisziplinen, die
immer wieder überraschende ästhetische und funktionale Novitäten
hervorbringt.

A chair, a table, a bed and a shelving unit – what more does anyone need?
And yet the world of furniture is truly immense, changes constantly,
reinvents itself and plays with volumes, materials, finishes and colours.
Furniture design is one of the most popular design disciplines of all
and yields an endless stream of surprising aesthetic and functional ideas.

5

GOLD — SITUP — MOBILE TRIBÜNENMODULE / MOBILE BLEACHER MODULES

JURY STATEMENT

Neue Ideen entstehen nicht im stillen Kämmerlein, sondern in kreativen Teams und wechselnden Konstellationen. Das Tribünensystem ist ein sehr praktisches Tool für solch inspirierende Gruppenprozesse – es ist variabel und frei nutzbar, leichtgewichtig und luftig in seiner optischen Erscheinung.

New ideas emerge not in isolation but in creative teams and changing constellations. The bleacher system is a very practical tool for such inspiring group processes – besides being variable and versatile, it's also lightweight and makes a pleasantly airy impression.

HERSTELLER / MANUFACTURER
System 180 GmbH
Berlin

DESIGN
Inhouse

VERTRIEB / DISTRIBUTOR
System 180 GmbH
Berlin

→ SEITE / PAGE
88–90, 92–93

Teamworking braucht einen Rahmen – räumlich, aber auch, was die Ausstattung betrifft. Die flexibel gruppierbaren Module des Tribünensystems können schnell temporäre oder auch dauerhafte Strukturen für Gruppenmeetings schaffen. Die Tribünenmodule übernehmen die bewährte Rohrstruktur anderer agiler Arbeitsmöbel des Herstellers. Mit den geraden, konvexen und konkaven, jeweils dreistufigen Modulen können rasch unterschiedlichste Tribünenformen geschaffen werden. Klettbänder, um die Rohrstruktur aus Edelstahl geschlungen, übernehmen die Verbindung. Trotz der filigranen Struktur ist jedes Modul mit maximal 400 Kilogramm belastbar, für die Sitzflächen stehen elf Unidekore zur Auswahl.

Teamworking needs the right setting – not just a space, but furnishings as well. The system's flexibly configurable modules are a quick way to create temporary or permanent structures for group meetings. The bleacher modules are based on the tried-and-tested tube structure familiar from the manufacturer's other furniture for agile working. The linear, convex and concave modules, each of which has three staggered levels, can be arranged in a wide range of different bleacher formations in next to no time and connected by means of Velcro straps wrapped around the stainless steel tubing. Despite the filigree design, each module can support a maximum load of 400 kilograms. The seats are available in a choice of 11 plain colours.

DIRK UPTMOOR **SENIOR DESIGNER, SYSTEM 180 GMBH**

»Designawards sind starke Motivationssignale für die Mitarbeiter*innen, die alle in einer bestimmten Form ihren besonderen Beitrag für die Produkte leisten.«

»Design awards send signals that have a strong motivational impact on employees, all of whom contribute to the products in some way or another.«

DIRK UPTMOOR

SENIOR DESIGNER, SYSTEM 180 GMBH

→ **Für welche Situationen oder Unternehmen sind die Tribünenmodule gedacht?**

Die SitUp-Tribünenfamilie setzt gezielt auf Kommunikation in einer kollaborativen Arbeitsumgebung, versteht sich also als ein Mindset für agile Arbeitsmethoden. Die Tribünenmodule unterstützen einen gemeinsamen Ideenaustausch im Rahmen informeller Treffen. Rollen verleihen Mobilität, dadurch ist das SitUp ortsungebunden und kann in Räumen flexibel eingesetzt werden. Die drei verschiedenen SitUp-Formen bieten, je nach Anforderung, eine Vielzahl an Möglichkeiten der Anordnung.

Welche Veränderungen bringt die Corona-Pandemie für dieses Nutzungskonzept?

Die Arbeitswelt von heute befand sich bereits vorher im Wandel. Neben eines generellen Change des Mindsets findet aktuell ein Umdenken in Bezug auf neue Arbeitsraumkonzepte statt. Auf der einen Seite werden in puncto Sicherheit neue Konzepte für den Einzelarbeitsplatz entwickelt, wie etwa Home Office oder isolierte Arbeitszonen, auf der anderen Seite stehen Firmenräume fortan verstärkt für einen Ausbau kollaborativer Raumbespielungen zur Verfügung. SitUp fügt sich spielerisch in diesen neuen Anforderungspool ein. Die Sitzanordnung mit auferlegten Abstandsregeln kann bereits bei zwei SitUps eingehalten werden. Die glatten, melaminbeschichteten Sitzflächen können problemlos mit einem wasserbasierten Desinfektionsmittel abgewischt werden.

Wie wichtig sind Designawards für den Erfolg Ihrer Produkte?

Designawards sind eine wichtige Message, sowohl für bestehende Partner*innen und Kund*innen als auch für Personen, die die Marke System 180 noch nicht kennen. Intern sind sie starke Motivationssignale für die Mitarbeiter*innen, die alle in einer bestimmten Form ihren Beitrag für die Produkte leisten. Auch wenn unsere Produkte im Nutzen, der Funktion und im Design für sich sprechen, können Designawards bei der einen oder anderen Kaufentscheidung den letzten Ausschlag geben.

Sie haben das Design intern entwickelt – warum nicht mit einem externen Designbüro?

System 180 steht seit Beginn seiner Firmengründung für eigenständiges Design, das stark aus seiner Funktion hergeleitet wird. Das über Dekaden erarbeitete und entwickelte Know-how ist unser Unique Selling Point, der uns von Wettbewerbern absetzt und von unseren Partner*innen geschätzt wird. System 180 öffnet sich bereits seit vielen Jahren dem Themengebiet Open Innovation, welches stetig weiter ausgebaut wird, um Partner*innen mit in den Entwicklungsprozess einzubeziehen.

Der erste Prototyp des multioptionalen Verbindungsprinzips geht auf das Jahr 1981 zurück. 1991 gegründet, wächst das Unternehmen seither kontinuierlich und baut das Möbel- und Raumsystem beständig aus. System 180 produziert ausschließlich in Berlin und erhielt bereits 2013 den Focus Open Silver für den Stehtisch der DT-Line.

www.system180.com

→ **What kind of situations or companies are the bleacher modules intended for?**

The SitUp bleacher family is specifically aimed at facilitating communication in a collaborative working environment; in other words, it sees itself as a mindset for agile working. The bleacher modules encourage a mutual exchange of ideas in the context of informal meetings. The casters add mobility, so SitUp can be rolled to wherever it's needed and used flexibly anywhere in the space. The three different shapes of the SitUp modules permit a multitude of different arrangements, depending on requirements.

How does the corona pandemic affect that usage concept? Does it change it in any way?

The world of work was already changing before corona struck. In addition to a general change of mindset, a change of thinking in relation to new workspace concepts is taking place right now as well. On the one hand, new concepts with an emphasis on safety are being developed for individual workstations, like the home office or isolated working zones, whereas on the other hand companies will have more in-house space available for expanding their collaborative working practices. SitUp is a good fit with this new pool of requirements and adds a playful touch. Even with just two SitUps, it's possible to create a seating arrangement that complies with the distancing rules. The smooth, melamine-coated seat surfaces can be wiped down with a water-based disinfectant without any problem at all.

How important are design awards for the success of your products?

Design awards send an important message, both for existing partners and customers and for people who aren't familiar with the System 180 brand yet. Internally, they have a strong motivational impact on employees, all of whom contribute to the products in some way or another. Even though the benefits, function and design of our products speak for themselves, design awards can sometimes be the factor that ultimately sways a customer's decision.

You developed the design internally – why not with an external design firm?

Ever since it was founded, System 180 has stood for independent design that is largely derived from its function. The know-how we've acquired and developed over the decades is our unique selling point – it's what sets us apart from our competitors and is valued by our partners. System 180 has been embracing the idea of open innovation for many years, and we're constantly expanding on it so as to involve our partners in the development process.

The first prototype of the multioptional connection principle dates back to 1981. Founded in 1991, the company has been growing steadily ever since and is constantly expanding its furniture and space configuration system. System 180 produces exclusively in Berlin. Its standing table for the DT-Line won a Focus Open Silver back in 2013.

www.system180.com

SILVER WINGS VORHANGSCHIENE / CURTAIN TRACK
→ SEITE / PAGE 104

SPECIAL MENTION — TÜBINGER STUHL 2.0 — STUHL / CHAIR

→ SEITE / PAGE 105

SPECIAL MENTION | TAO → SEITE / PAGE 106 | POLSTERMÖBEL UPHOLSTERED FURNITURE

SPECIAL MENTION — EXO — → SEITE / PAGE 107 — GAMING-STUHL / GAMING CHAIR — 98 / 99

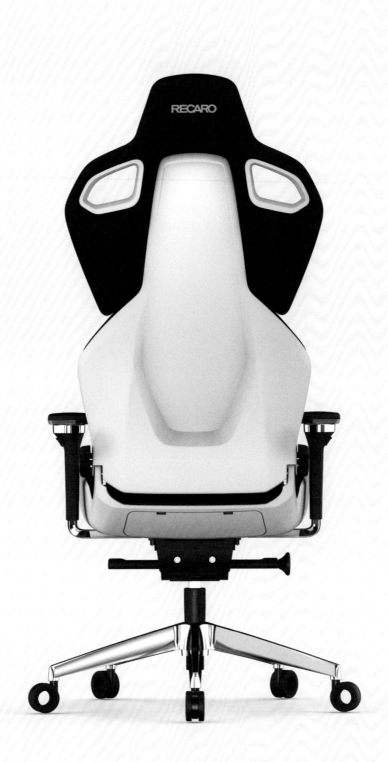

| SPECIAL MENTION | FRANK & FREI
→ SEITE / PAGE
108 | BETT
BED |

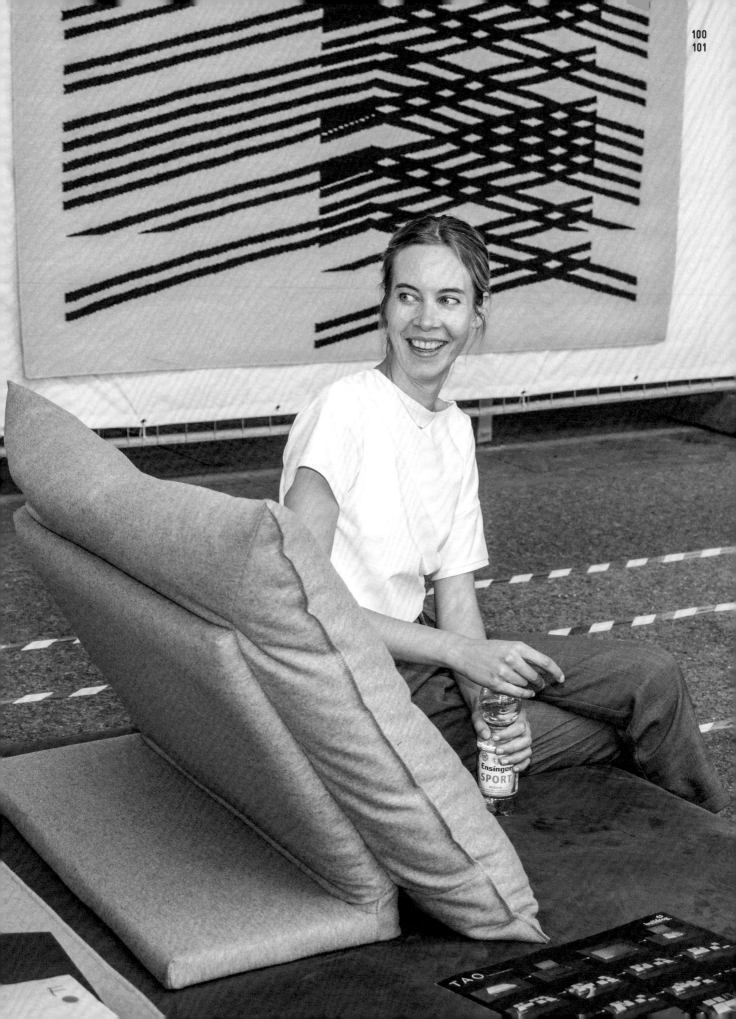

SILVER   MASTERLIFT 5   SCHREIBTISCH / DESK

JURY STATEMENT

Ein sehr sauber gestalteter Tisch mit einer interessanten Formgebung der Fußelemente. Gut gelöst wurden die direkte Integration von Leuchten und der Ansatz, lange und tiefe Einheiten zu schaffen. Damit lassen sich endlich Meetings im Stehen realisieren.

An immaculately designed desk with interestingly shaped feet. The direct integration of lighting and the possibility of creating long and deep units are compelling solutions. As a result, stand-up meetings are finally an option.

HERSTELLER / MANUFACTURER
Inwerk GmbH
Meerbusch

DESIGN
Inhouse
Karl Bell

VERTRIEB / DISTRIBUTOR
Inwerk GmbH
Meerbusch

→ SEITE / PAGE
94

Die schlanken Ausleger aus Vollstahl lassen das Tischgestell mit seiner elektrischen Höhenverstellung scheinbar schweben und verleihen ihm eine markante Optik. Die modulare Grundidee erlaubt neben der Einzelkonfiguration auch die Verkettung zu langen oder tiefen Kombinationen. Das ermöglicht auch Steh-Sitz-Konferenztische, die bis auf 134 Zentimeter Höhe ausfahrbar sind. Kabel, Steuereinheit und Steckdosen passen sich dabei der Verstellung an. Leuchten, Abschirmungen oder Ablagen können direkt angebaut werden.

The slender all-steel feet are reminiscent of outriggers, giving the electric height-adjustable desk frame a striking appearance and making it seem to hover in mid-air. Thanks to the modular concept, the basic unit can either be used on its own or combined to create long or deep configurations, permitting arrangements like sit-stand conference tables that can be raised to a height of up to 134 centimetres. The cable, control unit and sockets adjust to suit the change in height. Lamps, privacy panels or trays can be attached directly to the desk.

SILVER — POP-UP OFFICE — BÜROELEMENTE / OFFICE ELEMENTS

JURY STATEMENT

Ein sehr ehrliches System, das mit offenen Kanten und stets sichtbarem Material spielt. Anders als ähnliche Lösungen im Markt sind die Elemente leichter, flexibler nutzbar und versprühen einen optimistischen Charme. Die Usability stimmt, die Elemente sind multifunktional und bestehen aus nachhaltigen Werkstoffen.

A very honest system that puts its cards on the table and always leaves the material visible. As compared to similar solutions on the market, the elements are lighter, more flexible and full of optimistic charm. In addition to their convincing usability, the elements are multifunctional and made of sustainable materials.

HERSTELLER / MANUFACTURER
Ongo GmbH
Stuttgart

DESIGN
UP Designstudio GmbH & Co. KG
Stuttgart

VERTRIEB / DISTRIBUTOR
Ongo GmbH
Stuttgart

→ SEITE / PAGE
95

Unsere heutige Arbeitswelt befindet sich in rasantem Wandel. Während immer häufiger Roboter oder künstliche Intelligenz monotone Arbeitsabläufe übernehmen, werden die Mitarbeiter*innen von morgen kreativer, kollaborativer und agiler arbeiten – und dafür passende Konzepte und Strukturen benötigen. Das Pop-Up Office besteht aus einzelnen, beliebig erweiterbaren Bausteinen. Der mittels einer hydraulischen Hubsäule höhenverstellbare Schreibtisch aus Multiplex ist fahrbar. Ihm zur Seite steht der bewährte Hocker, der durch seinen gewölbten Fuß dynamisches Sitzen ermöglicht und dadurch nachweislich die Konzentration steigert. Der ebenfalls in der Höhe verstellbare Hocker kann mit einer Magnethalterung in eine Nut am Tisch eingehängt werden. Verschiedene Boards – neben extrem leichten Pin- und Whiteboards sind auch fahrbare Modelle sowie Monitorboards erhältlich – komplettieren das Office-Konzept.

The world of work is changing rapidly. While monotonous work routines are increasingly being taken over by robots or artificial intelligence, tomorrow's workforce will adopt more creative, more collaborative and more agile practices – and they'll need the right concepts and structures to create the appropriate environments. The Pop-Up Office consists of individual components that can be added to as required. Equipped with a hydraulic height-adjustment system, the multiplex desk is mobile and paired with the manufacturer's tried-and-tested stool, which has a domed base for active sitting and thus demonstrably improves concentration. The stool is also height-adjustable and can be hooked into a groove in the desk by means of a magnetic holder. Various boards – including extremely light pin- and whiteboards, as well as mobile models and monitor boards – put the finishing touches to the office concept.

SILVER WINGS VORHANGSCHIENE / CURTAIN TRACK

> **JURY STATEMENT**
>
> Der Y-förmige Querschnitt baut zur Decke hin eine visuell stabile Verbindung auf und leitet durch die Verjüngung formal sehr stimmig zum Vorhang über. Der Ansatz, eine Vorhangschiene nicht weiter zu entmaterialisieren, sondern sie als selbstbewusstes Element zu definieren, ist sehr erfrischend.
>
> Besides creating a sturdy-looking connection with the ceiling, the Y-shaped cross-section also ensures a harmonious transition to the curtain thanks to its tapering shape. Defining a curtain track as a self-assured element of the interior rather than dematerialising it to the max is a very refreshing approach.

Mit ihrem Y-förmigen Querschnitt präsentiert sich die Vorhangschiene trotz der reduzierten Formensprache markant im Raum. Innerhalb der beiden Schenkel platzierte Trägerelemente sorgen für den notwendigen Abstand von der Decke und gleichen Unebenheiten der Deckenfläche aus. Die Schiene ist für ein- und zweiläufige Vorhänge erhältlich und mit entsprechenden Trägervarianten auch wandseitig montierbar.

With its striking, Y-shaped cross-section, the curtain track cuts an eye-catching figure despite its understated design language. Mounting elements between the two arms of the Y ensure the necessary distance from the ceiling and even out any irregularities in its surface. Available with both single and double tracks, the product can also be attached to the wall by using different mounts.

HERSTELLER / MANUFACTURER
Zimmer + Rohde GmbH
Oberursel

DESIGN
Schmiddem Design
Berlin

VERTRIEB / DISTRIBUTOR
Artline
Oberursel

→ SEITE / PAGE
96

SPECIAL MENTION

TÜBINGER STUHL 2.0 — STUHL / CHAIR

JURY STATEMENT

Der Stuhl ist so schlicht wie funktional. Die Oberflächen sind fein gearbeitet, die Beine durchdringen die Sitzfläche und sind extrem stabil damit verbunden. Dank der Linoleumoberfläche entsteht eine interessante Haptik.

The chair is as straightforward as it is functional. The surfaces are finely crafted, the legs pierce the seat and are attached to it with extremely sturdy joints. The linoleum surface adds an interesting tactile quality.

HERSTELLER / MANUFACTURER
Pozsgai Möbelschreinerei
Heitersheim

DESIGN
Inhouse

VERTRIEB / DISTRIBUTOR
Pozsgai Möbelschreinerei
Heitersheim

→ SEITE / PAGE
97

Bis 1973 produzierte die Tübinger Stuhlfabrik Schäfer einfache, robuste und preiswerte Stühle für die Gastronomie. Der sogenannte Tübinger Stuhl geht auf einen Entwurf von Adolf Gustav Schneck zurück und wurde immer wieder leicht variiert.

Der Tübinger Stuhl 2.0 ist eine Neuinterpretation dieses Traditionsprodukts und basiert auf dem gleichen Konstruktionsprinzip der durchgestemmten Beine, das zugleich ein charakteristisches Gestaltungsmerkmal darstellt. Während die Beine aus geölter Eiche oder Esche bestehen, setzt sich die Sitzfläche aus mehrschichtigem Birkenholz und einer Oberfläche aus farbigem Linoleum zusammen. Für die Modernisierung des Klassikers gaben die Stuhlfabrikerben grünes Licht.

Up until 1973, the Schäfer chair factory in Tübingen produced simple, robust and inexpensive chairs for the food service sector. The model that became known as the Tübinger Stuhl (Tübingen Chair) can be traced back to a design by Adolf Gustav Schneck and was slightly modified numerous times over the years.

The Tübinger Stuhl 2.0 is a new interpretation of this tradition-steeped product and is based on the same construction principle of through-mortise legs that doubles as a distinctive feature of the design. The legs are made of oiled oak or ash, while the seat consists of multilayered birch topped with coloured linoleum. The modernisation of the classic design was given the green light by the chair factory's heirs.

SPECIAL MENTION   TAO   POLSTERMÖBEL
UPHOLSTERED FURNITURE

JURY STATEMENT

Trotz seiner Größe wirkt das Möbel leicht, ja geradezu schwebend. Das Konzept lädt ein, immer wieder andere Konfigurationen zu schaffen, was dank der leicht bedienbaren Mechanik und logischen Bewegungsabläufe tatsächlich auch so gelebt werden kann.

Despite its size, the furniture looks light and even appears to float in mid-air. The concept tempts users to keep trying out different configurations – and thanks to the easy-to-use mechanism and logical sequence of movements, there's nothing to stop them acting on their impulse.

HERSTELLER / MANUFACTURER
Bullfrog Marketing Design GmbH
Michelau

DESIGN
Studiobeier GmbH
Kurt Beier
Kati Quinger
Michelau

VERTRIEB / DISTRIBUTOR
Bullfrog Marketing Design GmbH
Michelau

→ SEITE / PAGE
98

Im Wohnbereich sind heute oftmals flexible und multifunktionale Lösungen gefragt. Mit seinen individuell konfigurierbaren Auf- und Anbaumöglichkeiten trifft das Polstermöbel den Nerv der Zeit. Die Grundkomponente besteht aus einem massiven, auf einer Stahlunterkonstruktion aufgebauten Holzplateau und einem Polsterelement. Ein 360-Grad-Dreh- und Schiebemechanismus ermöglicht unterschiedlichste Positionierungen des Polsters im Raum – bis zu 60 Zentimeter über die Plateaufläche hinaus. Bereits aus zwei Grundelementen lassen sich mit verschiedenen Zusatzfeatures wie aufstellbaren Rückenkissen, Armteilen und Hockern individuelle Wohnsituationen bis hin zur Nutzung als Schlafstätte gestalten.

Nowadays, flexible and multipurpose solutions are often sought after for living areas. So with its individually configurable layout and add-on options, this upholstered furniture is very much in tune with the times. The basic component consists of a solid wooden platform built on a steel substructure and topped with an upholstered element. A 360-degree swivel-and-slide mechanism means the cushion can be placed in all sorts of different positions – even protruding up to 60 centimetres beyond the platform. Just two basic elements with various additional features like fold-up back cushions, armrests and stools are all it takes to create individual living room arrangements or even a bed.

SPECIAL MENTION — EXO — GAMING-STUHL / GAMING CHAIR

JURY STATEMENT

Verglichen mit anderen Vertretern seines Genres präsentiert sich dieser Gaming-Stuhl wohltuend schlicht, dafür umso hochwertiger und im Detail durchdacht. Seine speziellen Einstelloptionen unterstützen die Zielgruppe sinn- und wirkungsvoll. Auch die Ästhetik und die formalen Ausprägungen passen letztlich zu den besonderen Erwartungen der Nutzer*innen.

Compared with other representatives of its genre, this gaming chair is refreshingly simple but far more upscale and meticulously designed right down to the last detail. Its special adjustment options provide meaningful and effective support for the target group, while the aesthetic and formal characteristics are a good fit with the special expectations of its users.

HERSTELLER / MANUFACTURER
Recaro Gaming GmbH & Co. KG
Stuttgart

DESIGN
Recaro Holding Inhouse Design
Stuttgart

VERTRIEB / DISTRIBUTOR
Recaro Gaming GmbH & Co. KG
Stuttgart

→ SEITE / PAGE
99

---

eGaming ist mittlerweile nicht nur eine beliebte Freizeitbeschäftigung, sondern ein professionell betriebenes, internationales Wettbewerbs-Business. Die Gamer*innen sitzen dabei oft stundenlang höchst konzentriert vor ihren Monitoren und benötigen speziell konzipierte Sitzgelegenheiten. Der Exo unterstützt während des Spiels und erleichtert die Erholung in den oftmals kurzen Pausen. Dafür bietet der Stuhl vier Positionen – der Attack-Modus entspricht etwa mit seiner nach vorne geneigten Rückenlehne der hohen Anspannung und Konzentration der Spieler*innen in dieser Phase des Spiels. Form und Kontur der Sitzschale sowie die fünffach justierbaren Armlehnen halten den Körper in optimaler Position, während die Seitenwangen am hohen Kopfteil die Gamer*innen von der Umgebung abschirmen. Die Formgebung und auch die Verstellung der Rückenlehne zitieren bewusst Elemente aus der Autositz-Sparte des Unternehmens.

Nowadays gaming isn't just a popular leisure activity, it's a professionally operated, international competition business as well. Because they often spend hours at a time in front of their monitors, deep in concentration, gamers need specially designed chairs. Exo provides support during play and makes it easier to relax during the often short breaks. The chair offers a choice of four different positions – including Attack mode, which tilts the backrest forward in keeping with the high level of tension and concentration during this phase of the game. Both the shape and contouring of the shell and the 5D armrests hold the body in the optimal position, while the projecting side bolsters on the high head section screen the gamer from their surroundings. Both the design and the adjustment of the backrest deliberately echo elements from the company's automotive seating division.

SPECIAL MENTION   FRANK & FREI   BETT / BED

JURY STATEMENT

Sehr gut umgesetzt ist hier der modulare Leitgedanke des Betts und die einfache Möglichkeit des Verbindens. Die Konstruktion ist sachlich, klar und prägnant, wobei die Lüftungsschlitze ein spielerisches Gegenmoment einbringen.

Both the modular guiding principle behind the bed and the simple solution for connecting the individual parts have been implemented very effectively. The construction is objective, clear and striking, while the ventilation slots add a playful counterpoint.

HERSTELLER / MANUFACTURER
Stadtnomaden GmbH
Riedhausen

DESIGN
Inhouse
Linda Krapf
Oliver Krapf

VERTRIEB / DISTRIBUTOR
Stadtnomaden GmbH
Riedhausen

→ SEITE / PAGE
100

Das variable Plattformbett lässt sich an unterschiedlichste Wohn- und Lebenssituationen anpassen und ist rasch und unkompliziert aufgebaut. Grundgerüst des Betts bilden vier Elemente aus Pappel-Sperrholz, die mittels Gurtverbindungen zwischen Kopf- und Fußteil eine stabile, dennoch luftig anmutende Auflage für Matratzen unterschiedlicher Breite schaffen. V-förmige Aussparungen in der Sperrholzfüllung sorgen für ausreichende Belüftung der Polsterauflage. Kopf- und Fußteil, Füße sowie die optional erhältliche Rückenlehne sind unter dem Aspekt der Langlebigkeit und Nachhaltigkeit aus Birkenholz gefertigt.

Das Bettenkonzept hält Lösungen von 90 bis zu 180 Zentimetern Matratzenbreite bereit, auch an unterschiedliche Matratzenlängen lässt es sich angleichen.

The variable platform bed can adapt to all sorts of different living settings and situations and is designed for quick and straightforward assembly. The basic framework consists of four elements made of poplar plywood and connected with belts between the head and foot sections to create a stable yet airy-looking platform for mattresses of different widths. V-shaped cutouts in the plywood panels ensure adequate ventilation. The head and foot sections, the legs and the optional headboard are made of birch and produced with a focus on durability and sustainability.

The bed concept provides solutions for mattresses between 90 and 180 centimetres wide and can also be adapted to mattresses of different lengths.

108
109

1 → SEITE / PAGE
112–117

2 → SEITE / PAGE
118, 122

3 → SEITE / PAGE
119, 123

4 → SEITE / PAGE
120, 124

LIFESTYLE, ACCESSOIRES
LIFESTYLE, ACCESSORIES

GOLD:
1 **COUGAR**
Papero
Markt Schwaben

SPECIAL MENTION:
2 **1247**
Belchengruppe GmbH
Basel

3 **LICHTSTAHL**
ArtenHaus
Wiernsheim

4 **MURG**
Rolf-Roland Wolf GmbH
Weißenbach a. Lech
Österreich / Austria

Sich mit positiven, sinnlich anregenden oder funktional durchdachten Dingen zu umgeben, macht den Alltag einfacher, facettenreich und inspirierend. Das gilt insbesondere für die kleinen Produkte, die uns durch den ganzen Tag begleiten, uns in bestimmten Situationen unterstützen, das Leben erleichtern oder ganz einfach zur Freude gereichen.

Surrounding oneself with positive things that appeal to the senses or are equipped with clever functions makes everyday life simpler, more varied and more inspiring. That particularly applies to little products that accompany us throughout the day, provide support in certain situations, make life easier or simply give us pleasure.

GOLD   COUGAR   RUCKSACK
BACKPACK

COUGAR

RUCKSACK

LIFESTYLE, ACCESSOIRES
LIFESTYLE, ACCESSORIES

FOCUS GOLD

GOLD COUGAR RUCKSACK BACKPACK

JURY STATEMENT

Der Rucksack überzeugt durch seine sensibel gestalteten Details, durch die gute Verarbeitung außen sowie innen und schließlich durch das verwendete Material. Die Haptik ist lederähnlich weich, die materialspezifische Knitteroptik lässt den Rucksack positiv altern. Zudem unterstreicht der Charity-Zusatz die Glaubwürdigkeit des Konzepts.

The sensitively designed details, good workmanship inside and out and, last but not least, the choice of material, add up to a highly compelling backpack. It has a soft, leather-like feel, while the crumpled look specific to the material means the product will age with dignity. In addition, the charitable donation underscores the project's credibility.

HERSTELLER / MANUFACTURER
Papero
Markt Schwaben

DESIGN
Inhouse

VERTRIEB / DISTRIBUTOR
Papero
Markt Schwaben

→ SEITE / PAGE
112–114, 115–117

Daypacks sind vor allem für ein junges Publikum zu einem unentbehrlichen Lifestyle-Accessoire geworden. Dieser Rucksack punktet nicht nur durch seine reduzierte, schnörkellose Form, sondern überzeugt vor allem durch sein Material: Er wird aus umweltverträglichem, reiß- und wasserfestem Kraftpapier gefertigt. Kraftpapier besteht zu fast 100 Prozent aus Zellulosefasern, die in diesem Fall aus nachhaltig bewirtschafteten Wäldern stammen.

Im Inneren bietet der vegane, mit Leinenfutter ausgekleidete Rucksack Platz für einen Laptop oder A4-Dokumente, in drei zusätzlichen Innentaschen finden weitere Utensilien Platz. Die Haupttasche lässt sich mit einem Zipper und Klettverschluss verschließen und so in der Größe anpassen. Für die Hersteller sind Nachhaltigkeit und Umweltschutz Teil ihrer Philosophie: Für jeden verkauften Rucksack geht ein Teil des Erlöses an ein Aufforstungsprojekt.

Daypacks have become a must-have lifestyle accessory, especially for youngsters. This backpack scores high marks not just for its understated, no-nonsense form but for its material too: it is made of eco-friendly, tear-resistant and waterproof Kraft paper, which consists almost entirely of cellulose fibres – in this case from sustainably managed forests.

Inside, the vegan, linen-lined backpack provides enough space for a laptop or A4 documents and has three additional pockets for utensils. The main compartment is closed with a zipper and features a variable Velcro fastening for adjusting the size. Sustainability and protecting the environment are a key part of the manufacturer's philosophy: for every backpack sold, the company donates a portion of the proceeds to a reforestation project.

JULIA RIEBE INHABER,
TIM RIEBE   PAPERO

»Wir sprechen Menschen an, die ihr Konsumverhalten und dessen Auswirkungen auf Mensch, Tier und Umwelt hinterfragen.«

»We appeal to people who reflect on their consumer behaviour and its impact on humans, animals and the environment.«

JULIA RIEBE
TIM RIEBE

OWNERS, PAPERO

→ **Mal etwas überspitzt formuliert: Rucksäcke hat die Welt mehr als genug – wieso braucht es da noch den Cougar?**

Rucksäcke werden gern genutzt, da sie praktisch und komfortabel zu tragen sind. Unsere Rucksäcke haben dazu noch ein außergewöhnlich schönes Design und bestehen aus dem nachwachsenden Material Kraftpapier. Tierwohl und Umweltschutz stehen bei uns an erster Stelle. Plastik- und chemiefrei, vegan und der Zero-Waste-Gedanke sind wesentliche Bestandteile unserer Unternehmensphilosophie, die wir leben. Im Cougar Rucksack sind alle guten Gründe vereint.

Ihr Grundmaterial wird in Deutschland produziert – wie wichtig sind Ihnen nachvollziehbare Lieferketten?

Wir legen großen Wert darauf, dass alle unsere Produkte stets gesundheits- und umweltverträglich sind. Das Holz, aus dem der Grundstoff für das Kraftpapier gewonnen wird, ist aus deutscher Waldwirtschaft und mit dem FSC-Siegel ausgezeichnet. Ebenso wichtig sind uns faire sowie ethische Arbeitsbedingungen bei der Produktion. Das Kraftpapier wird in Deutschland von einem alteingesessenen Unternehmen produziert, das sich auf die Herstellung von recyclebaren und nachwachsenden Materialien spezialisiert hat. Eine unabhängige Prüfkommission kontrolliert regelmäßig deren Arbeitsbedingungen.

An welche Zielgruppen wenden Sie sich mit Ihren Produkten?

Generell sind unsere Unisex-Rucksäcke für jede und jeden geeignet, der oder die auf der Suche nach einem leichten Begleiter für Alltag, Freizeit und Urlaub ist. Darüber hinaus sprechen wir Menschen an, die ihr Konsumverhalten und dessen Auswirkungen auf Mensch, Tier und Umwelt hinterfragen. Wir möchten gemeinsam mit unseren Kund*innen neue und langlebige Alltagslieblinge mit nachwachsenden Rohstoffen entwerfen. Für jeden Kauf einer Tasche oder eines Rucksacks spenden wir einen Teil an den gemeinnützigen Verein Primaklima e.V. für Aufforstungsprojekte.

Lassen sich die Produkte aus Kraftpapier reparieren – und wie steht es um die Langlebigkeit?

Reparaturen sind möglich. Das Kraftpapier ist robust und auch bei Regen bleibt der Inhalt trocken. Dennoch: Ein besonderes Material braucht manchmal auch eine achtsame Nutzung – dann hat man lange Freude an seinem Papero.

Die Idee zu ihrem Unternehmen kam Julia und Tim Riebe, als sie vergeblich nach einer robusten, veganen Tasche aus nachwachsenden Rohstoffen und dazu mit schöner Optik suchten. Sie nahmen die Sache selbst in die Hand und produzieren seit 2018 unter dem Label Papero Taschen und Rucksäcke aus dem Basisrohstoff Kraftpapier.

www.papero-bags.de

→ **Not to put too fine a point on it: the world has more than enough backpacks – why does it need the Cougar?**

People like using backpacks because they're practical and comfortable to carry. On top of that, our backpacks have an unusually attractive design and are made of Kraft paper, which is a renewable material. Animal welfare and protecting the environment are our top priorities. No plastics or chemicals, vegan, zero waste – those are the key components of our company philosophy and we live by its principles. All those good reasons come together in the Cougar backpack.

Your basic material is produced in Germany – how important are transparent supply chains to you?

We attach great importance to ensuring that all our products are eco-friendly and don't have any adverse impact on health. The wood that the raw material for the Kraft paper is obtained from is sourced from German forests and FSC-certified. And we consider fair and ethical working conditions in production just as important. The Kraft paper is produced in Germany by an old-established company that specialises in making recyclable and renewable materials. Their working conditions are regularly monitored by an independent auditing body.

What target groups are your products aimed at?

In general our unisex backpacks are suitable for anyone and everyone who's looking for a lightweight companion for everyday life, leisure time and holidays. We also appeal to people who reflect on their consumer behaviour and its impact on humans, animals and the environment. Together with our customers, we want to develop new, long-lasting everyday favourites made of renewable raw materials. We donate part of the proceeds from every bag or backpack sold to the Primaklima e.V. nonprofit for its reforestation projects.

Can the products made of Kraft paper be repaired – and how durable are they?

Repairs are possible. The Kraft paper is robust and the contents stay dry even when it rains. Even so: sometimes a special material calls for careful usage – then you'll get years of enjoyment out of a Papero.

The idea for founding their company came to Julia and Tim of Papero when they were looking for a robust, vegan bag made of renewable raw materials that was attractive to look at as well. They couldn't find one. So they took the matter into their own hands and have been producing bags and backpacks out of Kraft paper under the Papero label since 2018.

www.papero-bags.de

SPECIAL MENTION | 1247 → SEITE / PAGE 122 | ARMBANDUHREN WATCHES

SPECIAL MENTION — LICHTSTAHL → SEITE / PAGE 123 — KAPSELHEBER / BOTTLE OPENER

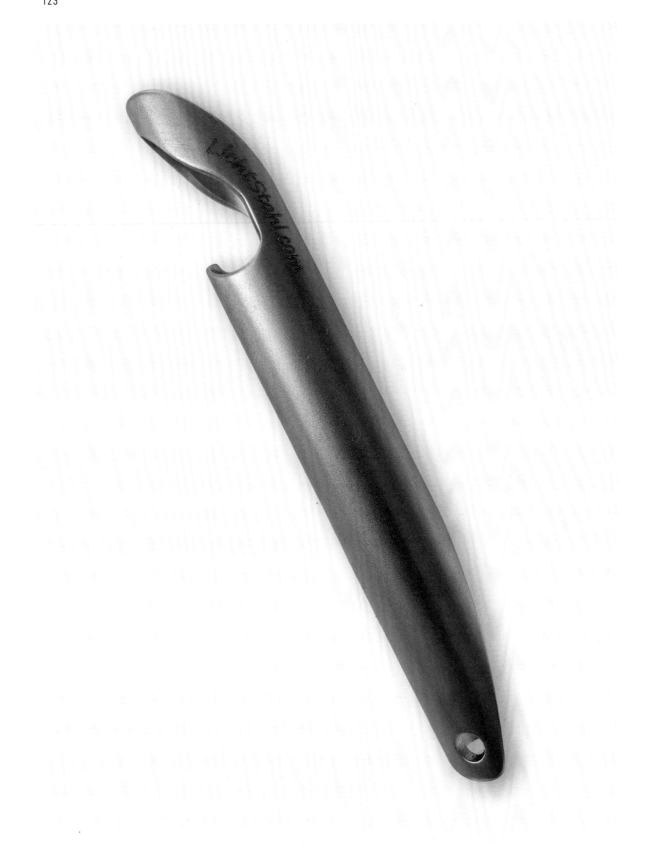

SPECIAL MENTION | MURG | BRILLENFASSUNG EYEWEAR FRAME
→ SEITE / PAGE
124

SPECIAL MENTION   1247   ARMBANDUHREN
                                WATCHES

> **JURY STATEMENT**
>
> Die beiden Armbanduhren sind trotz ihrer reduzierten Form sehr detailreich und markant gestaltet. Das besondere Augenmerk liegt natürlich auf den Zifferblättern, deren analoge Anzeige die Stunden vielleicht etwas entspannter und lässiger vergehen lässt.
>
> Despite their understated form, the two watches are richly detailed and strikingly designed. Particular attention has been paid to the dials, whose analogue displays might succeed in making wearers feel more relaxed and easygoing about the passing hours.

HERSTELLER / MANUFACTURER
Belchengruppe GmbH
Basel
Schweiz / Switzerland

DESIGN
Inhouse

VERTRIEB / DISTRIBUTOR
Belchengruppe GmbH
Basel
Schweiz / Switzerland

→ SEITE / PAGE
118

Die Gehäuseformen der mechanischen Armbanduhren orientieren sich an klassischen Mustern, zugleich betonen Kantigkeit und Facettierung die Eigenständigkeit des Entwurfs. Die Zifferblätter spielen ebenfalls mit der gewohnten Wahrnehmung: Das Modell 120° zeigt drei Kreisabschnitte, die für den Vormittag, den Nachmittag und den Abend stehen. Beim Zifferblatt Visuren wiederum lösen sich die Markierungen völlig von den gewohnten Positionen und erinnern an Sonnenstrahlen oder an die Sichtlinien zwischen den fünf Belchenbergen des Dreiländerecks um Basel. So verbinden die Uhren schweizerische Präzision mit Intuition und einem andersartigen Zeitgefühl.

Although the cases of the mechanical watches echo classic shapes, their angularity and faceting underscore the originality of the design. The dials likewise play with familiar perceptions: the 120° model divides the circle into three sections representing morning, afternoon and evening, whereas the markings on the Visuren dial detach themselves from their familiar positions completely and are reminiscent of sunbeams or the sightlines between the five mountains of the Belchen System in the tri-border area around Basel. The watches thus combine Swiss precision with intuition and a totally different sense of time.

SPECIAL MENTION — LICHTSTAHL — KAPSELHEBER / BOTTLE OPENER

JURY STATEMENT

Eigentlich gibt es schon genügend Kapselheber, doch dieses Exemplar, das immer nochmals verbessert wurde, vereint zwei wichtige Aspekte. Das Tool ist ganz einfach gedacht, zugleich aber hoch funktional. Und: Die Kronkorken werden nur gering geknickt, was das Wiederaufsetzen auf der Flasche ermöglicht.

Even though there are actually already enough bottle openers in the world, this specimen – which has undergone several updates – combines two important aspects. Although the tool's design is extremely simple, it is nevertheless highly functional. What's more, the cap is only slightly bent, enabling it to be put back on the bottle.

HERSTELLER / MANUFACTURER
ArtenHaus
Wiernsheim

DESIGN
Marco Jouvenal
Wiernsheim

VERTRIEB / DISTRIBUTOR
ArtenHaus
Wiernsheim

→ SEITE / PAGE
119

Ein unaufgeregter Alltagsgegenstand, der durch seinen clever durchdachten Hebemechanismus das Öffnen von Kronkorken zur wahren Freude werden lässt. Im Vergleich mit dem 2013 ebenfalls prämierten Vorgängermodell ist diese Version kürzer. So bleibt der Kronkorken beim Öffnen in der Hand – und kann entweder entsorgt oder wieder aufgesetzt werden. Die kufenförmigen, geschwungenen Auflageflächen sorgen für das exakte Ansetzen des Kapselhebers und verhindern, dass der Kronkorken zu stark knickt und so ein Wiederaufsetzen unmöglich wäre. Eine weitere Verbesserung ist der verbreiterte Schlitz im Mantel des Tools sowie die geschickte Gewichtsverteilung: Der Kapselheber verharrt so nach Gebrauch an Ort und Stelle.

A self-possessed everyday object with a cunningly devised lifting mechanism that turns opening crown caps into a pleasure. As compared to the predecessor model, which was likewise awarded a Special Mention back in 2013, this version is shorter. As a result, the cap stays in the hand as the bottle is opened – and can either be disposed of or replaced. The curved contact surfaces are shaped like sledge runners; besides ensuring the opener is correctly positioned, they also prevent the cap from getting too bent, in which case it couldn't be put back on the bottle. Another improvement is the wider slit along the length of the tool and the clever weight distribution, which ensures the bottle opener stays where it's put after use.

SPECIAL MENTION · MURG · BRILLENFASSUNG / EYEWEAR FRAME

JURY STATEMENT

Die verfahrenstechnisch bedingte raue Oberfläche, eigentlich ein Makel, wird hier nicht komplett gefinished, sondern bis zu einem gewissen Grad beibehalten und so geschickt in ein besonderes Merkmal verwandelt, das taktiles Interesse hervorruft. Auch in dieser Modellreihe ist die Scharnierlösung gekonnt umgesetzt.

Rather than being finished to perfection, the rough surfaces resulting from the manufacturing process – usually considered a flaw – are retained to a certain extent and thus cleverly transformed into a special feature that delivers an interesting tactile experience. In this series too, the hinge solution is expertly implemented.

HERSTELLER / MANUFACTURER
Rolf - Roland Wolf GmbH
Weißenbach a. Lech
Österreich / Austria

DESIGN
Inhouse

VERTRIEB / DISTRIBUTOR
Rolf - Roland Wolf GmbH
Weißenbach a. Lech
Österreich / Austria

→ SEITE / PAGE
120

Bisher trat das junge Unternehmen aus Österreich vor allem mit nachhaltig gefertigten Brillenfassungen aus Holz in Erscheinung. Das Basismaterial für die neue Substance-Kollektion ist ein Pulver, das aus dem Wunderbaum, einem schnell wachsenden Wolfsmilchgewächs, gewonnen wird. Wie alle Brillen der Kollektion wird auch Murg im 3D-Druckverfahren hergestellt. Das schraubenlos funktionierende, hochflexible Flexlock-Gelenk am Übergang vom Gestell zum Bügel wird als Teil der Brille gleich mitgedruckt. Verschiedene Schleifprozesse verfeinern die Oberflächen nach dem Druck so lange, bis sie sich haptisch angenehm anfühlen.

Jedes Brillenmodell wird am Standort in Tirol handgefertigt und erfüllt damit den Anspruch einer regionalen, nachhaltigen Produktion mit minimalem ökologischem Fußabdruck.

Up until now, the young Austrian company's market presence has mainly been defined by sustainably produced eyewear frames made of wood. In the case of the new Substance collection, the basic ingredient is a powder obtained from the castor oil plant, a fast-growing member of the spurge family. Like all the eyewear in the collection, Murg is 3D-printed. The screwless Flexlock hinge that attaches the temples to the frame is printed as part of the glasses. Various grinding processes are subsequently used to refine the surfaces until the finish is pleasant to the touch.

Every model is handcrafted at the company's Tyrol site and thus in keeping with its goal of regional, sustainable production with a minimal ecological footprint.

TINA KAMMER   **INTERIORPARK., STUTTGART**

»Im Sinne der Nachhaltigkeit muss man Produkte vom Grundentwurf her betrachten – Parameter, die während des Designs nicht berücksichtigt werden, lassen sich später nicht mehr ändern. Gestalter*innen sollten sich dieser Verantwortung bewusst sein, ihre Kundschaft beraten und auch ökonomische Aspekte erörtern können. Denn Nachhaltigkeit ist längst kein Wohlfühlthema mehr.«

»In the interests of sustainability, you have to consider products in terms of their basic design – parameters that aren't taken into account during the design phase can't be altered later on. Designers should be aware of that responsibility, advise their clients accordingly and be able to discuss economic aspects as well. Because the days when sustainability was a feel-good issue are long gone.«

Tina Kammer ist gelernte Möbelschreinerin und studierte Innenarchitektur in Mainz. Zunächst arbeitete sie im Londoner Architekturbüro Jestico + Whiles, anschließend betreute sie die Markenarchitektur von Firmen wie BMW, Mini oder IBM. Bei der Hugo Boss AG entwickelte sie Ladenkonzepte für den internationalen Markt. Zusammen mit Andrea Herold gründete Tina Kammer 2010 die Online-Plattform InteriorPark. in Stuttgart, die als Research- und Informationsquelle für ausgewähltes, nachhaltiges Design dient. Daneben ist das Unternehmen auch als Beratungs- und Planungsstudio für Innenraumkonzepte aktiv.

www.interiorpark.com

Tina Kammer is a qualified cabinetmaker and studied interior design in Mainz. Her first position was at London architectural practice Jestico + Whiles, after which she was responsible for the corporate architecture of firms like BMW, Mini and IBM. At Hugo Boss AG, she developed store concepts for the international market. Together with Andrea Herold, Tina Kammer founded InteriorPark. in Stuttgart in 2010. The online platform serves as a research and information source for select, sustainable design. The studio also provides consulting and planning services for interior concepts.

www.interiorpark.com

1   → SEITE / PAGE
    130–135

2   → SEITE / PAGE
    136, 138

3   → SEITE / PAGE
    137, 139

LICHT
LIGHTING

128
129

GOLD:
1 R-SL-16
   Corporate Friends GmbH
   Kamenz

SILVER:
2 **LIGHTING PAD LOUNGE**
   Nimbus Group GmbH
   Stuttgart

SPECIAL MENTION:
3 **PROFILE**
   Formagenda
   München / Munich

Licht aus der Leuchtdiode ist längst Standard – denn sie bietet nicht nur Energieeffizienz, sie ermöglicht auch ganzheitlich konzipierte Leuchtensysteme. Neben der Ergänzung mit zusätzlichen Features oder der faszinierenden Miniaturisierung bietet das Halbleiter-Leuchtmittel die Möglichkeit, auch einzelne Leuchten in digitale Steuerungssysteme zu integrieren.

Light-emitting diodes have long since become a standard light source – in addition to being energy-efficient, they permit holistically designed lighting systems as well. Besides enabling additional features and a fascinating degree of miniaturisation, the semiconductor light source also provides the option of integrating individual luminaires into digital control systems.

| GOLD | R–SL–16 | LED-LICHTLEISTE |
| | | LED LIGHT BAR |

R–SL–16

LED–
LICHTLEISTE

LICHT
LIGHTING

FOCUS GOLD

GOLD — R-SL-16 — LED-LICHTLEISTE / LED LIGHT BAR

JURY STATEMENT

Eine herausragende Konstruktion, sehr sauber gestaltet und technisch überzeugend. Besonders faszinieren die miniaturisierten und filigranen Komponenten, die gleichzeitig hoch funktional und variierbar sind. Interessant gelöst wurde die Dimmung der einzelnen Strahler mit einem magnetischen Stift.

An outstanding design with very clean lines and convincing technical solutions. The miniaturised and filigree components are not just fascinating, they're highly functional and variable as well. The magnetic pen used to dim the individual spotlights is an interesting touch.

HERSTELLER / MANUFACTURER
Corporate Friends GmbH
Kamenz

DESIGN
Inhouse

VERTRIEB / DISTRIBUTOR
Corporate Friends GmbH
Kamenz

→ SEITE / PAGE
130–132, 134–135

Speziell für den Einsatz in Vitrinen entwickelt, besteht das formal extrem reduzierte und miniaturisierte Lichtsystem aus zwei Grundelementen: dem eigentlichen Leuchtenprofil mit 16 Millimetern Durchmesser und den frei im Profil platzierbaren LED-Strahlern. Damit lässt sich sowohl eine Grund- als auch eine Akzentbeleuchtung mit nur einem integrierten System realisieren. Das um seine Längsachse drehbare Profil kann Optiken in zwei unterschiedlichen Höhen aufnehmen, wobei die Abstrahlwinkel dann zwischen 20 und 80 Grad variieren. Auch für die einzeln dimmbaren Miniatur-Strahler stehen verschiedene Linsen und Blenden zur Verfügung – so wird es möglich, die Lichtführung exakt auf die Exponate und das Präsentationskonzept anzupassen. Drei Lichtfarben stehen zur Verfügung, der Lichtstrom der Lichtleiste liegt bei 900 Lumen je laufendem Meter. Der Einbau lässt sich vertikal wie auch horizontal vornehmen.

Specially developed for use in showcases, the extremely reductive and miniaturised lighting system consists of two basic elements: the actual bar, which has a diameter of 16 millimetres, and LED spotlights that can be positioned as required. As a result, a single integrated system can be used to provide both basic and accent lighting. The profile rotates around its long axis and can accommodate optics at two different heights, in which case the beam angles vary between 20 and 80 degrees. Various lenses and adapters are available for the individually dimmable miniature spotlights too, enabling the light to be directed and modified to suit the precise requirements of the individual exhibits and presentation concept. Available in a choice of three light colours, the light bar produces luminous flux of 900 lumens per metre and is suitable for both vertical and horizontal installation.

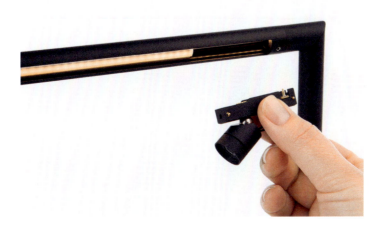

JAN EICKHOFF **GESCHÄFTSFÜHRER,
CORPORATE FRIENDS GMBH**

»Die Lichtleiste transportiert in ihrer extremen Reduktion den Charakter von Schlichtheit, Perfektion und Langlebigkeit.«

»Thanks to its extremely understated look, the light bar conveys simplicity, perfection and longevity.«

JAN EICKHOFF

MANAGING DIRECTOR, CORPORATE FRIENDS GMBH

→ **Die Lichtleiste ist mitsamt ihrer Strahler formal extrem reduziert. Wo bleibt da das Design?**

Die eigentliche Herausforderung liegt ja gerade darin, die beste Form für die gewünschte Funktion zu finden. Die Anforderungen an die Leuchte wie Größe und Aufgabe waren im Vorfeld klar definiert. Dafür galt es, eine Lösung zu finden. Die Formgebung bildet immer die große Klammer, die den Entwicklungsprozess begleitet und zusammenhält. Alles wird permanent hinterfragt, damit das finale Produkt nicht nur seine Funktion erfüllt, sondern benutzerfreundlich, wirtschaftlich und flexibel genug ist, um möglichst viele Anwendungen abzudecken. Dabei muss es im Erscheinungsbild der Produktfamilie und dem Anspruch an unsere Marke gerecht werden. Die Lichtleiste transportiert in ihrer extremen Reduktion auch den Charakter von Schlichtheit, Perfektion und Langlebigkeit.

Die Lichtleiste arbeitet mit 24 Volt und 12 Volt Gleichspannung – weshalb?

Das hat verschiedene Gründe. Die Lichtleiste kann mit einem LED-Band und zusätzlich mit mehreren LED-Strahlern bestückt werden – Grundlicht und Akzentlicht sind also in einem System miteinander kombiniert. Die Strahler werden unabhängig vom Grundlicht betrieben, sind einzeln dimmbar und können einzelne Exponate mit ihrem Licht genau akzentuieren. Da beide Systeme autark arbeiten, werden zwei Netzteile benötigt. Um die Wärmeentwicklung des LED-Strahlers möglichst gering zu halten, haben wir uns für eine Spannungsversorgung mit 12 Volt entschieden, während das LED-Band mit 24 Volt gespeist wird.

Worin lag die größte Herausforderung bei der Entwicklung des Systems?

Unser Ziel war es, eine Profil-Leuchte mit einem minimalen Durchmesser zu entwickeln, die gleichzeitig sowohl lineares als auch punktuelles Licht aufnehmen kann. Dabei sollte die Position der Strahler möglichst frei und schnell veränderbar sein – ohne die Leuchte dabei zu demontieren. Die Entwicklung hat über ein Jahr gedauert. Ein Großteil der Bauteile wurde speziell für die Leuchte angefertigt. Innerhalb dieser sehr engen Grenzen alle Funktionalitäten der Leuchte unterzubringen, war genauso herausfordernd, wie die Zulieferer für die extrem kleinen Bauteile zu finden.

Für welche Usecases ist das Lichtsystem gedacht?

Das Lichtsystem ist speziell für die Beleuchtung von Vitrinen entwickelt worden. Die aufsteckbaren, einzeln dimmbaren Einzelstrahler sind mit dem gesamten Zubehörprogramm wie Wabenraster oder Torblenden unserer C1-mini-Serie kompatibel.

Seit 2011 entwickelt Corporate Friends LED-Leuchten und Lichtsysteme für Museen, Architekten und Planer. Dabei hat sich das Unternehmen aus Kamenz vor allem auf flexible Lichtlösungen im Bereich der Vitrinenbeleuchtung spezialisiert. Eine hohe Material- und Oberflächenqualität stehen ebenso im unternehmerischen Fokus wie die nachhaltige, ökologische und regionale Fertigung der Leuchtenkomponenten.

www.corporatefriends.de

→ **The forms of both the light bar and its spotlights are reduced to the max. What scope does that leave for design?**

That's precisely the challenge: to find the best form for the desired function. The requirements the luminaire had to meet, like its size and purpose, were clearly defined beforehand. Then it was a case of finding an appropriate solution. The form is always the overarching consideration that accompanies the development process and holds everything together. Everything is questioned again and again to ensure that the final product doesn't just perform its function but is user-friendly, cost-efficient and flexible enough to cover as many applications as possible. At the same time, it has to be compatible with the visual identity of the product family and people's expectations of our brand. And thanks to its extremely understated look, the light bar conveys simplicity, perfection and longevity.

The light bar runs on 24 volt and 12 volt direct current – why?

There are various reasons. The light bar can be equipped with both an LED strip and several LED spotlights – i.e. ambient and accent lighting can be combined with one another in a single system. The spotlights are operated independently of the ambient lighting; they can be dimmed individually and used to accentuate individual exhibits with great precision. Because the two systems work independently of one another, two mains adapters are needed. To keep the heat generated by the LED spotlights to a minimum, we decided to use a 12-volt supply, whereas the LED strip has a 24-volt supply.

What was the biggest challenge when you were developing the system?

Our goal was to develop a profile-based luminaire with a minimal diameter that can accommodate both strip and spot lighting. At the same time, we wanted to ensure the position of the spotlights could be changed as freely and quickly as possible – without having to take the light apart. The development work took over a year. A lot of the components were custom-made. Accommodating all the light's functions within these very narrow limits was just as much of a challenge as finding suppliers for the extremely small components.

Which use cases is the lighting system intended for?

It was specially developed for illuminating display cases. The click-in, individually dimmable spotlights are compatible with the entire range of accessories for our C1-mini series, which includes honeycomb grids and barn door adapters.

Corporate Friends has been developing LED luminaires and lighting systems for museums, architects and planners since 2011. In particular, the Kamenz-based company specialises in flexible lighting solutions for illuminating display cases and attaches just as much importance to top-quality materials and finishes as it does to the sustainable, ecological and regional production of the components used to make its luminaires.

www.corporatefriends.de

SILVER **LIGHTING PAD LOUNGE**
→ SEITE / PAGE 138

PENDELLEUCHTE
PENDANT LUMINAIRE

SPECIAL MENTION
PROFILE
→ SEITE / PAGE 139
LEUCHTENFAMILIE
LIGHTING FAMILY

SILVER

LIGHTING PAD LOUNGE
PENDELLEUCHTE
PENDANT LUMINAIRE

JURY STATEMENT

Trotz ihres akustisch notwendigen Durchmessers wirkt die Pendelleuchte durchaus filigran. Das sichtbare Akustikmaterial ist Teil des Designkonzepts, genauso die holzsichtige Oberseite, aus der ein interessanter Materialkontrast resultiert. Während Baldachine häufig formal nicht überzeugen, ist dieser hier sehr sauber gestaltet.

Despite its large diameter, which is necessary for acoustic reasons, the pendant lamp makes an extremely slender and subtle impression. The visible acoustic material is part of the design concept, as is the wooden upper side – an interesting contrast of materials. And while unsatisfactory canopies are the norm, this one is as immaculate as the luminaire itself.

HERSTELLER / MANUFACTURER
Nimbus Group GmbH
Stuttgart

DESIGN
Inhouse

VERTRIEB / DISTRIBUTOR
Nimbus Group GmbH
Stuttgart

→ SEITE / PAGE
136

Speziell für das Private Living, aber auch für Loungebereiche in Hotels und Gastronomie wurde die Pendelleuchte entwickelt. Sie schafft mit ihrem blendfreien und fast unsichtbaren Lichtaustritt nicht nur atmosphärische Lichtinseln, sondern ist durch ein Formvlies auf der Unterseite auch akustisch wirksam. Kleine, in das Pad integrierte Hochleistungs-LEDs ermöglichen über so genannte Freiformlinsen eine Lichtausbeute von bis zu 5000 Lumen. Die Farbtemperatur lässt sich von Warmweiß bis Neutralweiß variieren. In die hölzerne, aufwendig in Form gebogene Oberseite der Leuchte sind ebenfalls LEDs integriert, die eine angenehme, indirekte Deckenaufhellung erzeugen. Unterschiedliche Farboptionen für das Akustikvlies und verschiedene Holzvarianten lassen viel Spielraum für individuelle Vorlieben.

Specially developed for private living spaces, the pendant luminaire is equally suitable for hotel lounges and restaurants. Besides conjuring up atmospheric islands of light with its glare-free and almost invisible light source, it provides acoustic benefits too thanks to the moulded fleece that covers its underside. The small high-performance LEDs that are integrated into the pad are equipped with free-form lenses that produce an output of up to 5,000 lumens. The colour temperature can be varied from warm to neutral white. LEDs are also integrated into the elaborately moulded wooden upper side of the luminaire and cast a pleasant, indirect glow on the ceiling. Different colour options for the acoustic fleece and various types of wood provide plenty of scope for individual preferences.

| SPECIAL MENTION | PROFILE | LEUCHTENFAMILIE / LIGHTING FAMILY |

JURY STATEMENT

Sowohl die Proportionen als auch die Oberflächen-Materialitäten sind sehr gelungen. Mit ihren klassischen Tastschaltern greifen die Leuchten die gelernte Bedienung auf. Sehr clever konzipiert ist das Strangpressprofil, aus dem sowohl die Leuchtenkörper wie auch die Baldachine gefertigt sind.

Both the proportions and the material qualities of the surfaces are very compelling. With their classic pushbutton switches, the luminaires are based on a learned control concept. The extruded profile that serves as both the body and the canopy is very cleverly designed.

HERSTELLER / MANUFACTURER
Formagenda GmbH
München / Munich

DESIGN
Christophe de la Fontaine
Neukirchen

VERTRIEB / DISTRIBUTOR
Formagenda GmbH
München / Munich

→ SEITE / PAGE
137

Bei dieser Leuchtenfamilie ist der Name Programm: Pendel-, Tisch- und Stehleuchte setzen mit ihren ausgeklügelten Profillösungen individuelle Statements. Die Formensprache ist sachlich und klar – gezielte Einschnitte und Abrundungen verleihen den Konturen der verschiedenen Leuchten dennoch einen eigenen, prägnanten Look. Je nach Ausführung lässt sich über das integrierte Bedienfeld an der Leuchte mittels eines Tasters das Licht dimmen oder die Farbtemperatur ändern. Für die Optik stehen von robuster Pulverbeschichtung über eloxierte Oberflächen bis hin zu einem veganen Lederbezug viele Möglichkeiten offen.

The name of this lighting family says it all: the suspension, table and floor luminaires use their ingenious profile solutions to make individual statements. The design language is clear and objective, while deliberately placed cutouts and curves nevertheless give the contours of the various lamps a distinctive, striking look. The integrated control panel on the luminaire features switches for dimming the light or, in the case of certain models, changing the colour temperature. Customers can choose from a wide range of different looks, from a robust powder-coated finish or anodised surfaces all the way to vegan leather.

1 → SEITE / PAGE 142–147

2 → SEITE / PAGE 148, 152

3 → SEITE / PAGE 149, 153

4 → SEITE / PAGE 150, 154

5 → SEITE / PAGE 151, 155

FREIZEIT, SPORT, SPIEL
LEISURE, SPORTS, PLAY

GOLD:
1 **EGGI**
  Einfach Gut Spielen
  Trebra

SILVER:
2 **HAVEN**
  BeSafe
  Krøderen
  Norwegen / Norway

SPECIAL MENTION:
3 **MICRO AIR HOPPER**
  Micro Mobility Systems AG
  Küsnacht
  Schweiz / Switzerland

4 **SWEET TREAT**
  Eis GmbH
  Bielefeld

5 **RHAPSODY**
  Carl Sauter Pianofortemanufaktur
  GmbH & Co. KG
  Spaichingen

Einst Leerraum für Entspannung, Rekreation und absichtsloses Sein, ist die Freizeit längst prall gefüllt mit Aktivitätsangeboten und entsprechenden Produkten für unterschiedlichste Neigungen, Altersgruppen und Erlebnisversprechen. Schön, wenn es da Dinge gibt, die keinen unmittelbaren Zweck erfüllen wollen – oder bewusst mehrdeutig sind.

Whereas free time was once a vacuum waiting to be filled with relaxation, recreation and delectable idleness, today it is crammed full with a vast spectrum of activity options and the corresponding products for diverse inclinations, age groups and experiences. Every now and again, it's nice when there are things that serve no direct purpose – or are deliberately ambiguous.

GOLD   EGGI   SPIELDING
                                                PLAYTHING

SPIEL—
DING

GOLD   EGGI   SPIELDING
                                                PLAYTHING

FREIZEIT, SPORT, SPIEL
LEISURE, SPORTS, PLAY

142
143

EGGI

EINFACH GUT spielen

FOCUS
GOLD

GOLD EGGI SPIELDING / PLAYTHING

JURY STATEMENT

Ein ganz simples Ding, irgendwie. Es entzieht sich tradierten Spielzeug-Kategorien. Aber einmal angestoßen, überrascht es mit seinen eigenwilligen Bewegungen und fordert selbst Erwachsene zum Spiel auf. Außerdem fasziniert das Spielding mit seiner samtigen, perfekten Holzoberfläche.

A very simple thing, somehow. It doesn't fit into any of the traditional toy categories. But once set in motion, it surprises users with its idiosyncratic movements and will make even adults want to play with it. The wooden object's velvety, perfect finish is no less fascinating.

HERSTELLER / MANUFACTURER
Einfach Gut Spielen
Trebra

DESIGN
Inhouse
Silke Kegeler
Trebra

VERTRIEB / DISTRIBUTOR
Einfach Gut Spielen
Trebra

→ SEITE / PAGE
142–144, 146–47

Nicht nur Kinder spielen gern – der kleine, eiförmige Körper spricht mit seiner Form und der haptisch angenehmen Oberfläche aus Holz Menschen jeden Alters an. Das »Spielding« ist aber viel mehr als ein fein gearbeiteter Handschmeichler – seine inneren Qualitäten treten zutage, wenn man ihn hinlegt und leicht anstößt. Dann erwacht Eggi zum Leben, bewegt sich autark und bringt es sogar fertig, aufrecht zu stehen. So schafft eine einfache Spielidee Gesprächsanreize und regt womöglich noch dazu an, über physikalische Phänomene nachzudenken. Das Spielding wird unter dem Aspekt der Nachhaltigkeit vom Entwurf bis zum fertigen Produkt in Deutschland gefertigt.

It's not just children who like to play – this little ovoid's shape and the pleasant feel of its wooden surface will appeal to people of all ages. But the »plaything« is much more than a finely crafted palm stone: putting it down and giving it a gentle tap reveals unforeseen inner qualities. Then Eggi comes to life, moves autonomously and even manages to stand upright. A simple play idea thus provides an interesting conversation starter and might even encourage users to reflect on physical phenomena. From the design to the finished product, the plaything is made in Germany with a focus on sustainability.

SILKE KEGELER   **INHABERIN, EINFACH GUT SPIELEN**

»Meine Spielideen entstehen, während ich selbst spiele.«

»My play ideas come to me while I'm playing myself.«

SILKE KEGELER

OWNER, EINFACH GUT SPIELEN

→ **Wie entstand die Idee zum Produkt?**

Meine Spielideen entstehen, während ich selbst spiele – mit Formen, Farben, Materialien, optischen Effekten, haptisch interessanten Angeboten und Bewegungen in der Natur. Kombiniert mit dem bewussten Sehen durch das Naturstudium schaffe ich mir bereits seit Jahrzehnten eine Gedächtnisbibliothek mit Formen und Funktionsprinzipien.

Das mechanische Grundprinzip von Eggi entdeckte ich bereits vor 40 Jahren. Damals baute ich es, winzig klein, mit den mir damals zur Verfügung stehenden Materialien und Mitteln. Heute, als ausgebildete Designerin, habe ich die Gestaltung dieses Spieldings optimal abgerundet.

Spielzeug muss unterschiedlichen Normen gerecht werden – welche galt es bei Eggi zu berücksichtigen?

Meine Ideen entstehen aus meiner ideellen Bibliothek. Danach lege ich fest, für welche Zielgruppe die Idee geeignet ist. Dementsprechend wird die Gestaltung an notwendige und für Spielzeug geltende Sicherheitsnormen geknüpft und realisiert. Da ich beim Spiel mit Eggi keine Alters- oder Entwicklungsgrenzen beobachten konnte, war das Ziel, das Spielding für Menschen jeden Alters ab drei Jahren ergonomisch handhabbar und sicher zu machen.

Nachhaltigkeit ist heute ein großes Thema – auch bei Spielzeug. Wie stellt man sicher, dass das Rohmaterial aus solchen Quellen kommt?

Nachhaltigkeit bedeutet für mich neben der Umsetzung ökologischer, ökonomischer und sozialer Aspekte hauptsächlich Sinnhaftigkeit. Das heißt: Ist das zu gestaltende Produkt notwendig, dient es einem positiven Zweck, ist es weitestgehend dauerhaft nutzbar? Ist es generationsübergreifend, besteht es überwiegend aus nachwachsenden Rohstoffen, und wenn nicht, sind sie recycelbar?

Wir produzieren in unserer eigenen Manufaktur, unsere Produkte werden aus heimischen, zertifizierten Hölzern und Farben hergestellt. Die Materialien beziehen wir von europäischen Herstellern und Händlern, mit denen wir in engem Kontakt stehen.

Wie bleibt man gegenüber Spielzeug aus Fernost konkurrenzfähig?

Unter dem preislichen und quantitativen Aspekt ist es natürlich für eine kleine Manufaktur, die hier in Deutschland produziert, schwierig, konkurrenzfähig zu sein. Entscheidender für mich sind aber die Fragen nach dem Spielwert, der Qualität, der Nachhaltigkeit und der Individualität. Die Palette unserer Entwürfe reicht von sehr individuellen Produkten, die durch einen hohen handwerklichen Anteil geprägt sind, bis hin zur bewusst spartanischen Gestaltung, die den funktionalen Charakter unterstützt und deshalb auch eine quantitativ höhere Serienproduktion zulässt.

Seit 1994 betreibt Produktdesignerin Silke Kegeler im thüringischen Trebra eine kleine Manufaktur, die sich auf die Herstellung von Holzspielzeug spezialisiert hat. Von der kreativen Idee bis zur Umsetzung in ein bespielbares Produkt geschieht alles vor Ort. Die Firma fertigt eigene Entwürfe, übernimmt aber auch die Produktion von Holzspielzeug für externe Auftraggeber.

www.einfach-gut-spielen.de

→ **Where did you get the idea for the product?**

My play ideas come to me while I'm playing myself – with shapes, colours, materials, optical effects, things with interesting tactile properties and movements in nature. Combined with the conscious way of seeing things I've learned from studying nature, that's enabled me to create a memory library of forms and functional principles over the decades.

I discovered the basic mechanical principle behind Eggi 40 years ago. Back then I made a tiny little version of it using the materials and means that were available to me at the time. Today, as a trained designer, I've been able to add the finishing touches and perfect the little plaything.

Toys have to meet various standards – which ones did you have to consider when designing Eggi?

My ideas come from my conceptual library. After that, I define which target group the idea is suitable for and match the design with the necessary product and toy safety standards accordingly before it's implemented. Because I didn't observe any age-related or developmental barriers to playing with Eggi, the goal was to make the plaything ergonomic and safe for people of all ages, from three years old upwards.

Sustainability is a major theme nowadays – does that go for toys too? How do you ensure that the raw materials come from appropriate sources?

To me, sustainability means more than factoring ecological, economic and social aspects into the equation; it's mainly about meaningfulness. In other words: is the product you want to design necessary, does it serve a positive purpose, is it as long-lasting as it can possibly be? Is it cross-generational, does it largely consist of renewable raw materials, and if not, are the materials recyclable?

We have our own boutique production operation, and our products are made of indigenous, certified wood and certified paints. We source our materials from European manufacturers and dealers that we're in close contact with.

How can you compete against toys from the Far East?

In terms of price and quantities, it's obviously difficult for a small boutique manufacturer that produces here in Germany to be competitive. But for me, it's things like play value, quality, sustainability and individuality that are the more crucial aspects. Our designs cover a broad spectrum, from very individual products that are largely handcrafted all the way to deliberately spartan design that underpins the functional character and is therefore suitable for higher-volume production.

Based in Trebra, Thuringia, product designer Silke Kegeler has been running a small boutique manufacturing company that specialises in wooden toys since 1994. Everything happens on site – from the creative idea all the way to its implementation in the form of a product that is genuinely fit for play. Besides producing its own designs, the firm also manufactures wooden toys for external clients.

www.einfach-gut-spielen.de

SILVER HAVEN BABYTRAGE BABY CARRIER
→ SEITE / PAGE 152

SPECIAL MENTION	MICRO AIR HOPPER → SEITE / PAGE 153	KINDERMOBILITÄT CHILD'S MOBILITY TOY	148 149

| SPECIAL MENTION | SWEET TREAT → SEITE / PAGE 154 | SEXTOY SEX TOY |

SPECIAL MENTION RHAPSODY KLAVIER / PIANO

→ SEITE / PAGE 155

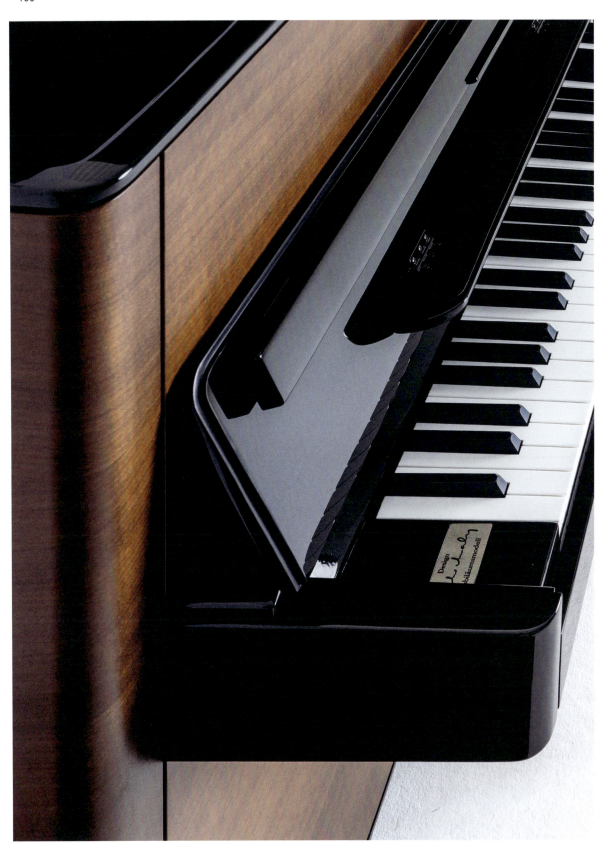

SILVER HAVEN BABYTRAGE / BABY CARRIER

JURY STATEMENT

Eine sehr gut gestaltete Alternative zu etablierten Produkten. Die weiterentwickelten Details, neue Funktionalitäten und Materialqualitäten kommen sowohl dem Baby wie auch dem Träger oder der Trägerin zugute.

A very well-designed alternative to established products. Both the baby and the wearer benefit from the sophisticated details, new functionalities and the properties of the materials.

HERSTELLER / MANUFACTURER
BeSafe
Krøderen
Norwegen / Norway

DESIGN
White Id
Schorndorf

VERTRIEB / DISTRIBUTOR
BeSafe
Krøderen
Norwegen / Norway

→ SEITE / PAGE
148

Im Körperkontakt mit ihren Eltern fühlen sich Babys und Kleinkinder sicher und geborgen. Auch die viel direktere Interaktion zwischen Vater, Mutter und Kind spricht für eine Babytrage. Mit drei verschiedenen Trageoptionen, eine davon für ältere Kinder auf dem Rücken, ist Haven sehr flexibel einsetzbar und dabei einfach und verständlich in der Handhabung. Die Trage passt sich an die Größe und den Körperbau der Eltern an, ein aufblasbares Luftkissen stützt das Baby und sorgt für eine gleichmäßige Gewichtsverteilung beim Tragen in Blickrichtung. Ohne Probleme kann die innen aus Tencel und Baumwolle, außen aus Polyester und Spandex bestehende Trage nach mehrmaligem Gebrauch in die Waschmaschine wandern.

Physical contact with their parents makes babies and infants feel safe and secure. The fact that a baby carrier permits much more direct interaction between father, mother and child is another point in its favour. With three different wearing options, including one on the back for older children, Haven is extremely flexible yet simple and intuitive to use. The carrier adapts to the size and build of the parent, while an inflatable air cushion supports the baby and ensures its weight is evenly distributed when carried in the outward-facing position. Made of Tencel and cotton on the inside and polyester and spandex on the outside, the carrier is simply cleaned in the washing machine after several uses.

SPECIAL MENTION — MICRO AIR HOPPER — KINDERMOBILITÄT / CHILD'S MOBILITY TOY

JURY STATEMENT

Die weiche, komplett runde Körperform weckt Assoziationen an ein freundliches Tier, wirkt sympathisch und baut keine Hürden zwischen Kind und Spielgerät auf. Die Gummilippe verhindert das Einklemmen zarter Kinderbeine und erhöht die Kippstabilität. Und wer die Ventilposition bemerkt, kann nochmals schmunzeln.

The soft, totally round shape of the body triggers associations with a friendly animal, looks endearing and doesn't create any barriers between the child and the toy. The rubber lip prevents little legs from getting pinched and increases stability. And last but not least, the position of the valve will bring a smile to your face.

Kinder haben einen natürlichen Bewegungsdrang und wollen mobil sein. Deshalb stehen Fahrzeuge mit Rollen, aber auch Hüpftiere und -bälle bei ihnen hoch im Kurs. Dem Micro Air Hopper gelingt es, beides in einem Gerät zu kombinieren. Ein aufblasbares Fantasietier in kindgerechter Form sorgt für das bekannte Hüpfgefühl. Es lässt sich mit einem Chassis verbinden, dessen 360-Grad-Rollen aus Polyurethan besonders leise sind. Das Spielgerät ist sowohl für den Gebrauch drinnen als auch für draußen konzipiert und kann schon bei den Allerkleinsten Koordinationsfähigkeit und Gleichgewichtssinn fördern.

Children have a natural urge to move and want to be mobile. That's why they love vehicles on casters so much, as well as bouncy animals and space hoppers. The Micro Air Hopper combines both types of toy. An inflatable fantasy animal with a child-friendly shape provides the familiar bouncing sensation and is combined with a chassis equipped with 360-degree polyurethane casters that are unusually quiet. The toy is intended for both indoor and outdoor use and can help even the very smallest children improve their coordination and balance.

HERSTELLER / MANUFACTURER
Micro Mobility Systems AG
Küsnacht
Schweiz / Switzerland

DESIGN
Inhouse

VERTRIEB / DISTRIBUTOR
Micro Mobility Systems D GmbH
Geislingen

→ **SEITE / PAGE**
149

SPECIAL MENTION

SWEET TREAT

SEXTOY
SEX TOY

JURY STATEMENT

Im Gegensatz zu anderen Vertretern dieser Produktgattung versprüht dieses kleine Intim-Spielzeug einen freundlichen Charme. Durch das assoziative Spiel mit dem Eistüten-Motiv wirkt es humorvoll und lädt zum vielfältigen Ausprobieren ein. Sehr gut gestaltet ist nicht nur die Verpackung dieses Gerätes, sondern aller Sextoys der aktuellen Serie.

Unlike other representatives of its product genre, this little toy radiates a friendly charm. The playful associations triggered by the ice-cream motif add a humorous touch and encourage experimentation. The packaging of both this device and all the other sex toys in the current series is very well designed.

Bunt, frech, süß – obwohl Sextoys schon lange der Schmuddelecke entwachsen sind, setzt dieser Auflegevibrator nochmals neue Maßstäbe und präsentiert sich ganz unverklemmt als hippes Vergnügungsspielzeug für Frauen, die ihre Sinnlichkeit selbstbewusst und unbeschwert leben. Die rotierenden Lamellen der Eiskugel sorgen, je nach Wahl der Rotationsstufe, für sanfte bis kräftige Stimulation der Klitoris. Die Steuerung verbirgt sich ebenso wie der aufladbare Geräteakku in der Eiswaffel. Das wasserdicht verarbeitete Toy besteht aus hautfreundlichem Silikon und lässt sich unkompliziert mit Wasser und Seife reinigen.

Colourful, cheeky, cute – even though sex toys came out of the closet long ago, this lay-on vibrator sets new standards and candidly presents itself as a hip pleasure toy for women who take a self-confident and carefree approach to exploring their sensuality. Depending on the setting selected, the rotating fins on the scoop of ice-cream provide gentle to powerful stimulation of the clitoris. Both the controls and the rechargeable battery are hidden in the cone. The waterproof toy is made of skin-friendly silicone and designed for easy cleaning with soap and water.

HERSTELLER / MANUFACTURER
Eis GmbH
Bielefeld

DESIGN
Inhouse

VERTRIEB / DISTRIBUTOR
Eis GmbH
Bielefeld

→ SEITE / PAGE
150

SPECIAL MENTION — RHAPSODY — KLAVIER / PIANO

JURY STATEMENT

Ein von Sehgewohnheiten bestimmtes Produkt wie ein Musikinstrument neu zu gestalten, ist in gewisser Hinsicht ein Wagnis. Dennoch, es kann gelingen, wie dieses Klavier zeigt. Dem monolithischen Korpus stehen abgerundete Kanten gegenüber, das Klavier scheint mit seinen filigranen Füßen über dem Boden zu schweben.

In a way, redesigning a product that's conventionally defined by ingrained expectations of its appearance – like a musical instrument – is a risky venture. But as this piano goes to show, that can be a successful undertaking too. The monolithic body is contrasted with rounded edges, while the filigree feet make the piano seem to hover above the floor.

HERSTELLER / MANUFACTURER
Carl Sauter Pianofortemanufaktur
GmbH & Co. KG
Spaichingen

DESIGN
Peter Maly
Aumühle

VERTRIEB / DISTRIBUTOR
Carl Sauter Pianofortemanufaktur
GmbH & Co. KG
Spaichingen

→ SEITE / PAGE
151

Im Erscheinungsbild ungewöhnlich, in der Materialität außergewöhnlich – das »Jubiläumspiano« zum 200-jährigen Bestehen der Traditionsfirma Carl Sauter bricht mit konventionellen Sehgewohnheiten. Die beiden sanft abgerundeten Korpusseiten umfassen die Vorderfront, wobei die horizontale Maserung des satinierten Nussbaumfurniers nur durch zwei Sichtfugen unterbrochen wird. Fast unvermittelt und im rechten Winkel zur Front springt der glänzend schwarz lackierte Spieltisch hervor. Der prägnante Materialkontrast wiederholt sich in den Böden, die den Korpus oben und unten einfassen. Mit seiner schlichten Eleganz, kombiniert mit feinster Klangtechnik und Mechanik, löst das Klavier den Anspruch, ein Meisterstück zu sein, ohne Weiteres ein.

Far from ordinary in its appearance, extraordinary in terms of its materiality – the »anniversary piano« launched to mark the 200th birthday of the tradition-steeped Carl Sauter company breaks with the usual visual conventions. The two gently rounded sides of the body embrace the front section, forming an expanse of satin-finish walnut veneer that is interrupted only by two visible joints. The gleaming, black-lacquered console juts out almost abruptly at a right angle to the front. This striking contrast of materials is repeated in the panels that cover the top and bottom of the body. With its simple elegance, combined with the finest sound and action, the piano easily fits the bill for a masterpiece.

REINHARD RENNER
TEAMS DESIGN GMBH, ESSLINGEN

»Produkte für den internationalen Markt müssen so konzipiert sein, dass sie auch überall funktionieren. In den USA beispielsweise wird in anderen Proportionen gedacht, Materialien und Konstruktionen sollten visuell Robustheit vermitteln. Es ist unglaublich spannend, diese Unterschiede zu sehen und mit Kolleg*innen aus anderen Kulturkreisen passende Lösungen zu finden.«

»Products for the international market have to be conceived in such a way that they work anywhere. In the USA, for instance, people think in different proportions, so materials and designs ought to convey robustness visually, too. It's incredibly exciting to see those differences and come up with suitable solutions with colleagues from different cultures.«

Reinhard Renner hat an der HfG Pforzheim studiert und ist Diplom-Industriedesigner (FH). 1978 kam er zum Büro Slany Design in Esslingen, 1987 wurde er zum geschäftsführenden Gesellschafter berufen und war federführend beim Aufbau von Teams Design sowie dessen internationaler Expansion. 2019 verabschiedete er sich aus der aktiven Rolle als Geschäftsführer, bleibt als Hauptgesellschafter aber nach wie vor dem Büro verbunden. Reinhard Renner war unter anderem Lehrbeauftragter an der TU Dresden.

www.teamsdesign.com

Reinhard Renner studied at Pforzheim University's School of Design and graduated as an industrial designer. He joined Slany Design in Esslingen in 1978, was appointed managing partner in 1987 and went on to oversee both the formation of Teams Design and its international expansion. In 2019 he retired from his active role as managing partner but is still associated with the company as its main shareholder. Among other things, Reinhard Renner taught as an associate lecturer at TU Dresden (Dresden University of Technology).

www.teamsdesign.com

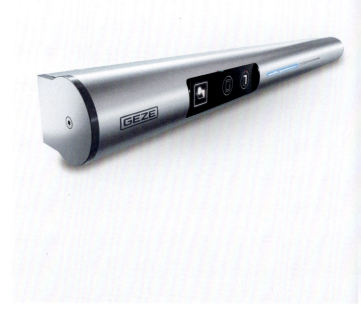

1 → SEITE / PAGE
160, 164

2 → SEITE / PAGE
161, 165

3 → SEITE / PAGE
162, 166

4 → SEITE / PAGE
163, 167

GEBÄUDETECHNIK
BUILDING TECHNOLOGY

SILVER:
1 **ROOMTOUCH 5"**
Busch-Jaeger Elektro GmbH
Lüdenscheid

SPECIAL MENTION:
2 **F1200+**
Geze GmbH
Leonberg

3 **ALTHERMA 3 HPC**
Daikin Europe N.V.
Oostende
Belgien / Belgium

4 **IP TOUCH 7"**
Busch-Jaeger Elektro GmbH
Lüdenscheid

Design unterstützt die Architektur in ihrem Bestreben, ästhetische und zugleich funktionale, effiziente und zukunftstaugliche Gebäude zu realisieren. Dazu gehören insbesondere die weiten Welten der Haustechnik samt Heizung und Kommunikation. Intelligentes Design erhöht deren Akzeptanz und Nutzerfreundlichkeit und baut emotionale Brücken zur reinen Funktionalität.

Design supports architecture in its endeavours to create aesthetic buildings that are nevertheless functional, efficient and futureproof. This particularly applies to the broad field of domestic technology, including heating and communication. Intelligent design increases acceptance, enhances user-friendliness and builds emotional bridges that make pure functionality more accessible.

SILVER ROOMTOUCH 5" GEBÄUDESTEUERUNGSPANEL
→ SEITE / PAGE BUILDING CONTROL PANEL
164

SPECIAL MENTION | ALTHERMA 3 HPC
→ SEITE / PAGE 166
WÄRMEPUMPENKONVEKTOR
HEAT PUMP CONVECTOR

SPECIAL MENTION | IP TOUCH 7" | GEBÄUDESTEUERUNGSPANEL / BUILDING CONTROL PANEL

→ SEITE / PAGE 167

SILVER ROOMTOUCH 5" GEBÄUDESTEUERUNGSPANEL / BUILDING CONTROL PANEL

JURY STATEMENT

Nicht nur die Hardware mit ihrem schlanken und gebürsteten Edelstahlrahmen ist sorgfältig gestaltet, auch das Interface besticht durch eine grafisch sehr klare und sich erklärende Symbolik. Das erleichtert nicht nur die Nutzung, sondern unterstützt ebenso die Langlebigkeit des Steuerungspanels.

The meticulous design extends beyond the slender, brushed stainless steel frame of the hardware to the interface itself, which features crystal clear and self-explanatory icons. Besides simplifying usage, that also benefits the control panel's longevity.

Das mit dem KNX-Standard kommunizierende Touchpanel dient zur Steuerung unterschiedlicher Funktionen im Smart Home. Das Bedienkonzept basiert auf von Smartphones erlernten Gesten und erlaubt das intuitive Abrufen von Funktionen oder ganzen Raumszenen. Ein integrierter Sensor aktiviert das Panel, wenn sich eine Person nähert, ein anderer Sensor passt die Hinterleuchtung des Displays an die Raumhelligkeit an. Dank einer speziellen Unterputzdose ragt das rechteckige Panel nur elf Millimeter über die Wandoberfläche und lässt sich waagerecht oder senkrecht anbringen.

The touch panel communicates via the KNX standard and is used to control various functions in the smart home. The UI concept is based on the gestures learned from smartphones and provides intuitive access to functions or entire room scenarios. An integrated sensor activates the panel when it detects somebody approaching, another sensor adapts the backlighting of the display to the brightness in the room. Thanks to a special flush-mounted box, the rectangular panel only protrudes 11 millimetres from the surface of the wall and can be fitted vertically or horizontally.

HERSTELLER / MANUFACTURER
Busch-Jaeger Elektro GmbH
Lüdenscheid

DESIGN
Inhouse
Dörte Thinius

VERTRIEB / DISTRIBUTOR
Busch-Jaeger Elektro GmbH
Lüdenscheid

→ SEITE / PAGE
160

SPECIAL MENTION F1200+ FENSTERANTRIEB / WINDOW DRIVE

JURY STATEMENT

Ein sauber gestaltetes Produkt, das sich auch additiv einsetzen lässt, sich also formal bewusst zurücknimmt. Das ist erfrischend für ein technisches Produkt, das eine rein dienende Funktion übernimmt.

A meticulously designed product that is also suitable for retrofitting and therefore deliberately understated. That's refreshing for a technical product that performs a purely auxiliary function.

HERSTELLER / MANUFACTURER
Geze GmbH
Leonberg

DESIGN
Inhouse

VERTRIEB / DISTRIBUTOR
Geze GmbH
Leonberg

→ SEITE / PAGE
161

Für die Fassade als Visitenkarte eines Gebäudes sind raumhohe Fenster- und Türelemente heute ein wichtiger Bestandteil. Doch die schweren Fenster und Türen wollen auch geöffnet, geschlossen oder gekippt werden. Hier setzt der Antrieb an, dessen kraftvoller Motor Fenster bis zu 200 Kilogramm drehen und kippen kann. Ein Näherungssensor aktiviert das im schlanken Gehäuse integrierte Bedienfeld. Die Steuerung erfolgt über kapazitative Touchbuttons, eine LED-Anzeige gibt Auskunft über den Status des Antriebs und die Öffnungsweite des Fensters.

Nowadays floor-to-ceiling window and door elements are an important feature of the facade, which serves as the calling card of a building, so to speak. But the heavy windows and doors have to be opened, closed or tilted too. This is where the electric drive comes in: its powerful motor can turn and tilt windows weighing up to 200 kilograms. A proximity sensor activates the control panel integrated into the slender housing. The interface consists of capacitive touch buttons and an LED display that indicates the status of the drive and the opening width of the window.

SPECIAL MENTION   ALTHERMA 3 HPC   WÄRMEPUMPENKONVEKTOR
HEAT PUMP CONVECTOR

JURY STATEMENT

Geschwungene und glatte Front, flache Bauweise, kaum sichtbare Öffnungen: Das Gerät überzeugt durch seine zurückhaltende Präsenz, die sich bestens in das Wohnumfeld einpasst.

A smooth, contoured front, a flat design, barely visible openings: its inconspicuous presence ensures the convector merges with its domestic setting.

HERSTELLER / MANUFACTURER
Daikin Europe N.V.
Oostende / Ostend
Belgien / Belgium

DESIGN
Yellow Design GmbH
Pforzheim

VERTRIEB / DISTRIBUTOR
Daikin
Airconditioning Germany GmbH
Unterhaching

→ SEITE / PAGE
162

Der Wärmepumpenkonvektor ist eine gute Alternative zu herkömmlichen Radiatoren und versorgt den Raum nicht nur mit warmer, sondern nach Wunsch auch mit kühler Luft. Er arbeitet geräuscharm, wärmt oder kühlt äußerst effektiv bereits bei sehr niedrigen Systemtemperaturen und verbraucht dadurch wenig Energie. Mit einer Tiefe von lediglich 135 Millimetern lässt er sich in so gut wie jede Raumsituation integrieren. Das Bediendisplay fügt sich unauffällig in die Oberseite des Geräts ein.

The heat pump convector is a good alternative to conventional radiators; besides supplying warm air, it can also be used to cool the room if required. It runs quietly, warms or cools extremely effectively even at very low system temperatures and therefore consumes less energy. With a depth of just 135 millimetres, it can be integrated into virtually any interior.
The control display blends in unobtrusively with the top of the convector.

SPECIAL MENTION — IP TOUCH 7" — GEBÄUDESTEUERUNGSPANEL / BUILDING CONTROL PANEL

JURY STATEMENT

Das große Display erlaubt viele Funktionalitäten auf dem Screen übersichtlich abzubilden, was den Umgang mit der Haussteuerung erheblich vereinfacht. Der Edelstahlstreifen unterstreicht sowohl die Wertigkeit des Geräts als auch die klare Formensprache.

Thanks to the big display, a large number of functionalities can be clearly depicted on the screen, considerably simplifying the handling of the smart home technology. The stainless steel strip underscores both the premiumness of the device and the clear design language.

Die mit einem hochauflösenden Touch-Display ausgestattete Steuerungszentrale für das Smart Home arbeitet mit dem KNX-Standard und integriert 480 unterschiedliche KNX-Bedienelemente. Trotz der Komplexität und des großen Funktionsumfangs – auch die Türkommunikation lässt sich integrieren – ist das Bedienkonzept auf intuitiven Zugang ausgelegt. Zudem ist das Panel hörgerätekompatibel, lässt sich per LAN oder WLAN in das Hausnetz integrieren und baut bei Unterputzmontage gerade einmal 7,8 Millimeter auf der Wand auf.

Equipped with a high-resolution touch display, the central control unit for the smart home works with the KNX standard and integrates 480 different KNX control elements. Despite the complexity and the wide range of functions – even the door communication system can be integrated – the UI concept is designed to be intuitively accessible. In addition, the panel is compatible with hearing aids, can be integrated into the home network via LAN or WLAN and projects just 7.8 millimetres from the wall when installed in a flush-mounted box.

HERSTELLER / MANUFACTURER
Busch-Jaeger Elektro GmbH
Lüdenscheid

DESIGN
Inhouse
Dörte Thinius

VERTRIEB / DISTRIBUTOR
Busch-Jaeger Elektro GmbH
Lüdenscheid

→ SEITE / PAGE
163

 1 → SEITE / PAGE 170–175

 2 → SEITE / PAGE 176, 182

 3 → SEITE / PAGE 177, 183

 4 → SEITE / PAGE 178, 184

 5 → SEITE / PAGE 179, 185

 6 → SEITE / PAGE 180, 186

 7 → SEITE / PAGE 181, 187

PUBLIC DESIGN, URBAN DESIGN

Gestaltung für die Öffentlichkeit ist immer auch von der Inszenierung geprägt – besonders Ausstellungskonzepte mit ihren multimedialen Präsentationen von Exponaten und Geschichten bedienen sich dieses Prinzips. Aber auch der öffentliche Raum gewinnt durch gestalterisch durchdachte Systeme an Attraktivität, Transparenz und Vielfalt.

Design for the public is always influenced by the need to stage things to some extent – exhibition concepts are particularly likely to adopt this principle in the form of multimedia exhibits and narratives. But well-designed systems add to the attractiveness, transparency and diversity of the public space too.

GOLD:
1 QUICKMODUL FAZILA
Schreiber Innenausbau GmbH
Geyer

SILVER:
2 AOK PROJEKTHAUS
AOK Baden-Württemberg
Stuttgart

3 CITYDECKS
Livable Cities GmbH
Mannheim

4 CL3710 SLEEPING COMFORT
Recaro
Aircraft Seating GmbH & Co. KG
Schwäbisch Hall

5 KTM MOTOHALL
KTM AG
Mattighofen
Österreich / Austria

SPECIAL MENTION:
6 TROY
StadtPalais Stuttgart –
Museum für Stuttgart
Stuttgart

7 AKTIVE BAHNHÖFE
Internationale Bauausstellung –
IBA Basel 2020
Basel
Schweiz / Switzerland

PUBLIC DESIGN, URBAN DESIGN
PUBLIC DESIGN, URBAN DESIGN

FOCUS GOLD

GOLD

QUICKMODUL FAZILA
GLASVITRINE / GLASS DISPLAY CASE

JURY STATEMENT

Schlanker und filigraner geht es kaum noch. Die Vitrine ist optisch kaum vorhanden, ihre Konstruktion bis ins Detail durchdacht und optimiert. Dank des modularen Konzepts lässt sich die Vitrine schnell aufbauen und anpassen. Nicht nur für Wechselausstellungen ist das ein großer Vorteil.

It doesn't get more slender and filigree than this! Visually, the display case is barely there at all – every detail of the design has been thought through and optimised. Thanks to the modular concept, it's also quick to assemble and adapt – a major benefit, not just for temporary exhibitions.

HERSTELLER / MANUFACTURER
Schreiber Innenausbau GmbH
Geyer

DESIGN
Inhouse

VERTRIEB / DISTRIBUTOR
Schreiber Innenausbau GmbH
Geyer

→ SEITE / PAGE
170–172, 174–175

Die modular aufgebaute und zerlegbare Glasvitrine lässt sich unter anderem für temporäre Ausstellungen in Museen nutzen, da sie demontiert und platzsparend gelagert werden kann. Der Auf- und Abbau geht rasch vonstatten, denn die Montage verlangt lediglich eine Verschraubung horizontaler Profile, während die Senkrechten der Scheiben profillos direkt per Gehrung aufeinander stoßen. Das Ergebnis ist eine rahmenlose, quasi entmaterialisierte Glasvitrine, die das Auge des Betrachtenden nicht ablenkt. Die horizontalen Profile sind mit zehn Millimetern Höhe extrem minimiert und mit den Glasscheiben flächenbündig verklebt. Zum Schutz sensibler Exponate ergänzt man die Vitrine mit einem eigens entwickelten Klimamodul.

Modular and designed for easy disassembly, the glass display case can be taken apart for space-saving storage – making it suitable, among other things, for temporary exhibitions in museums. Setting up and dismantling it takes next to no time, because assembly only involves screwing horizontal profiles together; the vertical edges of the glass panes are mitred so that they are in direct contact with one another. The result is a frameless, virtually dematerialised glass cabinet with nothing to distract the viewer's eye from the exhibits. The extremely slender horizontal profiles are just 10 millimetres high and glued flush with the glass panels. The display cases can be supplemented with a specially developed climate-control module to protect sensitive exhibits.

BERND SCHREIBER GESCHÄFTSFÜHRER,
SCHREIBER INNENAUSBAU GMBH

»Das Quickmodul-Vitrinensystem ist für Sonder- und Wechselausstellungen ebenso ideal wie bei schwierigen Raumsituationen.«

»The Quickmodul display case system is ideal for special and temporary exhibitions, as well as for difficult spaces.«

BERND SCHREIBER

MANAGING DIRECTOR, SCHREIBER INNENAUSBAU GMBH

→ **Wie lange dauerte die Entwicklung des Vitrinensystems?**
Alles zusammengerechnet dürften Konzeption und Umsetzung schnelle sechs Monate beansprucht haben.

Was unterscheidet das Quickmodul von anderen Vitrinen?
Die Grundidee war, den Museen und anderen Kunden ein wiederverwertbares Vitrinensystem anzubieten. Es sollte auch für Laien ohne spezielles Werkzeug schnell sowie unkompliziert aufbau- und zerlegbar sein. Die Vitrinen sollten eine platzsparende Aufbewahrung ermöglichen, gleichzeitig sollte das System nur wenige Einschränkungen in Bezug auf Größe und Zusätze wie Licht bieten. Das System ist auf Nachhaltigkeit ausgelegt – falls beispielsweise eine Scheibe beschädigt ist, kann diese leicht getauscht werden. Bei normalen Vitrinen muss dann die gesamte Vitrine entsorgt werden. Ebenso kann mit dem Nachkauf einzelner Glasscheiben die Vitrine einfach vergrößert oder verkleinert werden.

Welche Herausforderungen gab es bei der Entwicklung zu meistern?
Das Einfassprofil ist die entscheidende Komponente. Das nur zehn Millimeter hohe Profil sollte viele Funktionen gewährleisten: die Stabilität des Glases, die flächenbündigen Übergänge von Glas zum Einfassprofil, die Standsicherheit der Vitrine und die Integration von Zubehör wie Licht, Einlegeböden, Grafikflächen und Klimatisierung. Außerdem sollte die Montage einfach und schnell mit maximal zwei Personen machbar sein. Durch mehrmaligen Musterbau konnte ich immer wieder Elemente ergänzen und erweitern. So bin ich am Ende bei diesem patentierten System angekommen.

Für welche Usecases ist das System gedacht?
Das System ist nicht nur für Museen gedacht, sondern auch für Privatsammler oder Ausstellungshäuser. Insbesondere kann es gut bei schwer zugänglichen Räumen eingesetzt werden. Für Sonder- und Wechselausstellungen, bei denen immer wieder andere Vitrinengrößen benötigt werden, ist das System perfekt geeignet. Die Quickmodul-Vitrine kann bis fünf Zentimeter unter die Deckenhöhe bequem aufgebaut werden. Übrigens lassen sich mit nur einer Eckverbindung auch Raumteiler oder Tastschutzelemente herstellen.

Wie wichtig sind Designawards für den Erfolg Ihrer Produkte?
Durch die Teilnahme an den Wettbewerben ist es mir möglich, einen größeren internationalen Bekanntheitsgrad zu erreichen. Zudem erfolgt eine Produktbewertung von einer unabhängigen Jury, was bei Kund*innen zu einer positiven Kaufentscheidung führen kann.

Die Schreiber Innenausbau GmbH mit Sitz im sächsischen Geyer agiert deutschlandweit als Spezialist für Museumseinrichtungen und Ladenbau. Der handwerkliche Meisterbetrieb konzentriert sich dabei insbesondere auf den Bau hochwertiger Schaukästen und Vitrinen für den Ausstellungsbereich – mit Schwerpunkt auf professionellen Lösungen für Sondervitrinen.

www.schreiber-innenausbau.de

→ **How long did the development of the display case system take?**
In total, I'd say six quick months for the concept and its implementation.

What sets the Quickmodul apart from other display cabinets?
The basic idea was to offer museums and other customers a reusable display case system. We wanted to come up with something that even an amateur can assemble or take apart quickly and easily, without the need for special tools. The cabinets were designed for space-saving storage, and at the same time the system was meant to impose as few restrictions as possible in terms of size and add-ons like lighting. The whole system is designed with an eye to sustainability – if one of the glass panels gets damaged, for instance, it's easy to replace. With a normal cabinet, you have to throw the whole thing away. The display cases can also be made bigger or smaller simply by purchasing individual glass panels at a later date.

What challenges did you have to overcome during the development stage?
The profile that surrounds the top and bottom of the cabinet is the crucial component. It's only 10 millimetres high but has to perform a lot of different functions: it has to guarantee the stability of the glass, the flush transitions between the glass and the surrounding profile, the steady footing of the cabinet and the integration of accessories, including lighting, shelves, graphic elements and climate control. In addition, we were aiming for quick and easy assembly with a maximum of two people. Making several prototypes enabled me to keep enhancing and perfecting certain elements. That's how I eventually arrived at this patented system.

What use cases is the system intended for?
Besides museums, the system is also intended for private collectors or exhibition venues. It's particularly suitable for awkward spaces, as well as being perfect for special and temporary exhibitions, which call for all sorts of different cabinet sizes. The Quickmodul cabinet can easily be built to within five centimetres of the ceiling. And it only takes one corner connection to create room dividers or elements that protect the exhibits from being touched.

How important are design awards for the success of your products?
Taking part in competitions enables me to achieve greater international awareness. On top of that, the product is assessed by an independent jury, which can have a positive impact on customers' purchase decision.

Schreiber Innenausbau GmbH is based in Geyer in Saxony. The company specialises in museum and shop fittings and is active all over Germany. In particular, the craft enterprise builds premium display cases and cabinets for the exhibition sector – with a focus on professional solutions for custom cabinets.

www.schreiber-innenausbau.de

SILVER CL3710 SLEEPING FLUGZEUGSITZ
COMFORT AIRCRAFT SEAT
→ SEITE / PAGE
184

SPECIAL MENTION | TROY → SEITE / PAGE 186 | AUSSTELLUNGSKONZEPTION EXHIBITION CONCEPT

SPECIAL MENTION AKTIVE BAHNHÖFE ERSCHEINUNGSBILD / VISUAL IDENTITY
→ SEITE / PAGE 187

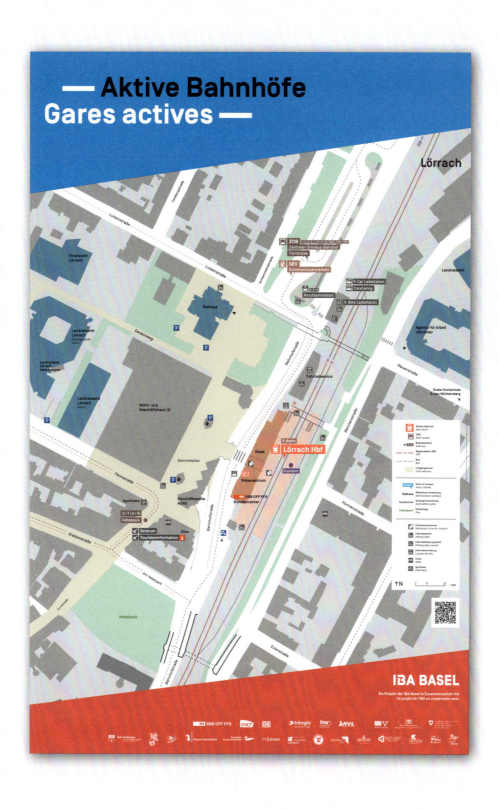

SILVER

AOK PROJEKTHAUS

LEITSYSTEM
ORIENTATION SYSTEM

> **JURY STATEMENT**
>
> Ein für eine Krankenkassen-Institution ungeheuer mutiges Projekt, das dem Unternehmen frische Impulse aus der eigenen Mitarbeiter*innen-Ebene bringen soll. Das Leitsystem weist die einzelnen Zonen aus, ist aber nicht starr, sondern assoziativ gedacht – und entspricht damit der Idee, eine Kultur des offenen Denkens zu schaffen.
>
> The project is an incredibly bold undertaking for a health insurance provider and aims to give the company fresh, employee-driven impetus. The orientation system identifies the individual zones but takes an associative rather than a rigid approach – and is thus in keeping with the idea of creating a culture of open thinking.

AUFTRAGGEBER / CLIENT
AOK Baden-Württemberg
Stuttgart

DESIGN
Typenraum GmbH & Co. KG
Stuttgart

FOTOS / PHOTOS
Joachim Grothus

→ SEITE / PAGE
176

Mit dem Projekthaus erkundet die AOK Baden-Württemberg prototypisch, wie das Arbeitsumfeld der Zukunft aussehen könnte. Auf den rund 1500 Quadratmetern einer ehemaligen Fabriketage gruppieren sich unterschiedlichste Zonen: offene Bereiche, Lounges für den Austausch sowie Module für konzentriertes Arbeiten. Mitarbeiter*innen der Krankenkasse sind dort für etwa sechs Monate aktiv, um die neuen Arbeitsformen zu erkunden, zu bewerten und weiterzuentwickeln.

Das parallel entwickelte Leitsystem ermöglicht, die offene Raumstruktur intuitiv zu erfassen. Es nimmt den überlagernden Charakter der Zonierung auf und differenziert in Form amorpher Farbflächen die verschiedenen Bereiche. Am Eingang überlagern und verdichten sich die Farben zu einer polychromen Wolke.

The Projekthaus for health insurance company AOK Baden-Württemberg is a prototype for exploring what tomorrow's workspaces might look like. The approx. 1,500 square metres of space on a former factory floor are occupied by a grouping of highly diverse zones: open areas, lounges for lively exchanges and modules for concentrated work. The health insurer's staff are active there for around six months in order to explore, evaluate and fine-tune the new ways of working.

The orientation system developed parallel to the project enables occupants to understand and use the open-plan structure intuitively. It echoes the overlapping character of the zoning and uses amorphous colour fields to differentiate the various areas. At the entrance, the colours overlap and condense into a polychrome cloud.

SILVER — CITYDECKS
PARKLET-MODULSYSTEM / MODULAR PARKLET SYSTEM

JURY STATEMENT

Eine sehr schöne und frische Lösung für ein ganz aktuelles urbanes Thema. Die Module bestechen durch ihre Einfachheit und ihre freie Zusammenstellung. Damit muss das Parklet nicht in jeder Kommune neu erfunden werden, die Stadt kann wieder menschengerechter werden.

A highly attractive and refreshing solution for a very topical urban issue. The simplicity and combinability of the modules is impressive. As a result, the parklet idea doesn't need to be reinvented for every municipality and cities can become more people-friendly again.

HERSTELLER / MANUFACTURER
Livable Cities GmbH
Mannheim

DESIGN
Yalla Yalla!
Mannheim

VERTRIEB / DISTRIBUTOR
Livable Cities GmbH
Mannheim

→ SEITE / PAGE
177

Viele Städte versuchen, den öffentlichen Raum neu aufzuteilen und hinterfragen die Dominanz des Autos. Dafür werden Parkplätze temporär oder dauerhaft umgewidmet – mit sogenannten Parklets, die einfach in den Straßenraum gestellt werden. Das 15-teilige Modulsystem erleichtert diesen immer wieder kontrovers diskutierten Schritt: Es bietet vorkonfigurierte Elemente, die mal Deck, mal Bank, mal Fahrradhalter, mal Sitztreppe, Stehtheke oder Pflanzbereich sind. Zwei Meter tief und 1,2 Meter breit, passen die Module exakt auf Parkflächen und erlauben ganz individuelle Kombinationen: Begegnungszonen beispielsweise, Aktionsflächen oder einfach nur Bereiche für die offene Aneignung.

Many cities are trying to reallocate public space and are questioning the dominance of the car. That means repurposing parking spaces on a temporary or permanent basis – with parklets that are simply placed in the street space. The 15-piece modular system makes this controversial step considerably easier by providing preconfigured elements that can serve as a deck, a bench, a bike stand, tiered seating, a stand-up counter or a planter. Two metres deep and 1.2 metres wide, the modules fit perfectly onto parking spaces and permit all sorts of individual combinations: home zones or interactive spaces, for instance, or simply areas for people to use however they like.

SILVER

CL3710 SLEEPING COMFORT
FLUGZEUGSITZ / AIRCRAFT SEAT

JURY STATEMENT

Mehr Komfort für die Economy Class im Flugzeug ist schon lange überfällig. Mit dem neuen Sitz kommt man dem Ziel, das Fliegen entspannter zu machen, ein großes Stück näher – trotz des geringen Spielraums, den die ökonomischen Rahmenbedingungen bieten. Allein die Kopfstütze wünscht man sich nicht nur auf Langstreckenflügen.

More comfort in economy class is long overdue. The new seat brings the goal of a more relaxing flying experience within reach – despite the narrow scope remaining in the light of economic considerations. The headrest would be a great addition to any seat – not just on long-haul flights.

HERSTELLER / MANUFACTURER
Recaro
Aircraft Seating GmbH & Co. KG
Schwäbisch Hall

DESIGN
Inhouse

VERTRIEB / DISTRIBUTOR
Recaro
Aircraft Seating GmbH & Co. KG
Schwäbisch Hall

→ SEITE / PAGE
178

Langstreckenflüge in der Economy Class sind keine Vergnügungsreisen, weil die Sitze dort keine wirkliche Schlafposition zulassen. Das soll der neue Sitz nun ändern: Seine ergonomisch anpassbare Kopfstütze hält den Kopf in einer individuell angenehmen Schlafposition, das Rückenpolster lässt sich umklappen und damit die Unterstützung verändern. Und schließlich ist die eigentliche Sitzfläche mittels eines hochklappbaren Zusatzes verlängerbar, wodurch entspanntere Sitzpositionen möglich werden. Da der Sitz auf der Standardvariante des CL3710 basiert und damit nur wenige neue Strukturelemente benötigt, bleibt der zusätzliche Wartungsaufwand für die Airlines überschaubar.

Long-haul flights in economy class are anything but a pleasure trip because the seats don't permit a proper sleeping position. This new seat aims to change that: its ergonomically adjustable headrest holds the head in whatever sleeping position is most comfortable for the individual passenger, and the backrest cushion can be folded down to support the lumbar region. Last but not least, the seat itself can be extended by means of a fold-up add-on that allows more relaxed sitting positions. Because the seat is based on the standard version of the CL3710 and only a few new structural elements have been added, only a moderate amount of additional maintenance is required on the part of the airlines.

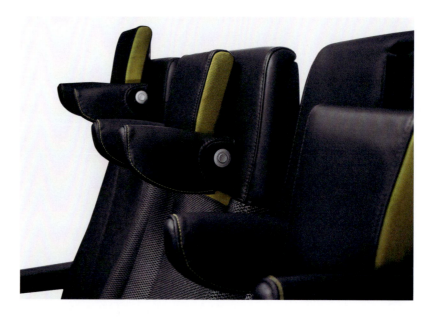

SILVER — KTM MOTOHALL — AUSSTELLUNGSKONZEPTION / EXHIBITION CONCEPT

JURY STATEMENT

Die emotional sehr aufgeladene Schau dürfte die Zielgruppe rundum begeistern. Die Ausstellung ist kein Showroom, sondern eine Erlebnistour auf den Spuren der Herkunft und der besonderen Werte der Marke. Insgesamt farbig stark reduziert, wird die Markenfarbe Orange umso prägnanter erlebbar.

The emotionally charged showcase will no doubt thrill the target group in every respect. The exhibition isn't a showroom but an experience, taking visitors on a tour that maps out the brand's heritage and special values. The otherwise understated use of colour makes the brand's trademark orange stand out all the more.

AUFTRAGGEBER / CLIENT
KTM AG
Mattighofen
Österreich / Austria

DESIGN
Atelier Brückner GmbH
Stuttgart

→ SEITE / PAGE
179

Auf rund 3000 Quadratmetern inszeniert das Ausstellungskonzept die Markenwerte des Motorradherstellers KTM. Im Vordergrund steht dabei der Rennsport. Mehr als 100 Original-Bikes zelebrieren diesen, unterstützt von Medienstationen, Projektionen und Zitaten aus der Rennwelt. Die drei Ebenen des ellipsoiden Baus zeigen neben der Firmengeschichte, die in den 1950er-Jahren beginnt, auch den Ablauf des Designprozesses eines Motorrads im Detail. Ihren Höhepunkt erreicht die Ausstellung mit einer Art Heldenschau, die legendäre Bikes von Rennfahrern mit deren Ausrüstungen zeigt und von einer 360-Grad-Projektion in ein immersives Erlebnis verwandelt wird.

The exhibition concept stages the brand values of motorcycle manufacturer KTM in a show covering approx. 3,000 square metres. The focus is on the brand's motorsports heritage, which is celebrated by more than 100 original bikes in conjunction with media stations, projections and quotes from the world of racing. In addition to the company's history, which begins in the 1950s, the three levels of the ellipsoidal building also detail the design process behind a motorcycle. The exhibition culminates in a kind of hall of fame that showcases legendary racing bikes along with their riders' gear and is transformed into an immersive experience by a 360-degree projection.

SPECIAL MENTION **TROY** **AUSSTELLUNGSKONZEPTION
EXHIBITION CONCEPT**

> **JURY STATEMENT**
>
> Eine Ausstellung weitab von der sonst üblichen musealen Aufbereitung, sehr emotional, sehr persönlich. Das passt zur Band, die bei der Konzeption involviert war und nach wie vor aktiv ist. Nicht nur, aber vor allem Fans des schwäbischen Phänomens dürften hier große Freude haben.
>
> A very different kind of exhibition to what is usually seen in museums, very emotional, very personal. That's in keeping with the band, which was involved with the concept and is still active today. A special treat for fans of the hip hop phenomenon from southwest Germany, and well worth a visit for anyone else.

Die Fantastischen Vier sind bereits eine Legende der Musikwelt – vor 30 Jahren in Stuttgart gegründet, hat die Band den deutschen Hip-Hop zu Höhenflügen gebracht. Mit der Ausstellung verwandelt sich das Stuttgarter Stadtpalais in einen temporären Kosmos rund um die Musiker. Natürlich startet die Schau dort, wo alles begann: Im nachgestellten Kinderzimmer von And.Ypsilon, in welchem sich die jungen Künstler erstmals formierten. Dioramen bestimmen auch die weitere Ausstellung, die betretbaren Schaukästen sind inspiriert von den größten Hits der Band. Um die immersiv angelegten Dioramen herum legt sich eine weitere Schicht musealer und doch emotionaler Inszenierungen.

Die Fantastischen Vier are already a legend in the music world – founded in Stuttgart 30 years ago, the four-strong band took German hip hop to new heights. The exhibition transforms the Stadtpalais museum in Stuttgart into a temporary cosmos that covers every aspect of the musicians' story. The show kicks off where everything began: in a replica of band member And.Ypsilon's childhood room, where the young artists first formed. Dioramas dominate the rest of the exhibition too – the walk-in showcases are inspired by the band's greatest hits. Another layer of more conventional but nevertheless emotional displays is wrapped around the immersive dioramas.

AUFTRAGGEBER / CLIENT
StadtPalais Stuttgart –
Museum für Stuttgart
Stuttgart

DESIGN
Jangled Nerves GmbH
Stuttgart

FOTOS / PHOTOS
Jens Lyncker / Jangled Nerves

→ SEITE / PAGE
180

SPECIAL MENTION   AKTIVE BAHNHÖFE   ERSCHEINUNGSBILD
                                        VISUAL IDENTITY

JURY STATEMENT

Die Arbeit greift ein ganz wichtiges Thema auf, nämlich ein ÖPNV-Leitsystem zu schaffen, das ganze Regionen einheitlich erschließt und darstellt. Die Arbeit zeigt, wie komplex diese Aufgabe ist, zugleich aber auch, wie gut sie sich bewältigen lässt. Ein tolles Beispiel, das Schule machen sollte.

The design takes up a very important issue: the creation of a signage system for local public transport that covers and depicts entire regions consistently. The example shows just how complex a task that is, but also how well it can be accomplished. An exemplary approach that will hopefully catch on.

AUFTRAGGEBER / CLIENT
Internationale Bauausstellung – IBA Basel 2020
Basel
Schweiz / Switzerland

DESIGN
Lengsfeld Designkonzepte GmbH
Basel
Schweiz / Switzerland

→ SEITE / PAGE
181

Die Internationale Bauausstellung Basel 2020 zielt vor allem auf eine bessere Verbindung des Zusammenlebens im Dreiländereck ab. Ein Aspekt betrifft die grenzüberschreitende öffentliche Mobilität, die ein gemeinsames Erscheinungsbild erhalten sollte. Das Konzept bezieht die 14 aktiven Bahnhöfe der Schweiz, Deutschlands und Frankreichs in der Region mit ein; bestehendes Material wurde dabei integriert und besser zugänglich gemacht. Den zusammenhängenden visuellen Rahmen liefern dynamische Keile in einem prägnanten, rotblauen Farbklang. Das Erscheinungsbild soll zum einen die Orientierung erleichtern, zum anderen die länderübergreifende Identität stärken.

The main aim of the IBA Basel 2020 is to ensure better connections for the people of three nations who live in the tri-border area. One aspect of that is cross-border public mobility, which was to be given a communal visual identity. The concept covers the region's 14 active stations in Switzerland, Germany and France; existing material was integrated and made more user-friendly. The information is framed by dynamic wedges in eye-catching shades of red and blue. Besides providing orientation, the aim is to strengthen the region's cross-border identity.

MEIKE HARDE

STUDIO MEIKE HARDE, KÖLN / COLOGNE

»Langlebigkeit ist eine wesentliche Voraussetzung für nachhaltigere Produkte. Neben den technischen Parametern wie Reparierbarkeit ist auch die ästhetische Seite gefragt. Aus meiner Sicht ist eine gewisse formale Neutralität und ein emotionaler Anknüpfungspunkt wichtig. Damit gelingt es, einen persönlichen Bezug zum Produkt aufzubauen, sodass man es nicht mehr hergeben möchte.«

»Longevity is a crucial requirement for more sustainable products. Besides technical parameters like repairability, the aesthetic side plays a role in that too. In my opinion, a certain neutrality of form and an emotional tie-in are important. That enables users to build a personal connection with the product, with the result that they don't want to part with it.«

Nach einem Hochschulstudium in Saarbrücken und kurzer Tätigkeit bei Benjamin Hubert in London gründet die in Köln ansässige Produktdesignerin Meike Harde 2013 ihr Studio. Zu Beginn ihrer Selbstständigkeit erhielt sie einige Newcomer Preise und nahm an zahlreichen Ausstellungen teil. Seit ca. 2015 platziert sie Möbel und Leuchten bei namhaften Firmen. Bis zu ihrem Umzug nach Köln 2017 arbeitete sie zudem als Lehrbeauftrage an der Universität des Saarlandes und der HBK Saarbrücken.

www.meikeharde.com

After studying in Saarbrücken and a brief period with Benjamin Hubert in London, Cologne-based product designer Meike Harde founded her own studio in 2013. She received several newcomer awards early on in her freelance career and has taken part in numerous exhibitions. She has been placing her furniture and lighting designs with prestigious companies since approx. 2015. Until moving to Cologne in 2017, she was also an associate lecturer at Saarland University and HBKsaar (Saar Academy of Fine Arts and Design) in Saarbrücken.

www.meikeharde.com

1 → SEITE / PAGE
192–197

MOBILITÄT
MOBILITY

GOLD:
1 M99 MINI PRO B54
Supernova Design GmbH & Co. KG
Gundelfingen

Die individuelle Mobilität steht vor der großen Herausforderung eines Systemwechsels. Besonderer Gewinner ist der Radverkehr – nicht nur durch die elektrische Unterstützung der Fahrer*innen. Gerade in der Rad-branche zeichnen sich rasante Innovationsschübe ab, die das Fahrrad sicherer, attraktiver und zuverlässiger machen.

Individual mobility is facing the major challenge of a system change. Cycling is emerging as one of the big winners – and not just because of the electrical assistance now available to riders. Especially in the bike sector, the innovation boom is rapidly resulting in safer, more attractive and more reliable products.

12

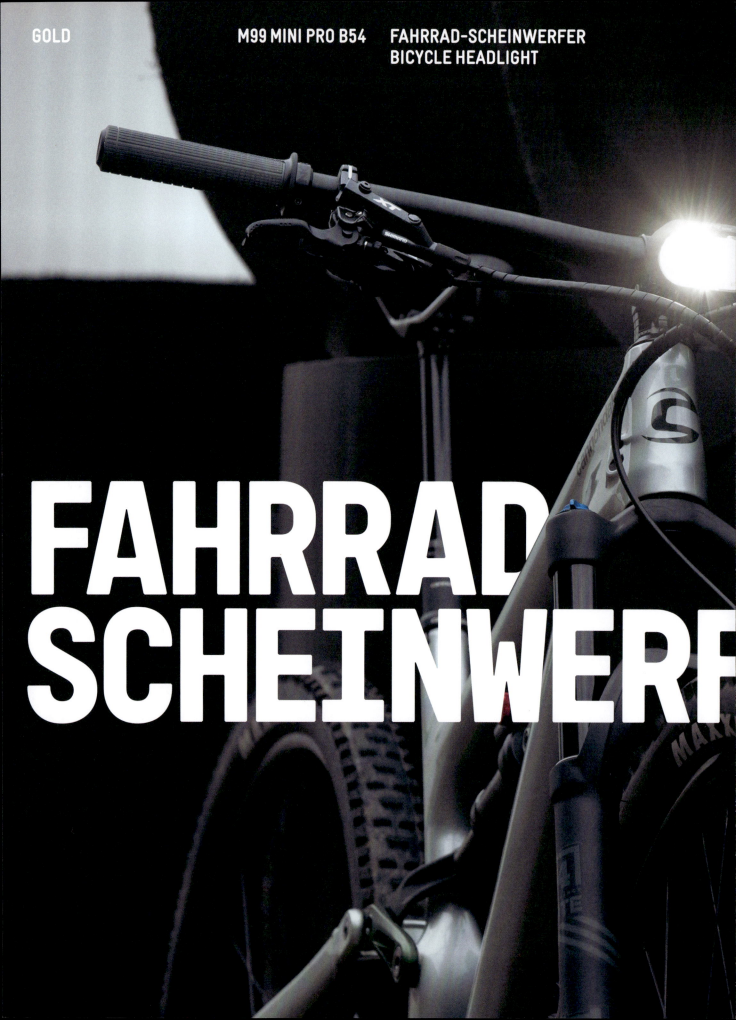

MOBILITY
MOBILITY

M99 MINI PRO B54

ER

FOCUS GOLD

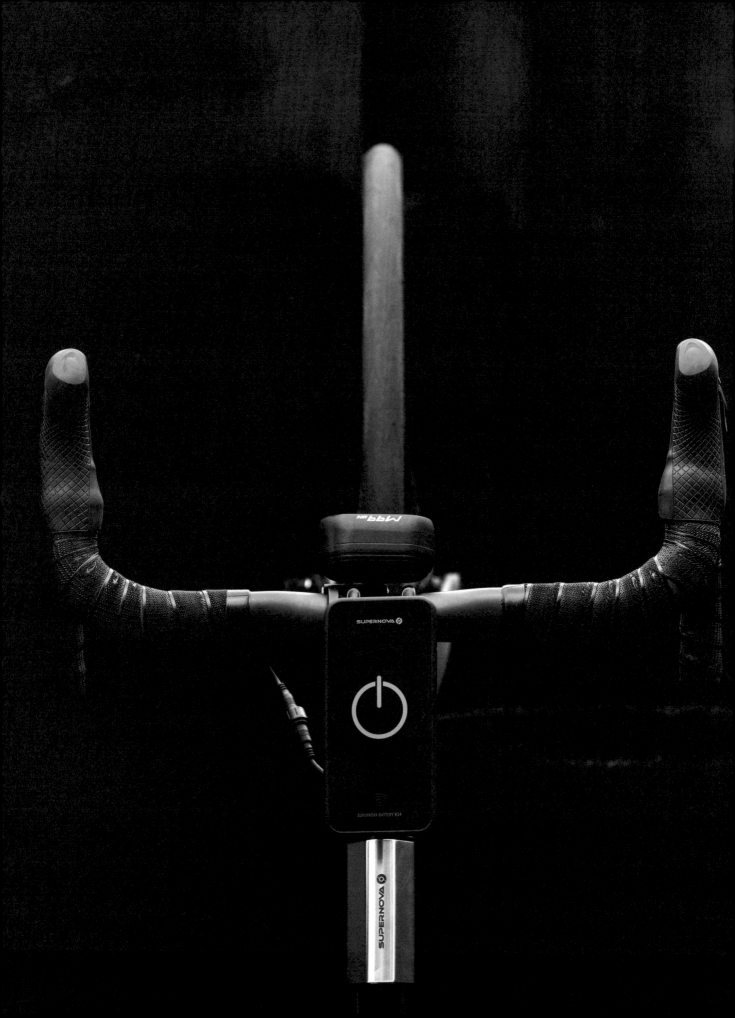

GOLD — M99 MINI PRO B54 — FAHRRAD-SCHEINWERFER / BICYCLE HEADLIGHT

JURY STATEMENT

Endlich steht auch sportlichen Radler*innen eine adäquate Lichtanlage zur Verfügung. Mit dem Scheinwerfer lassen sich auch nächtliche Fahrten auf Waldwegen sicher bewältigen. Das schlichte Design macht Akku und Scheinwerfer kompatibel zu allen Radmodellen. Gut gelöst ist die freie Platzierbarkeit des Fernlicht-Tasters und die App, mit der sich der Ladezustand minutengenau ablesen lässt.

Finally: an adequate lighting system that meets the needs of sporting cyclists too. With this headlight, even night rides on forest trails are safe. Thanks to the simple design, the battery and light are compatible with any bike model. The freely positionable high beam switch and an app that displays the charge status to the exact minute are equally convincing.

HERSTELLER / MANUFACTURER
Supernova Design GmbH & Co. KG
Gundelfingen

DESIGN
Inhouse

VERTRIEB / DISTRIBUTOR
Supernova Design GmbH & Co. KG
Gundelfingen

→ SEITE / PAGE
192–194, 196–197

Wer in der Dunkelheit mit dem Fahrrad unterwegs ist, weiß einen lichtstarken und zuverlässigen Scheinwerfer zu schätzen. Je zügiger das Tempo und unübersichtlicher die Wegeführung, desto mehr Licht ist notwendig – dann schlägt die Stunde des Fernlichts. Die Umschaltung von Abblend- auf Fernlicht mit maximal 1600 Lumen erfolgt ganz einfach durch Tastendruck am Lenker. Das Fernlicht ist so optimiert, dass die Leuchtweite auch bei eingetauchter Federgabel ausreichend groß ist. Der zugehörige, beheizte und nur 300 Gramm schwere Akku mit 54 Wh Kapazität liefert bis zu 50 Stunden Energie – was besonders Vielfahrer*innen interessieren dürfte. Sensoren schalten den Scheinwerfer automatisch ab und aktivieren ihn, wenn das Umgebungslicht schwächer wird. Natürlich verfügt die Lichtanlage über eine StVZO-Zulassung.

Anybody who rides a bike in the dark appreciates the importance of a bright and reliable headlight. The faster you cycle and the harder it is to see where you're going, the more light you need – time to turn the high beam on! Simply pushing a button on the handlebars switches the headlight from low beam to high beam mode, which provides a maximum output of 1,600 lumens. The high beam is optimised to ensure sufficient range even when the fork dives. The accompanying 54 Wh battery is heated, weighs just 300 grams and provides up to 50 hours of power – making it particularly interesting for those who cycle a lot. Sensors automatically switch the headlight off and activate it if lighting conditions deteriorate. It goes without saying that the light has been approved as road-legal under German regulations.

MARCUS WALLMEYER   CEO UND HEAD OF DESIGN,
SUPERNOVA DESIGN GMBH & CO. KG

»Coole Produkte brauchen
ein gutes Design, weil es deren
Message, begehrenswert
und attraktiv zu sein, verstärkt.«

»Cool products need a good design
because it reinforces the message that
they're desirable and attractive.«

MARCUS WALLMEYER — CEO AND HEAD OF DESIGN, SUPERNOVA DESIGN GMBH & CO. KG

→ **Welche Bedeutung hat das Design in der Fahrradbranche heute?**

Design ist in der Fahrradindustrie wichtiger denn je. Das Image des Fahrrads hat sich in den letzten Jahren grundlegend verändert. Noch nie war es so cool wie jetzt, mit einem stylischen Rad unterwegs zu sein. Coole Produkte brauchen natürlich auch ein gutes Design, weil es deren Message, begehrenswert und attraktiv zu sein, verstärkt.

Der E-Bike-Markt boomt, trotzdem haben Sie eine Scheinwerfervariante für motorlose Fahrräder entwickelt. Warum?

Mit Leuchten für E-Bikes kann man natürlich aktuell deutlich mehr Umsatz machen, aber ich finde es wichtig, auch im Bereich der motorlosen Fahrräder die Entwicklung von innovativen Lichtsystemen voranzutreiben. Supernova entwickelt sehr oft Produkte, die ich mir aus meiner persönlichen Erfahrung heraus tatsächlich selbst wünsche. Das ist aus betriebswirtschaftlicher Sicht nicht immer sofort verständlich, aber in den letzten Jahren lag ich eigentlich ganz gut mit meinem Bauchgefühl, was Radfahrende so brauchen.

Wie würden Sie die Zielgruppe des Produktes beschreiben?

Wir haben verschiedene Zielgruppen. Viele unserer Kund*innen sind Pendler*innen, die bei Wind und Wetter zur Arbeit fahren und auf der Suche nach langlebigen Produkten sind. In einer weiteren Zielgruppe mischen sich Hobbyfahrer*innen und Extremsportler*innen, die den Scheinwerfer auf dem Mountainbike oder Rennrad nutzen. Hobbyfahrer*innen können mit einem hellen Lichtsystem ihre Fahrradsaison bis in den Herbst und Winter verlängern. Extremsportler*innen erfreut die bis zu 50 Stunden lange Leuchtzeit und die minutengenaue Leuchtzeitangabe. Zuverlässigkeit ist zudem ein wichtiger Faktor, wenn man sich teilweise jahrelang auf eine Weltumrundung vorbereitet hat.

Akkus, LEDs und Steuerungschips kommen in der Regel von internationalen Zulieferern – wie anfällig sind diese Lieferketten – etwa vor dem Hintergrund der Corona-Pandemie?

Bisher gab es bei uns nur geringe »coronabedingte« Verzögerungen. Wir haben unsere Lieferketten sehr gut im Griff und sichern unsere Bedarfe bis über ein Jahr im Voraus. Zusätzlich haben wir ein Notlager von allen wichtigen Mikrochips, LED-Treibern und LEDs angelegt, für die es keine Alternativen gibt. Akkuzellen haben wir ebenfalls frühzeitig reserviert. Hier hatten wir vor Jahren böse Erfahrungen gemacht, als uns Tesla alle Panasonic-18650-Zellen vor der Nase weggeschnappt hat.

Seinen ersten Fahrrad-Scheinwerfer baute sich der Gründer und Radrennfahrer Marcus Wallmeyer 1995 – aus einer Tomatenmarkdose und einer Motorradbatterie, um auch in der Nacht lange trainieren zu können. Inzwischen entwickelt und produziert das Unternehmen mit über 50 Mitarbeiter*innen im industriellen Maßstab Hochleistungs-Lichtanlagen für Fahrräder mit und ohne elektrische Motorisierung. Daneben betreut Supernova nach wie vor auch Designaufträge von Drittkunden.

www.supernova-lights.com

→ **How important is design in today's bike sector?**

Design is more important in the bike industry than ever before. There have been fundamental changes in the image of the bicycle in recent years. Riding a stylish bike has never been as cool as it is today. And cool products need a good design because it reinforces the message that they're desirable and attractive.

The e-bike market is booming, but that didn't stop you developing a version of the headlight for motorless bikes. Why?

In today's market, you can obviously sell a lot more product if you make lamps for e-bikes, but I think it's important to drive the development of innovative lighting systems for motorless bikes too. Very often, the products Supernova develops are things I want to have myself, based on my personal experience. That doesn't always immediately make sense from a business perspective, but in recent years my gut feeling as to what cyclists need has actually been pretty accurate.

How would you describe the product's target group?

We cater to various target groups. A lot of our customers are commuters who cycle to work in all weathers and are looking for products that will last a long time. Another of our target groups is a mix of hobbyists and extreme athletes who use the headlight on their mountain or racing bikes. For hobbyists, bright lights mean they can prolong their cycling season into the autumn and winter, whereas extreme athletes love the fact that the system gives them up to 50 hours of light and displays the charge status to the exact minute. And if you've invested years in preparing to cycle round the world, reliability is obviously an important factor too.

As a rule, rechargeable batteries, LEDs and chips are sourced from international suppliers. How vulnerable are those supply chains – for instance in the light of the corona pandemic?

Up until now, we've only had minimal delays because of corona. We stay on top of our supply chains and secure our needs in good time, sometimes more than a year in advance. In addition, we have emergency stocks of all the important microchips, LED drivers and LEDs that there are no alternatives for. We also reserved a good supply of rechargeable cells early on. That was something we had a really bad experience with years ago, when Tesla snapped up all the Panasonic 18650 cells from under our nose.

Because he wanted to be able to train for extended periods at night too, founder and racing cyclist Marcus Wallmeyer built his first bicycle headlight back in 1995 – out of a tomato puree can and a motorbike battery. Nowadays the company employs over 50 people and produces high-performance light systems for bikes with and without an electric motor on an industrial scale. In addition, Supernova continues to take on design assignments from third-party customers.

www.supernova-lights.com

1 → SEITE / PAGE
200–205

2 → SEITE / PAGE
206–211

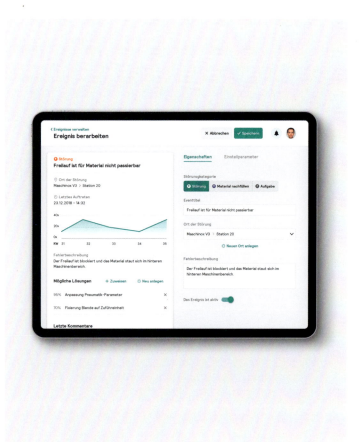

3 → SEITE / PAGE
212, 213

SERVICE DESIGN
SERVICE DESIGN

GOLD:
1 **BOSCH BRAND GUIDE ONLINE**
Robert Bosch GmbH
Gerlingen

2 **HORST FX**
Fruitcore Robotics GmbH
Konstanz / Constance

SPECIAL MENTION:
3 **DIE INTELLIGENTE FABRIK**
Plus 10 GmbH
Augsburg

Die Digitalisierung von Produkten und Dienstleistungen schreitet voran –
die nutzerzentrierte Gestaltung von Interfaces und Bedienlogiken
sorgt dafür, dass die Services in ihrer Tiefe und Funktionalität zu intuitiven
Tools werden, die sowohl im virtuellen wie realen Kontext ihren eigentlichen Wert entfalten können.

The digitalisation of products and services is progressing – the user-
centric design of interfaces and operating logics makes the depth
and functionality of services accessible by turning them into intuitive tools
that can demonstrate their true value in both a real and virtual context.

13

GOLD BOSCH BRAND GUIDE ONLINE MARKEN- UND DESIGNPLATTFORM BRAND AND DESIGN PLATFORM

SERVICE DESIGN
SERVICE DESIGN

FOCUS
GOLD

GOLD

BOSCH BRAND GUIDE ONLINE

MARKEN- UND DESIGNPLATTFORM
BRAND AND DESIGN PLATFORM

JURY STATEMENT

Ein sehr gutes Tool, global gedacht und intuitiv nutzbar. Die Online-Plattform hat konzernweite Geltung und verdeutlicht den Stellenwert eines durchgehenden Designs im Unternehmen. Zudem ist die grafische Qualität des Guides ebenso hoch wie die der dort auffindbaren Elemente.

A very good tool, designed with a global audience in mind and intuitive to use. The online platform is valid across the group and illustrates just how important consistent design is for a company. In addition, the quality of the guide's graphics matches that of the elements it contains.

HERSTELLER / MANUFACTURER
Robert Bosch GmbH
Gerlingen

DESIGN
Inhouse
Bosch Corporate Design Team und /
and United Digital Group
Gerlingen

VERTRIEB / DISTRIBUTOR
Robert Bosch GmbH
Gerlingen

→ SEITE / PAGE
200–202, 204–205

Unternehmen mit internationaler Präsenz und diversifizierten Geschäftsbereichen kämpfen in der Regel mit der Konsistenz ihrer Markenerscheinung. Bosch hat dafür einen Online-Guide geschaffen, auf den Mitarbeiter wie externe Dienstleister sofort Zugriff haben und über nutzerspezifische Direkteinstiege schnell die passenden Bausteine und Richtlinien finden. Dazu gehören Styleguides, Icons und Vorlagen für Druckerzeugnisse, Messeauftritte und für digitale Präsentationen ebenso wie Frontend-Kits für die Gestaltung von Websites oder Interfaces. Die zentrale Marken- und Designplattform reduziert den Arbeitsaufwand, verringert Anwendungsfehler und die Verwendung nicht mehr aktueller Vorgaben – damit sichert der Online-Guide die Identität und das Image des Unternehmens. Die Entwicklung des Guides basiert auf einer ausführlichen Nutzer*innenbefragung und Usability-Testings.

Generally speaking, companies with an international presence and diversified business units struggle with the consistency of their brand's visual identity. That's why Bosch has developed an online guide that staff and external service providers can access immediately; user-specific direct entry points provide a fast route to the appropriate building blocks and guidelines. The materials include style guides, icons and templates for printed materials, trade show appearances and digital presentations, as well as front end kits for designing websites or interfaces. The central brand and design platform reduces the amount of work involved and cuts down both on application errors and the use of obsolete guidelines, thereby safeguarding the company's identity and image. The development of the online guide is based on a comprehensive UX survey and usability testing.

EVA SANDNER　　PROJEKTMANAGEMENT BOSCH CORPORATE DESIGN DIGITAL
GREGOR SCHILLING　HEAD OF BOSCH CORPORATE DESIGN

»Unser Bosch Brand Guide ist die zentrale Designplattform und schafft ein einzigartiges Nutzererlebnis mit unserer Marke über alle Touchpoints weltweit.«

»Our Bosch Brand Guide is the central design platform and creates a unique user experience with our brand across all touchpoints worldwide.«

EVA SANDNER
GREGOR SCHILLING

PROJECT MANAGEMENT, BOSCH CORPORATE DESIGN DIGITAL
HEAD OF BOSCH CORPORATE DESIGN

→ **Was gab den Impuls für die Entwicklung des Online-Brand-Guides?**

Wir wollten eine weltweit zentrale Anlaufstelle für alle Themen rund um die marken- und designrelevanten Inhalte schaffen. Aus insgesamt vier Plattformen, zahlreichen PDFs und Büchern haben wir eine neue Plattform geschaffen, die alle Inhalte in digitaler Form und immer auf dem aktuellsten Stand bereithält – und zudem in Echtzeit weiterentwickelt werden kann. Diese Form der Dokumentation ermöglicht, digitale Assets und Libraries in unsere Style-Guides sinnvoll zu integrieren, beispielsweise UI-Patterns für die Programmierung von digitalen Interfaces, einen Logo-Konfigurator oder eine Icon Library. Die umfasst mittlerweile rund 1.500 Icons, wird von allen Geschäftsbereichen genutzt und befüllt. Allein das spart erhebliche Kosten.

Über welchen Zeitraum lief die Realisierung?

Von der Konzeption bis zur Liveschaltung dauerte es etwa 18 Monate. Wir sind seit Januar 2019 online, seitdem werden die Inhalte und Templates kontinuierlich weiterentwickelt und optimiert.

Wann ist ein solcher Online-Brand-Guide prinzipiell sinnvoll?

Eine solche Lösung ist aus unserer Sicht ein Muss für jedes größere Unternehmen, um unter dem Dach einer zentralen Markenführung einen weltweit einheitlichen und professionellen Markenauftritt sicherzustellen.

Und wie relevant ist für Bosch ein einheitlicher Auftritt über alle Sparten hinweg?

Sehr relevant – letztlich ist das Corporate Design Teil der Unternehmensidentität. Die Marke Bosch bildet einen Vertrauensvorschuss in den Herzen und Köpfen unserer Kund*innen, Mitarbeiter*innen und und der Öffentlichkeit. Der Kunde kauft Bosch, für ihn spielt es keine große Rolle, aus welchem unserer Geschäftsbereiche die Lösung kommt – es wird ein Produkt gekauft, verbunden mit allen Assoziationen und auch Erwartungen, die mit der Marke Bosch verknüpft werden. Die Marke stellt über ihre Reputation sicher, dass auch neue Geschäftsfelder mit den positiven Eigenschaften verknüpft werden. Diese Reputation wird auch durch einen wiedererkennbaren und professionellen Markenauftritt gestützt – der eben übergreifend weltweit derselbe sein muss, um seine Kraft zu entwickeln und prägend zu sein.

Der Brand-Guide stellt die Basiselemente und deren Anwendungsdefinitionen zentral zur Verfügung, die Geschäftsbereiche können sich aus diesem Fundus bedienen. Das führt in der Folge zu einer schnellen Umsetzbarkeit der Kommunikation auch durch unsere Geschäftsbereiche mit der Sicherheit, markenkonform aufzutreten.

→ **What was the driving force behind the development of the online brand guide?**

We wanted to create a central global resource for all content-related topics that impact brand and design. Based on a total of four platforms, numerous PDFs and books, we created a new platform that provides all the content in digital form and always in the most up-to-date version. What's more, it can be expanded in real time. This type of documentation enables us to integrate digital assets and libraries into our style guides in a meaningful way, like UI patterns for programming digital interfaces, a logo configurator or an icon library. There are now around 1,500 icons in the library; it's used and stocked by all divisions, and that alone results in considerable cost savings.

How long did it take to implement?

Between the concept and going live, about 18 months. We've been online since January 2019, and the content and templates have been expanded and optimised continuously ever since.

In principle, when does this kind of online brand guide make sense?

In our opinion, a solution like this is a must for any sizeable company that wants to ensure a globally consistent and professional brand identity under the umbrella of central brand management.

And how important is it for Bosch to have a consistent look across all divisions?

Very important – ultimately, the corporate design is part of the corporate identity. The Bosch brand creates a trust advantage in the hearts and minds of our customers, employees and the general public. The customer buys Bosch; it doesn't really matter to them which of our divisions the solution comes from – they buy a product that they connect with all the associations and expectations that go hand in hand with the Bosch brand. Through its reputation, the brand ensures that even new areas of business are associated with those same positive attributes. A recognisable and professional brand identity also plays a role in underpinning this reputation – and it has to be the same all over the world in order to unfold its power and have a formative influence.

The brand guide makes the basic elements and the definitions of their applications available on a central basis, so the business divisions can help themselves from this pool of resources. As a result, communications can be implemented quickly, including by our business divisions, with the certainty that they're on brand.

Die Bosch-Gruppe ist ein international führendes Technologie- und Dienstleistungsunternehmen mit weltweit rund 400.000 Mitarbeiter*innen. Sie erwirtschaftete im Geschäftsjahr 2019 einen Umsatz von 77,7 Milliarden Euro. Die Aktivitäten gliedern sich in die vier Unternehmensbereiche Mobility Solutions, Industrial Technology, Consumer Goods sowie Energy and Building Technology.

www.bosch.com

The Bosch Group is a leading global supplier of technology and services that employs approx. 400,000 people worldwide. In 2019, it generated sales of 77.7 billion euros. Its activities are divided into four business sectors: Mobility Solutions, Industrial Technology, Consumer Goods and Energy and Building.

www.bosch.com

SERVICE DESIGN
SERVICE DESIGN

FOCUS
GOLD

HORST FX

BEDIENOBERFLÄCHE / USER INTERFACE

JURY STATEMENT

Die Hürde, einen kollaborativen Roboter zu nutzen, ist enorm, wenn spezielle Programmierkenntnisse vonnöten sind. Doch die Bedienoberfläche hier zeigt, dass es anders geht: Sie ist grafisch sehr klar aufgebaut und einfach zu nutzen. Das Anlernen des Automaten braucht keine abstrakten Codes, Aktionen werden bildhaft dargestellt und in schlüssige Abläufe eingebunden. Zudem ein interessanter Ansatz: Für Usability-Tests arbeitete man mit Kindern.

There are huge barriers to using a collaborative robot if it calls for special programming skills. But this user interface shows that there's another way: its graphics are very clearly structured and the software is easy to use. No abstract codes are required to train the automaton, and the actions are displayed very vividly and incorporated into logical processes. Another interesting approach: the developers worked with children for the usability tests.

HERSTELLER / MANUFACTURER
Fruitcore Robotics GmbH
Konstanz / Constance

DESIGN
Solidfluid
Konstanz / Constance

VERTRIEB / DISTRIBUTOR
Fruitcore Robotics GmbH
Konstanz / Constance

→ **SEITE / PAGE**
206–208, 210–211

Ein Roboter allein ist noch keine Hilfe im Unternehmen – erst seine Programmierung macht ihn zu einem wirtschaftlichen Faktor. Damit dieser Vorgang so einfach wie möglich ablaufen kann, entwickelte das Unternehmen die intuitiv bedienbare Software Horst FX. Sie setzt keine Programmierkenntnisse voraus und reduziert die Komplexität der Robotersteuerung so, dass die Automatisierung auch für kleine und mittlere Betriebe interessant wird. Die Benutzeroberfläche auf dem 13,3-Zoll-Touchscreen teilt sich in drei Bereiche: In der Mitte wird der Roboter in seiner realen Stellung gezeigt, rechts davon befindet sich die Aktionskonsole mit den Schritt für Schritt abrufbaren Aktionen. Die linke Seite macht den daraus folgenden Ablauf des Programms im Detail sichtbar.

Zunächst für den Roboter Horst gedacht, soll die Bedienoberfläche alle künftig hinzukommenden Roboter einschließen und sogar externe Maschinen einbinden können.

A robot alone is no help to a company – it's only the right programming that turns it into an economic factor. In order to ensure that process runs as smoothly as possible, the company has developed an intuitive software by the name of Horst FX. It works on the assumption that the user has no programming expertise and reduces the complexity of controlling the robot so effectively that automation becomes an interesting option even for small and medium-sized enterprises. The user interface on the 13.3-inch touchscreen is divided into three areas. The middle section shows the robot in its real-time position, while the console on the right provides step-by-step instructions for the preset actions. The left-hand side displays the details of the resulting program flow.

Initially designed for use with the company's Horst robot, the user interface is intended to be compatible with any future robots and even communicate with external machines.

JENS RIEGGER UND PATRICK ZIMMERMANN   **GESCHÄFTSFÜHRER, FRUITCORE ROBOTICS GMBH**

»HorstFX eignet sich für Einsteiger genauso wie für Experten und sorgt durch intelligente Features für Transparenz und Digitalisierung in der Produktion.«

»HorstFX is just as suitable for newcomers as it is for experts and uses intelligent features to ensure transparency and digitalisation in production operations.«

JENS RIEGGER AND PATRICK ZIMMERMANN

MANAGING DIRECTORS, FRUITCORE ROBOTICS GMBH

→ **Wieso benötigt ein Industrieroboter eine eigene Bedienoberfläche?**

Alle Industrieroboter von Fruitcore Robotics arbeiten mit der Software HorstFX. Unser Ziel heißt: einfache Handhabung und wirtschaftliche Robotik für alle Unternehmensgrößen. Die Software reduziert die Komplexitätsanforderungen für den Bedienenden auf ein Minimum, Programmierkenntnisse sind nicht nötig.

Welche Funktionalitäten deckt die Oberfläche ab?

Die Oberfläche steuert den Industrieroboter Horst. Über die grafische Programmierung lassen sich, dank der industriellen Schnittstellen, auch externe Maschinen ansteuern. HorstFX verwaltet und steuert die Abläufe von einfachen Bewegungsabläufen bis zu komplexen Palettieranwendungen. Der Übergang zur Programmierung komplexer Prozesse ist fließend. Beispielsweise können grafisch programmierte Abläufe mit einem Klick in Programmcodes konvertiert werden. HorstFX eignet sich für Einsteiger genauso wie für Experten und sorgt durch intelligente Features für Transparenz und Digitalisierung in der Produktion.

Durch das Hinzufügen von Aktionen kann der Nutzer seine Programmabläufe erstellen, er wird Schritt für Schritt durch vordefinierte Features wie zum Beispiel Palettieranwendungen geführt. Zusätzlich bietet die Aktionskonsole immer die Möglichkeit, Fehler zu beheben und eine Eingabe rückgängig zu machen.

Sie sind einen interessanten Weg für das User Testing gegangen. Warum?

Gestartet sind wir mit der bekannten User Journey und haben dann eine erste Version der Softwareoberfläche entwickelt. Damit war es möglich, den Roboter zu bewegen und einfache Programmabläufe zu erstellen. Für das User Testing haben wir zum einen verschiedene Kund*innen involviert, zum anderen Personen, die nichts mit Robotik und Automatisierung zu tun haben. Auch Schüler*innen und Auszubildende haben wir in das User Testing aufgenommen. Mit dem breit gefächerten Feedback konnten wir die Software weiterentwickeln und optimieren.

Welche Bedeutung hat Design für Fruitcore Robotics?

Zum einen verleiht Design unseren Produkten ein wiedererkennbares Gesicht, gerade in unserer Branche ist das eine absolute Notwendigkeit. Dadurch unterstreichen wir auch unsere Alleinstellung. Zum anderen sehen wir, gerade in der Softwareoberfläche HorstFX, was Design leisten kann. Es geht darum, komplexe Funktionen und Zusammenhänge so zu strukturieren und zu visualisieren, dass sie für Anwender*innen leicht benutzbar und zugänglich sind.

> Fruitcore Robotics GmbH mit Sitz in Konstanz wurde 2017 gegründet und ist spezialisiert auf Entwicklung, Herstellung und Vermarktung technisch herausragender und einfach zu bedienender Industrieroboter. Die Robotersysteme für Unternehmen aller Größen sind Made in Germany, von der Hardware bis zur Software.
>
> **www.fruitcore-robotics.com**

→ **Why does an industrial robot need its own user interface?**

All of Fruitcore Robotics' industrial robots work with the HorstFX software. Our goal is to ensure simple handling and cost-efficient robotics for companies of any size. The software reduces the complexity requirements for the user to a minimum, no programming skills are necessary.

Which functionalities does the interface cover?

The interface controls the industrial robot Horst. And thanks to the industrial interfaces, the graphic programming can be used to control external machines as well. HorstFX manages and steers the processes – from simple movement sequences all the way to complex palletising applications. The transition to programming complex processes is fluid. Processes that have been created graphically can be converted into program codes with a single click, for instance. HorstFX is just as suitable for newcomers as it is for experts and uses intelligent features to ensure transparency and digitalisation in production operations.

Users can create their program flows by adding actions, they're guided through predefined features like palletising applications step by step. In addition, the action console always provides the possibility of correcting mistakes and undoing an entry.

You took an unusual path when it came to user testing. Why?

We started off with the familiar user journey and then developed an initial version of the software interface that made it possible to move the robot and create simple program flows. Two groups of people were involved in the user testing process: various customers on the one hand, and people who have nothing to do with robotics and automation on the other. We included school students and trainees in the user testing as well. The wide-ranging feedback enabled us to refine and optimise the software.

How important is design for Fruitcore Robotics?

On the one hand, design gives our products a recognisable face, and that's an absolute necessity, especially in our sector. It also enables us to underline our uniqueness. On the other hand, especially in the case of the HorstFX software interface, we're very much aware of what design can achieve. It's all about structuring and visualising complex functions and connections in such a way that they're easy to use and access.

> Founded in 2017, Fruitcore Robotics GmbH is based in Constance and specialises in the development, production and marketing of technically outstanding and easy-to-operate industrial robots. From the hardware to the software, its robot systems for companies of all sizes are made in Germany.
>
> **www.fruitcore-robotics.com**

SPECIAL MENTION | DIE INTELLIGENTE FABRIK | MULTIPLATTFORM-APPLIKATION / MULTIPLATFORM APPLICATION

→ SEITE / PAGE 213

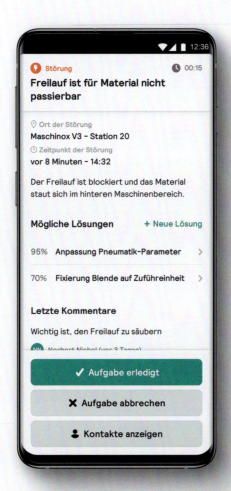

SPECIAL MENTION

DIE INTELLIGENTE FABRIK
MULTIPLATTFORM-APPLIKATION / MULTIPLATFORM APPLICATION

JURY STATEMENT

Eine sehr übersichtlich gestaltete App, sachlich klar und logisch im Aufbau, sodass sie auch von ungelernten Mitarbeiter*innen genutzt werden kann. Das Prozessoptimierungs-Tool setzt dabei auf direkte Kommunikation und Einbindung der Mitarbeiter*innen, nicht nur bei der Störungsbeseitigung.

A very clearly designed app with an objective and logical structure that means even unskilled staff can use it. The process optimisation tool relies on direct communication and staff participation, not just when it comes to troubleshooting.

Die Software des Start-ups überwacht Maschinen in der Produktion und analysiert sowie kategorisiert die erhobenen Daten mittels Machine Learning. Die Prozesse werden auf diese Weise transparenter und effizienter – weil das System nicht nur akute Störungen erkennt, sondern auch Probleme, bevor sie auftreten. In solchen Fällen bietet die Software über mobile Endgeräte oder stationäre Terminals den Mitarbeiter*innen vor Ort passende Lösungen an. Außerdem baut die Applikation einen Wissenspool auf, den die Belegschaft über Schichtgrenzen hinweg nutzen kann.

The software developed by the startup monitors production machinery and uses machine learning to analyse and categorise the gathered data. This makes the processes more transparent and more efficient – because besides detecting acute malfunctions, the system also identifies problems before they occur. In such cases, the software offers on-site staff appropriate solutions via mobile devices or stationary terminals. In addition, the application builds up a pool of knowledge that the entire workforce can use across different shifts.

HERSTELLER / MANUFACTURER
Plus 10 GmbH
Augsburg

DESIGN
F209 GmbH
Heidelberg

VERTRIEB / DISTRIBUTOR
Plus 10 GmbH
Augsburg

→ SEITE / PAGE
212

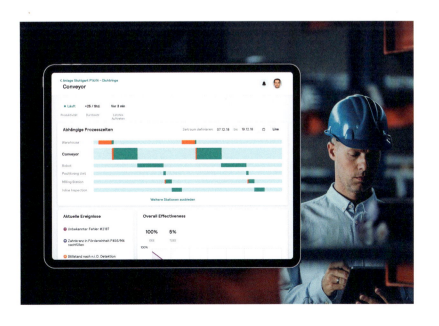

LUCIANA SILVARES   **MAZDA MOTOR EUROPE GMBH, OBERURSEL**

»Die Jurierung des Focus Open ist auch ein Austausch mit Kolleginnen und Kollegen, die in anderen Designsparten arbeiten. Für mich ist dies sehr bereichernd. Der Award an sich eignet sich besonders für Newcomer*innen, weil er transparent und erschwinglich ist – sowohl bei der Anmeldung und auch dann, wenn man ausgezeichnet wurde.«

»Judging the Focus Open competition is also an opportunity to exchange views and ideas with fellow designers who work in different fields. I find that extremely rewarding. The award itself is particularly suitable for newcomers because it's transparent and affordable – both in terms of registration and what happens if you're among the winners.«

Luciana Silvares hat an der Mackenzie Universität in São Paulo Architektur und Städtebau studiert, danach ein Industriedesign-Masterstudium an der Hochschule für angewandte Wissenschaften in München angeschlossen und an der britischen University of Warwick einen postgradualen Master of Business Administration in General Management erworben. Seit 2000 arbeitet Luciana Silvares bei Mazda Europe, zunächst als Senior Designer in der Abteilung für Farben und Materialien. Seit 2017 ist sie dort für das Brand Style Management und die Strategische Entwicklung für Produkte/ Merchandising verantwortlich.

www.mazda.de

Luciana Silvares studied architecture and urban planning at Mackenzie University in São Paulo, earned a master's degree in industrial design at Munich University of Applied Sciences and an MBA in general management from the University of Warwick in the UK. She has been working at Mazda Europe since 2000, initially as a senior designer in the colours and materials department. Since 2017, she has been responsible for brand style management and strategic development for products/merchandising.

www.mazda.de

1   → SEITE / PAGE
    218–223

2   → SEITE / PAGE
    224, 226

3   → SEITE / PAGE
    225, 227

MATERIALS & SURFACES

GOLD:

1 **LIGNO AKUSTIK NATURE 3D**
Lignotrend Produktions GmbH
Weilheim

SPECIAL MENTION:

2 **FORUM FOR GREAT IDEAS**
Object Carpet GmbH
Denkendorf

3 **3:CYCLING, ELIADE, SMART FINISH**
Rökona Textilwerke GmbH & Co. KG
Tübingen

Technik beeinflusst schon immer das Design, auch Werkstoffe tun dies mehr denn je. Materialien mit innovativen Eigenschaften eröffnen Nutzungsszenarien, die zu mehr Nachhaltigkeit, geringerem Ressourcenverbrauch oder optimierter Funktionsintegration leiten.

Technology has always influenced design, and materials are having a greater impact than ever before. Materials with innovative properties open up usage scenarios that lead to greater sustainability, reduced resource consumption or the optimised integration of functions.

14

GOLD LIGNO AKUSTIK NATURE 3D AKUSTIKPANEEL ACOUSTIC PANEL

LIGNO AKUS
NATURE 3D

AKUSTI
PANEEL

GOLD

LIGNO AKUSTIK NATURE 3D
AKUSTIKPANEEL / ACOUSTIC PANEL

220
221

JURY STATEMENT

Auf den ersten Blick wirkt die Idee, Holzleisten aneinanderzureihen, recht simpel. Aber wer genau hinschaut, erkennt die Raffinesse des einfachen Aufbaus. Verwendet werden nur hölzerne Materialien, die Reihung der unterschiedlichen Leisten erzeugt ein belebtes Deckenprofil mit warmer, natürlicher Anmutung. Damit profitieren Räume nicht nur akustisch von den Paneelen, sondern auch ästhetisch.

At first glance, the idea of creating rows of wooden slats seems very simple. But on closer inspection, you realise just how sophisticated this straightforward structure is. The panels consist entirely of wood-based materials. The juxtaposition of differently sized slats creates a vivid profile with a warm, natural look. As a result, the panels deliver aesthetic benefits as well as enhancing the acoustics of a space.

HERSTELLER / MANUFACTURER
Lignotrend Produktions GmbH
Weilheim

DESIGN
Inhouse

VERTRIEB / DISTRIBUTOR
Lignotrend Produktions GmbH
Weilheim

→ **SEITE / PAGE**
218–220, 222–223

Minimalistisch ausgestattete Interiors mit schallharten Oberflächen mögen zwar das Auge erfreuen, nicht aber das Ohr – es wird mit Nachhall, Reflektionen und Überlagerungen konfrontiert. Damit sich die Hörsamkeit solcher Räume verbessert, treten Akustikdecken in Aktion, die meist abgehängt und visuell wenig inspirierend sind. Lebendig hingegen wirken die knapp drei Meter langen Paneele, bestehend aus einer hölzernen Tragstruktur, schallabsorbierenden Holzfaserplatten und darüberliegenden, sichtbaren Leisten. Durch die Varianz der Leistenbreiten und -höhen entsteht ein dreidimensionaler, natürlicher Effekt. Das verwendete Weißtannen- oder Eichenholz ist astfrei, optisch homogen und stammt aus PEFC-zertifizierten Quellen. Die Verklebung der einzelnen Elemente basiert auf den baubiologischen Kriterien von Natureplus. Dank der großen Paneelformate wird die Wiederholung des Streifenmusters kaum wahrgenommen.

Minimalist interiors with acoustically hard surfaces might be easy on the eye but not on the ear – they confront those using the room with reverberations, reflections and superpositions. The acoustic ceilings that are deployed to improve the audibility of such spaces are usually suspended and not particularly inspiring to look at. By contrast, these panels are extremely vivid: almost three metres in length, they consist of a wooden backing structure, sound-absorbing fibreboard and visible slats. The varying widths and heights of the slats create a natural, three-dimensional effect. The silver fir or oak used for the panels is knot-free, looks homogeneous and is sourced from PEFC-certified forests. The way the individual elements are glued together meets the sustainable building criteria of the Natureplus ecolabel. Thanks to the large format of the panels, the repetition of the striped pattern is barely noticeable.

RALF HARDER   **MARKETINGLEITER,
LIGNOTREND PRODUKTIONS GMBH**

»Bei unseren Akustikpaneelen aus Holz steht immer im Vordergrund, neue Designvarianten anzubieten, die materialgerecht sind.«

»When it comes to our wooden acoustic panels, the focus is always on creating new design variants that are appropriate to the material.«

RALF HARDER

HEAD OF MARKETING, LIGNOTREND PRODUKTIONS GMBH

→ Akustikdecken für schallharte Interiors sind nicht neu – was ist an Ihrer Lösung anders gedacht?

Natürlich sind Akustikdecken keine Produktneuheit, auch solche nicht, die aus dem nachwachsenden Rohstoff Holz bestehen. Unser Ansatz ist, die Verarbeitungstiefe des Rohstoffs Holz gering zu halten. Die Akustikpaneele Ligno Akustik light bestehen aus gewachsenen Echtholzlagen, bei denen das jeweils sortentypische Maserungsbild erhalten ist. Die nun ausgezeichnete Variante Ligno Akustik nature:3D bringt zusätzlich eine belebende Tiefe ins Spiel: Die Leisten variieren in der Breite und in der Höhe, vergleichbar mit dem Wuchsbild des Baumes, der schmalere und breitere Jahresringe hat. Durch die große Elementbreite fällt die Musterwiederholung nicht auf. Obwohl betont natürlich, zeigt die fertige 3D-Fläche durch die Astfreiheit eine edle Schlichtheit.

Die Aufbauhöhe von Akustikdecken ist ein wichtiges Thema – wie groß ist die bei Lignotrend?

Je nach Einsatz startet die typische Aufbauhöhe eines 3D-Paneels inklusive Unterkonstruktion bei 66 Millimetern. Häufig, vor allem im Objektbereich, werden aber abgehängte Decken mit größerem Hohlraum ausgeführt – um darin Leitungen zu führen oder die Schallabsorption weiter zu verbessern.

Was stand am Anfang der Entwicklung? Die Idee, mit dem Material zu arbeiten oder die besondere Optik?

Wir arbeiten ausschließlich mit dem Material Holz. Im Vordergrund steht also die Absicht, neue materialgerechte Designvarianten anzubieten.

Stammt das Holz aus zertifizierten Quellen oder welche Kriterien liegen der Rohstoff-Auswahl zugrunde?

Ja, wir achten auf zertifizierte Holzquellen, unsere Produktion trägt das PEFC-Zertifikat. Viel wichtiger, weil deutlich strenger und ambitionierter, ist aber die Natureplus-Zertifizierung, die nicht nur ökologische Maßstäbe an Herkunft und Gewinnung des Ausgangsmaterials Holz anlegt, sondern auch baubiologische und funktionale Kriterien an das fertige Produkt. Die Kleber und Holzfaser-Akustikabsorber etwa müssen hinsichtlich gesundheitlicher Kriterien höchsten Standards entsprechen.

Werden keine besonderen Anforderungen gestellt, können wir übrigens auch auf den verbreiteten Einsatz von mineralischen Fasern als Absorber verzichten – wir bleiben mit ebenso wirksamen Holzfaserabsorbern für die Raumakustik beim nachwachsenden Rohstoff Holz.

→ Suspended ceilings for acoustically hard interiors are nothing new – how is the concept behind your solution different?

Obviously acoustic ceilings aren't new, not even ones made of renewable raw materials like wood. Our approach is to ensure the timber only undergoes a low level of processing. The Ligno Akustik light panels consist of layers of natural real wood that preserves the grain pattern typical of the respective species. The variant that's been presented with the award – Ligno Akustik nature:3D – adds a vivid sense of depth to the overall effect: the slats are different widths and heights, a bit like the ring pattern of a tree, in which some rings are narrower, some wider. Because the element is so wide, you don't notice the repetition of the pattern. And although the finished 3D surface is emphatically natural, it also has a simple elegance because there are no knots in the wood.

Dropped ceilings mean sacrificing a certain amount of height – how much ceiling height is lost with Lignotrend?

Depending on the assignment, the typical depth of a 3D panel including the substructure starts at 66 millimetres. But it's quite common – especially in the contract sector – to leave a bigger void when fitting suspended ceilings because it can be used to conceal the mechanical and electrical services or further improve sound absorption.

What was the starting point for the development? The idea of working with the material or the special visual effect?

Since wood is the only material we use, the focus is always on creating new design variants that are appropriate to the material.

Does the wood come from certified sources or which criteria do you base your choice of raw materials on?

Yes, we use wood from certified sources, our production is PEFC-certified. But the Natureplus certification is much more important because it's a lot stricter and more ambitious: besides defining ecological standards for the origin and harvesting of the basic raw material – wood in this case – it also specifies sustainable and functional criteria that the finished product has to meet. Take the adhesive and the wood fibre acoustic absorbers, for instance: they have to comply with the very highest health standards.

By the way: if there are no special requirements, we can dispense with the common practice of using mineral fibre absorbers – wood fibre absorbers are just as effective and mean we can stick to a renewable material for the room acoustics.

Das 1991 gegründete Unternehmen Lignotrend setzt als Hersteller konfigurierbarer Brettsperrholzelemente auf Designorientierung beim Bauen mit Holz. Die Produktpalette erstreckt sich über Lösungen für Konstruktion, Innenausbau und Fassade und fokussiert auf hohe architektonische, bautechnische und nachhaltige Qualität.

www.lignotrend.de

Founded in 1991, Lignotrend produces configurable cross-laminated timber elements and considers design a top priority for timber products used in construction. The product range includes solutions for construction, interiors and facades and focuses on top architectural and structural quality paired with sustainability.

www.lignotrend.de

| SPECIAL MENTION | FORUM FOR GREAT IDEAS → SEITE / PAGE 226 | TEXTILE BODENBELÄGE TEXTILE FLOOR COVERINGS |

SPECIAL MENTION — 3:CYCLING, ELIADE, SMART FINISH → SEITE / PAGE 227

TECHNISCHE TEXTILIEN
TECHNICAL TEXTILES

SPECIAL MENTION

FORUM FOR GREAT IDEAS

TEXTILE BODENBELÄGE
TEXTILE FLOOR COVERINGS

JURY STATEMENT

Die Kollektion zeigt sehr mutige, selbstbewusste Designs, der Boden wird mehr denn je zu einer ganz eigenständigen Gestaltungsebene im Raum. Trotz der visuellen Opulenz stimmen die technischen Aspekte: Die Beläge enthalten weder PVC, Latex oder Bitumen, dem Recycling steht also nichts entgegen.

The collection features very bold, self-confident designs – in keeping with the fact that, more than ever before, the floor is becoming a design arena in its own right. Despite the visual opulence of the design, the technical aspects are compelling: the carpeting contains no PVC, latex or bitumen, meaning nothing stands in the way of recycling.

Ein neues Kreativkonzept ermöglicht es Architekten und Interiordesignern, auf raumgreifenden Flächen innerhalb von Geschäften, Lobbys, Büros oder Hotels eigene Designideen zu verwirklichen – wahlweise als Bahnenware, Akustikfliese oder Einzelteppich. Innovative Produktionstechniken machen es möglich, eigenständige Unikate als Sonderanfertigungen zu realisieren. Als Inspirationsquelle dienen dabei 18 unterschiedliche Designs, die von Flower-Power-Motiven über organische Farb- und Formmuster bis hin zu puristischer Strenge reichen. Neben der gestalterischen Vielfalt punkten die textilen Bodenbeläge mit Strapazierfähigkeit und einer Rückenausführung, die aus recyceltem PET-Material besteht.

A new creative concept that enables architects and interior designers to implement their own design ideas over extensive areas in stores, lobbies, offices or hotels – with sheet carpeting, acoustic tiles or individual rugs. Innovative production methods make it possible to create distinctive, custom-made one-offs. Inspiration is provided by 18 different designs, ranging from flower-power motifs and organic colour and shape patterns all the way to puristic severity. In addition to their creative diversity, the textile floor coverings score high marks for durability and a backing made of recycled PET.

HERSTELLER / MANUFACTURER
Object Carpet GmbH
Denkendorf

DESIGN
Kathrin Patel
Mark Patel
Bremen

VERTRIEB / DISTRIBUTOR
Object Carpet GmbH
Denkendorf

→ SEITE / PAGE
224

SPECIAL MENTION

3:CYCLING, ELIADE, SMART FINISH

TECHNISCHE TEXTILIEN
TECHNICAL TEXTILES

JURY STATEMENT

Die Sortenreinheit der Materialien ist ein guter Ansatz zu mehr Nachhaltigkeit und geringerer Umweltbelastung bei der Produktion und beim Recycling. Die taktile Anmutung entspricht derjenigen von Naturmaterialien. Die visuelle Erscheinung überrascht durch interessante Effekte, beispielsweise Farbverläufe.

The fact that the products are monomaterials is a good approach for greater sustainability and less environmental impact with regard to both production and recycling. The tactile qualities resemble those of natural materials. The appearance of the materials is also surprising thanks to interesting effects such as colour gradients.

Die drei Materialien stehen stellvertretend für eine ganze Reihe textiler Werkstoffe, die der Hersteller für unterschiedlichste Anwendungen im Fahrzeug-Interior entwickelt. Alle Mitglieder dieser gewirkten 2D- und 3D-Textil-Familie sind automotive-konform und zudem möglichst nachhaltig konzipiert. 3:Cycling steht für ein sortenreines, aus Polyester bestehendes 3D-Material, das keine zusätzliche Hinterschäumung verlangt. Eliade wiederum bietet eine Haptik wie Leder. Smart Finish reduziert die Umweltauswirkungen durch spezielle Fertigungsverfahren und reduziert gleichzeitig später stattfindende Prozessschritte.

The three materials stand for a whole series of textiles that the manufacturer develops for a wide range of different applications in vehicle interiors. All the members of this family of knitted 2D and 3D textiles are compatible with the automotive sector and designed for maximum sustainability. 3:Cycling stands for a 3D polyester mono-material that doesn't require an additional foam backing. Eliade feels like leather, and Smart Finish uses special production processes to reduce climate impacts while simultaneously reducing the number of process steps required later on.

HERSTELLER / MANUFACTURER
Rökona Textilwerke GmbH & Co. KG
Tübingen

DESIGN
Inhouse

VERTRIEB / DISTRIBUTOR
Rökona Textilwerke GmbH & Co. KG
Tübingen

→ SEITE / PAGE
225

MIA SEEGER PR. 2020

MIA SEEGER PR. 2020

Jährlicher Wettbewerb der Mia Seeger Stiftung
für junge Designerinnen und Designer
mit Unterstützung der Hans Schwörer Stiftung und
des Rat für Formgebung

The Mia Seeger Foundation's annual
competition for young designers,
sponsored by the Hans Schwörer Foundation
and the German Design Council

| 1 | → SEITE / PAGE 232–233 | 2 | → SEITE / PAGE 234–235 | 3 | → SEITE / PAGE 236–237 |

| 4 | → SEITE / PAGE 238–239 | 5 | → SEITE / PAGE 240 | 6 | → SEITE / PAGE 241 |

| 7 | → SEITE / PAGE 242 | 8 | → SEITE / PAGE 242 | 9 | → SEITE / PAGE 243 |

| 10 | → SEITE / PAGE 243 | 11 | → SEITE / PAGE 243 | 12 | → SEITE / PAGE 243 | 13 | → SEITE / PAGE 243 |

MIA SEEGER PREIS 2020
MIA SEEGER PRIZE 2020

AMUV
1 Maximilian Holstein

FORTSCHREITER
2 Ruben Geörge

AUVIS
3 Lara Laddey

INFEKTIONSSCHUTZ BEI ENDEMIEN EPIDEMIEN UND PANDEMIEN
4 Nadja Skorov

ANERKENNUNG
HIGHLY COMMENDED

PROTHESE 2.0
5 Lucas Balcilar

LETZTER ABSCHIED
6 Lena Jacobi

JOI
7 Elisabeth Klug
und / and
8 Marius Greiner

CAPTIN_KIEL
9 Simeon Ortmüller
10 Vincent Steinhart-Besser
11 Jingyue Chen
12 Yigang Shen
13 Tobias Gehrke

MIA SEEGER PREIS 2020 FÜR JUNGE DESIGNERINNEN UND DESIGNER
MIA SEEGER PRIZE 2020 ANNUAL COMPETITION FOR YOUNG DESIGNERS

JURY
PROF. ANNE BERGNER
Designerin, Akademie der Bildenden Künste Stuttgart / Designer, Stuttgart Academy of Art and Design

MATTHIS HAMANN
Designer, Managing Partner, Fluid GmbH, München / Designer, managing partner, Fluid GmbH, Munich

STEFAN LIPPERT
Designer, UP Designstudio, Stuttgart, Mia Seeger Preisträger 1993 und Stipendiat / Designer, UP Designstudio, Stuttgart, Mia Seeger prize winner 1993 and scholarship winner

ARMIN SCHARF
Freier Journalist, Tübingen / Freelance journalist, Tübingen

OLIVER STOTZ
Industriedesigner, stotz-design.com, Wuppertal, Mia Seeger Preisträger 1992 / Industrial designer, stotz-design.com, Wuppertal, Mia Seeger Prize winner 1992

ELKE WEISER
Designerin, Weiser_Design, Stuttgart, Mia Seeger Preisträgerin 1993 / Designer, Weiser_Design, Stuttgart, Mia Seeger Prize winner 1993

Alles wie gehabt? – Eben nicht. Gerade war wieder der Mia Seeger Preis 2020 mit 10.000 Euro ausgeschrieben, da brach Corona herein. Die Stiftung verlegte sich aufs Digitale. Einreichungen nur noch per Internet, Terminverschiebungen, Einrichten von Datenspeichern, Jurieren unterm Bildschirm. Ohne die Hilfe von außen wäre es nicht gegangen. Allen, die sich ins Zeug gelegt haben (siehe Jury und Impressum), sei von Herzen gedankt. Die Mühe hat sich gelohnt: 115 Anmeldungen aus 30 Hochschulen – so viele wie nie zuvor. An die eingereichten Arbeiten hatte die Jury neben den üblichen Qualitätsmaßstäben den des sozialen Nutzens anzulegen. Resultat: vier Preise und vier Anerkennungen.

The same procedure as always? Not this time! The Mia Seeger Prize 2020 had just been announced with prize money of 10,000 euros when corona hit. The foundation shifted to digital mode. Entries could only be submitted online, deadlines were postponed, data stores set up, the judging took place on screen. It wouldn't have been possible without external help – which is why we'd like to say a big thank you to everyone who made it happen (see Jury and Publishing Details). But all the effort was well worth the trouble: the foundation received 115 entries from 30 colleges and universities – more than ever before. In addition to the usual quality criteria, the jury also assessed the works submitted on the basis of their benefit to society. The result: four prizes and four Highly Commended distinctions.

Die Jury am 15. Juli 2020. Von links nach rechts: Elke Weiser, Stefan Lippert, Anne Bergner, Oliver Stotz, Armin Scharf. Nicht im Bild: Matthis Hamman; er war per Video zugeschaltet.

The jury on 15 July 2020. From left to right: Elke Weiser, Stefan Lippert, Anne Bergner, Oliver Stotz, Armin Scharf. Not pictured: Matthis Hamman, who joined the other judges via video.

© Florin Betz

MIA SEEGER PREIS 2020
MIA SEEGER PRIZE 2020

JURY STATEMENT

Ja, genau, so könnte es gehen, dass eine – auch deutlich aufgefächerte – medizinische Versorgung in die Fläche kommt und mit der Zeit die überlaufene und schlecht erreichbare Landarztpraxis ablöst. Alles richtig gemacht, gut recherchiert und schlüssig bedacht. Es ging ja nicht nur um den Entwurf eines selbstfahrenden Kabinenwagens und dessen höchst zweckmäßiger Inneneinrichtung, sondern auch darum, eine Versorgungsstruktur zu konzipieren, die eine ganze Fahrzeugflotte bereithält und dafür Wartung, Ausrüstung und Logistik braucht.

Yes, this could well be the answer to providing even specialised healthcare in rural areas. Over time, it could gradually replace country doctors' practices, which are often overrun and difficult to reach. Everything has been done right, thoroughly researched and logically thought through. After all, it wasn't just a case of designing an autonomous pod and its highly practical interior, but of developing a supply structure that keeps an entire fleet of vehicles on hand and ensures the necessary maintenance, equipment and logistics are available.

AMUV — AUTONOMOUS MEDICAL UTILITY VEHICLE

ENTWERFER / DEVELOPER
Maximilian Holstein
maximilianholstein@gmx.net

STUDIUM / DEGREE COURSE
Industrie-Design, Diplom FH
Hochschule Darmstadt

BETREUUNG / SUPERVISOR
Prof. Tom Philipps

Herr K., gebrechlich und nicht gesund, muss zum Arzt. Vom Dorf in die Stadt schafft er es nicht mehr, nur noch bis zum Gemeindehaus. Dort erwartet ihn das Sprechstunden-Mobil. Zur Tagestour über die Dörfer war das Gefährt nachts in der Zentrale mit den erforderlichen Modulen ausgestattet worden, so dass auch für Herrn K., wenn die Pflegekraft ihn umsorgt, das richtige dabei ist. Bei Bedarf zieht sie den Arzt per Video hinzu. Nachdem alle, die angemeldet waren, behandelt sind und vielleicht noch etwas Zeit für Nachzügler war, geht es weiter zur nächsten Station.

Mr Bloggs, frail and unwell, needs to see a doctor. He can't make it all the way into town, the village community centre is the farthest he can manage. When he gets there, the mobile treatment room is waiting for him. In preparation for its daytime tour of the local villages, the vehicle spent the night at base, where it was equipped with the modules the nurse will need to take care of Mr Bloggs when he arrives. If necessary, she can consult the doctor remotely. After everybody with an appointment has been treated and possibly allowing a little extra time for latecomers, the AMUV departs for its next stop.

MIA SEEGER PREIS 2020
MIA SEEGER PRIZE 2020

JURY STATEMENT

Nichts ist in der Bachelor Thesis ausgelassen, nicht die Erfolgsgeschichte vom Sneaker und nicht das zugehörige Sündenregister, in das sich Industrie, Handel und Kundschaft eingetragen haben. Am Kreislauf der Materialien will der Verfasser mit seinem Reformwerk ansetzen, und der Knoten scheint geplatzt, als er auf die Idee mit der rahmengesteckten Machart kommt. Von da aus erschließt er sich den weiteren Weg zu Langlebigkeit und sortenreiner Zerlegbarkeit und schafft es, dass der Schuh ökologisch weniger drückt und doch unverkennbar Sneaker bleibt. Respekt.

The bachelor's thesis doesn't leave anything out – neither the success story of sneakers' rise to popularity nor the catalogue of sins committed by industry, retailers and consumers in the process. The developer takes closed loop recycling as the starting point for his reforms – and cuts the Gordian knot by coming up with the idea of click-in welts. From there, he continues on the path towards product longevity and separable components made of monomaterials, ensuring that the shoe is a comfortable fit with sustainability while nevertheless incontestably remaining a sneaker. Well done!

FORTSCHREITER
ÖKOLOGISCHER SCHUHABDRUCK
ECOLOGICAL SHOEPRINT

ENTWERFER / DEVELOPER
Ruben Geörge
rubengeoerge@yahoo.de

STUDIUM / DEGREE COURSE
Produktgestaltung BA,
Strategische Gestaltung MA
Hochschule für Gestaltung
Schwäbisch Gmünd

BETREUUNG / SUPERVISORS
Prof. Gabriele N. Reichert
Prof. Gerhard Reichert

Fortschritt sieht hier so aus: Der Sneaker ist aus Einzelteilen aufgebaut, ohne Kleber. Nur re- und upgecycelte Materialien kommen in Frage. Schaft und Sohlen sind in rahmengesteckter (nicht: rahmengenähter) Machart verbunden. Abgenutzte Komponenten lassen sich austauschen. Ein verschmutzter Innenschuh kommt einfach in die Waschmaschine. Ausgediente Schuhe werden vollständig zerlegt und ihre Bestandteile dem Recycling zugeführt. Bauart, Austauschbarkeit und die Produktion im 3D-Drucker begünstigen die Individualisierung und damit die Wertschätzung.

A big step forward: the sneaker is put together out of individual parts – without adhesive. Only recycled and upcycled materials come into question for its production. The welt that connects the upper with the sole is clicked into place (not sewn or glued!). Worn-out components can be replaced. A dirty inner shoe can be put in the washing machine. And when the shoes have had their day, they're taken apart so that their individual components can be recycled. The way they're made, their interchangeable parts and the fact that the components are 3D-printed mean the shoes are easy to personalise, increasing the chances that their owners will value them.

MIA SEEGER PREIS 2020
MIA SEEGER PRIZE 2020

JURY STATEMENT

Warum zum Knie? – Die Designerin beruft sich auf eine Pilotstudie, in der herausgefunden worden sei, dass ein gesundes Knie anders knirscht als eines im Frühstadium der Arthrose. Daher das Abhören der Gelenke in die Vorsorge einzubeziehen wäre. Klar, dass sich dann die Zweiteilung des Stethoskops als ganz praktisch erwiese, die diagnostischen Vorteile der Digitalisierung noch gar nicht gerechnet. Indem das neue Stethoskop die Grundgestalt des alten übernimmt, profitiert es von dessen Symbolkraft.

Why would the doctor want to listen to the patient's knee? The designer cites a pilot study that found a healthy knee makes different grating noises than one in the early stages of arthrosis. It would therefore make sense to listen to the patient's joints during a check-up too. And then separating the stethoscope into two parts would obviously be extremely practical, not to mention the diagnostic benefits of its digitalisation. The new stethoscope benefits from the symbolic power of its predecessor by retaining its familiar basic form.

ENTWERFERIN / DEVELOPER
Lara Laddey
laraladdey@gmail.com

STUDIUM / DEGREE COURSE
Industriedesign (Master Medical Design)
Muthesius Kunsthochschule Kiel

BETREUUNG / SUPERVISOR
Prof. Detlef Rhein

Ein Stethoskop ohne Schläuche. Wie soll das gehen? – Im Sensorkopf ist die druckempfindliche Membran durch eine Art Mikrophon ersetzt. Ein kleiner Prozessor stellt sich auf die zu erwartenden Frequenzen ein, verstärkt charakteristische Geräusche, filtert störende heraus und sendet die Daten an den Empfänger im Hörrohr, wo sie klar und deutlich mittels geeigneter Mikro-Lautsprecher ans Ohr der Ärztin dringen. Sie kann jetzt das Gerät in ihrer Hand, ohne durch einen Schlauch inkommodiert zu sein, von Brust oder Rücken des Patienten kurzerhand zu seinem Knie führen.

A stethoscope with no tubes – how's that supposed to work? By replacing the pressure-sensitive diaphragm with a kind of microphone in the sensor head! A small processor tunes itself to the expected frequencies, amplifies characteristic sounds, filters out interfering noises and sends the data to the receiver in the headset, where it reaches the doctor loud and clear thanks to the micro-speakers in the earpieces. As a result, the doctor can move the sensor from the patient's chest or back to their knee without being inconvenienced by a tube.

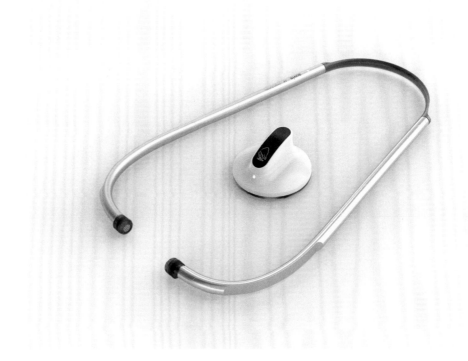

MIA SEEGER PREIS 2020
MIA SEEGER PRIZE 2020

JURY STATEMENT

Sicherheit geht vor. Dieser Maxime folgt die Designerin im Ganzen und in vielen Details, ohne detailversessen zu sein. Daher ihr Anliegen, den Körper vollständig zu bedecken. Von ihrer Maxime lässt sie sich auch bei Kompromissen leiten. Den Ehrgeiz, alles selber zu zeichnen, hat sie nicht. Lieber kümmert sie sich bei übernommenen Teilen, Handschuhen zum Beispiel, darum, dass der Anschluss zum Overall stimmt. Gelassen nimmt sie eine additive Gestaltung in Kauf. Allein das Farbkonzept – Weiß nach außen, Orange nach innen – stiftet Einheit.

Safety first. The designer adheres to this maxim in both her overall approach and in many of its details, without becoming obsessive. That's why she's so intent on covering the body completely. And it's that same maxim that guides her approach to compromises. She does not aspire to design everything herself. Instead, she prefers to use bought-in parts, gloves for instance, and ensure that they interface perfectly with the overall. She is quite content to accept an additive solution. The colour concept – white goes on the outside, orange on the inside – is the only unifying element.

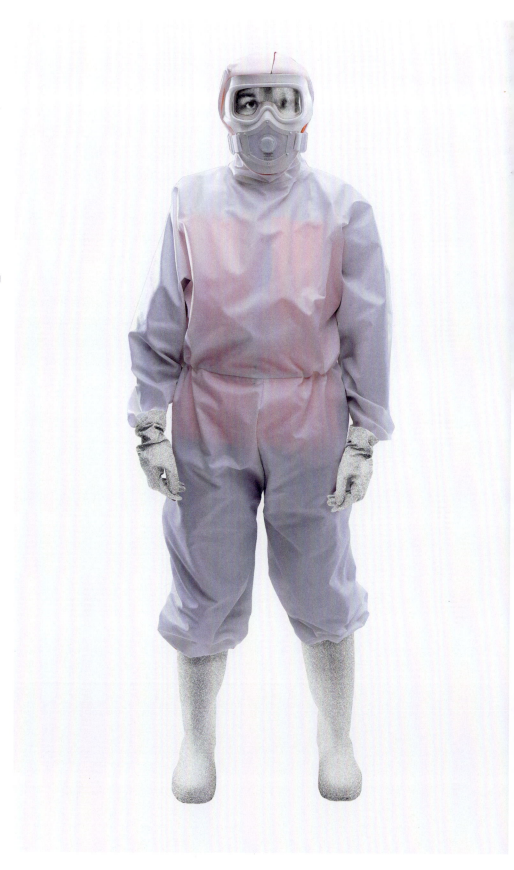

INFEKTIONSSCHUTZ BEI ENDEMIEN, EPIDEMIEN UND PANDEMIEN
PROTECTION FROM INFECTION IN ENDEMICS, EPIDEMICS AND PANDEMICS

ENTWERFERIN / DEVELOPER
Nadja Skorov
nadiaskorov@gmail.com

STUDIUM / DEGREE COURSE
Industrial Design, Bachelor of Arts
Hochschule für Technik und Wirtschaft
Berlin

BETREUUNG / SUPERVISORS
Prof. Pelin Celik
Prof. Sebastian Feucht

So richtig gut schützen Infektions-Schutzanzüge noch nicht. Der hier vorgeschlagene verbessert vieles. Die wichtigsten Errungenschaften sind eine Gesichtsmaske, in die sich Brille und Mundschutz passgenau einfügen, eine lückenlose Verbindung von Maske und Kapuze, auffällige Markierungen in Orange, die fehlerhaftes Anlegen des Anzugs erschweren, und eine Kühlweste mit Taschen für Cool-Packs. Materialien, Zuschnitte oder Zukaufteile sind auf geringe Kosten für Produktion, Abfall, Verschnitt, Lagerhaltung oder Verfügbarkeit berechnet.

Right now, PPE overalls are not that effective when it comes to protecting the wearer from infection. This suit makes a number of improvements. The most important achievements are a face shield that the goggles and mask fit into perfectly, a continuous join between the mask and hood, conspicuous orange markings that make it harder to put the overall on incorrectly, and a cooler waistcoat with pockets for cold packs. The materials, cuts and bought-in parts are designed to keep costs for production, waste, offcuts, storage and availability as low as possible.

ANERKENNUNG
HIGHLY COMMENDED

PROTHESE 2.0

PROSTHETIC ARM

JURY STATEMENT
Für die Handhabung ist ein Schritt weiter gewonnen. Was an Mikroelektronik, Sensorik, Netzwerktechnik und einschlägigen Forschungsergebnissen verfügbar und geeignet erscheint, ist der Prothese mit Gewinn einverleibt, in der Form- und Farbgestalt sichtbar gemacht und zum Teil offengelegt in den Durchbrüchen an Arm, Handrücken und Fingern. Dem technikaffinen Nutzer mag die androide Cyborg-Ästhetik zusagen. Für den, der mit seiner Behinderung eher zurückhaltend umgeht, sind textile Überzüge passend zur übrigen Kleidung konzipiert.

A step forward for the handling of such prostheses. Along with relevant research findings, the prosthesis incorporates and benefits from any currently available microelectronic, sensor and network technology that seems fit for purpose, uses form and colour to visualise it and in some cases puts it on full display through apertures in the arm, the back of the hand and the fingers. Technophile users will no doubt find the androidal cyborg aesthetic appealing. But for those with reservations about calling attention to their disability, the concept includes textile coverings that blend in with the wearer's clothes as well.

ENTWERFER / DEVELOPER
Lucas Balcilar
balcilar.lucas@gmail.com

STUDIUM / DEGREE COURSE
Industrial Design, Bachelor of Arts
Hochschule für Technik und Wirtschaft
Berlin

BETREUUNG / SUPERVISORS
Prof. Pelin Celik
Prof. Birgit Weller

Einfach die Hand ausstrecken und zugreifen? Mit den Armprothesen von heute geht es noch nicht. Hier schon. Im Handgelenk sind Kameras eingebaut. Die ihnen hinterlegte KI-Technik erkennt das anvisierte Objekt und wählt den passenden Griff-Typ aus. Ein Muskelzucken und die Hand schließt sich. Sensoren in den Fingern registrieren den Andruck. Deren Daten und die der Handbewegungen geben, zu Vibrationsmustern umgerechnet und an geeignete Muskeln im Stumpf übertragen, dem Träger die Illusion, selber zu greifen. Das Fremdkörpergefühl schwindet.

Simply reaching for something and picking it up isn't possible with the prosthetic arms currently available. But with this one it is. Cameras are integrated into the wrist. The AI technology that powers them identifies the object the wearer is aiming for and selects the type of grip required accordingly. A muscle signal is all it takes to close the hand. Sensors in the fingers register the amount of pressure applied. The data from the sensors and hand movements is converted into vibration patterns that are relayed to the relevant muscles in the stump, giving the wearer the illusion of gripping the object themselves and minimising the sensation of operating a foreign body.

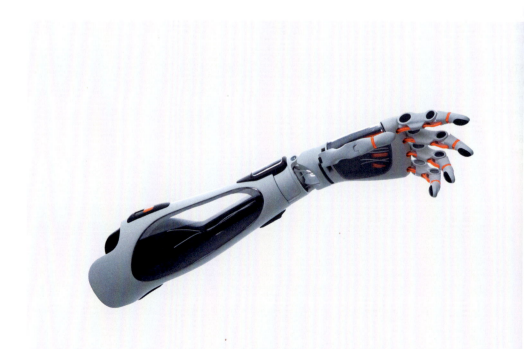

ANERKENNUNG / HIGHLY COMMENDED

LETZTER ABSCHIED / SHROUD

240 241

JURY STATEMENT

Würde und Pietät prägen den Entwurf. Von muslimischen Leichentüchern abgeleitet, löst er viele Probleme, wie Stoffersparnis, einheitlicher Zuschnitt für alle Körpergrößen, Vorrichtung zum Tragen, Infektionsschutz oder Identifikation. Er zeigt sich neutral gegenüber religiösen Riten und gibt den Hinterbliebenen ihr Recht auf Abschied. Für den Fall überschaubarer Katastrophen ist die Lösung überzeugend – und wertvoll als Aufruf, nicht erst in der Not über Alternativen zum üblichen Sarg aus Holz nachzudenken.

Dignity and piety are the defining influences behind the design. Derived from Muslim shrouds, it provides a solution to all sorts of problems: it saves fabric, is cut so that one size fits any body, is equipped with loops that serve as carrying handles, provides protection from infection and permits identification. It takes a neutral position on religious rites and grants the bereaved their right to say goodbye. A compelling solution for catastrophes on a limited scale – and a valuable approach that calls on us to think about alternatives to conventional wooden coffins before disaster strikes.

ENTWERFERIN / DEVELOPER
Lena Jacobi
lena.jacobi@mail.de

STUDIUM / DEGREE COURSE
Industrial Design, Bachelor of Arts
Hochschule für Technik und Wirtschaft Berlin

BETREUUNG / SUPERVISORS
Prof. Sebastian Feucht
Prof. Pelin Celik

Etwas Besseres als ein Plastiksack findet sich allemal, auch im Katastrophenfall: eine Schutzhusse wie diese, aus Tuch, oval zugeschnitten, mit Bändern, Schlaufen und einer kleinen Tasche versehen, darin der Leichnam eingeschlagen wird. Der Verstorbene liegt auf einer Hanfmatte, die Flüssigkeiten absorbiert und mit Pilzsporen zur Zersetzung von Keimen präpariert ist. Bei hoher Infektionsgefahr ist er zusätzlich in eine transparente Schutzfolie aus Bio-Plastik gehüllt. Zum Identifizieren und bei Abschiedszeremonien kann der Kopf frei bleiben.

There has to be something better than a plastic sack, even in a disaster situation: a shroud like this to wrap the body in, made of cloth, oval in shape, equipped with loops and ties and a little pocket. The deceased lies on a hemp mat that absorbs fluids and is treated with fungal spores that combat bacteria. As an additional precaution when there is a high risk of infection, the body is wrapped in a transparent protective foil made of bioplastic as well. The head can be left uncovered for identification purposes or during mourning ceremonies.

ANERKENNUNG
HIGHLY COMMENDED

JOI

ÜBUNGSGERÄT FÜR PARKINSONKRANKE
TRAINING DEVICE FOR PARKINSON'S SUFFERERS

JURY STATEMENT
Sensorbasierte Gestenerkennung – was bei Computerspielen geht, könnte auch für die Therapie klappen. An die Stelle von Gesten treten gymnastische Bewegungen, die es digital zu überwachen gilt. Mit Rücksicht auf die Erkrankung ist die Bedienerführung einfach und unmittelbar verständlich gefasst, desgleichen die bildhafte Rückmeldung. Alle Funktionen sind auf den einen therapeutischen Zweck fokussiert, und doch ist das Spielerische dabei nicht vergessen.

Sensor-based gesture recognition – if computer games can do it, why not use the technology for therapeutic purposes as well? Instead of gamers' gestures, the device monitors the gymnastic performance of Parkinson's sufferers. In view of the impairments associated with the disease, navigation is simple and easy to understand, as is the pictorial feedback. And while all the functions focus on achieving the therapeutic goals, the play aspect is by no means ignored.

Unter den Bedingungen von Parkinson reicht kein Video, es müsste schon so etwas wie »Joi« sein: ein interaktives Wandgerät, das zum Üben aufruft, anzeigt, welche Übung dran ist, und die Ausführung kontrolliert. Das Strichmännchen macht die Übung vor. Was Patientin oder Patient nachmachen, registriert die Gestenerkennung. Was sie zeitgleich auf die Wand projiziert sehen, will sie in ihrem Tun bestätigen und bestärken oder sie zur Korrektur anhalten. Aus der Aufzeichnung der Bewegungsdaten erhält das betreuende Personal Aufschlüsse über therapeutische Fortschritte.

Given the conditions associated with Parkinson's disease, a video simply isn't enough, only something along the lines of »Joi« can really help: an interactive, wall-mounted device that encourages sufferers to exercise, shows them what they should be doing and monitors how they do it. The matchstick man demonstrates the exercise. Gesture recognition technology detects how well the patient follows his lead. The projections on the wall either provide approval and encouragement or make suggestions for improvements. The recorded data informs caregivers of the progress the patient is making as a result of the therapy.

ENTWERFER*IN / DEVELOPERS
Elisabeth Klug
elisabeth.klug@stud.hs-coburg.de
und / and
Marius Greiner
marius.greiner@stud.hs-coburg.de

STUDIUM / DEGREE COURSE
Integriertes Produktdesign (Bachelor)
Hochschule Coburg

BETREUUNG / SUPERVISOR
Prof. Wolfgang Schabbach

ANERKENNUNG / HIGHLY COMMENDED

CAPTIN_KIEL — AUTONOMOUS FERRY CONCEPT

JURY STATEMENT

Zwei ungleiche Schwestern laufen vom Stapel: Die eine macht das Übersetzen über die Förde zu einem unvergesslichen Seh-Erlebnis; die andere will ihren Passagieren eine schwimmende und schützende Brücke sein (daher das Gewölbe). Sehr früh hat damit Design in einem großen Forschungs- und Entwicklungsprojekt zwei grundsätzliche Richtungen vorgezeichnet. Man darf gespannt sein, wie die Kieler sich entscheiden. Am liebsten so, dass, wer nach Kiel kommt, unbedingt mit der neuen Fähre fahren will.

The concept launches two very different sisters: one of them turns crossing the Kiel fjord into an unforgettable sightseeing experience, the other serves as a floating and protective bridge (hence its arched shape). As a result, design has succeeded in predetermining two basic directions for a major research and development project. It will be interesting to see how the citizens of Kiel decide. Hopefully their preferred option will ensure that anybody who visits Kiel will put the new ferry on their »must-do« list.

Im Rahmen von »CAPTin Kiel« haben die Studierenden ein Gestaltungskonzept für sauberen autonomen Fährverkehr auf der Kieler Förde entwickelt. Genau genommen: zwei Konzepte. In vielen Renderings befreiten sie sich von maritimen Klischees wie Ausflugsdampfer oder Schnellboot und fanden – zwischen Pflichtenheft und Sehnsucht nach Außergewöhnlichem – zu zwei neuartigen Typen: »Floating Platform« und »Passage«. Beide bauen nach Art des Katamarans auf doppelt angelegten Schwimmkörpern auf, die hier mit Wasserstoff betrieben sind.

The students who contributed to the »CAPTin Kiel« project developed a concept for a clean, autonomous ferry service for the Kieler Förde inlet. Or to be more precise, two concepts. In their many renderings, they liberated themselves from maritime clichés such as pleasure steamers and speedboats and – by balancing the requirements set out in the scope statement with their desire to create something out of the ordinary – came up with two new types of craft: »Floating Platform« and »Passage«. Both models are based on the catamaran principle and have twin hulls – in this case powered by hydrogen.

ENTWERFER / DEVELOPERS
Simeon Ortmüller
Vincent Steinhart-Besser
Jingyue Chen
Yigang Shen
Tobias Gehrke
captin.muthesius@outlook.de
simeon.ortmueller@arcor.de

STUDIUM / DEGREE COURSE
Industriedesign (Master)
Muthesius Kunsthochschule Kiel

BETREUUNG / SUPERVISORS
Prof. Detlef Rhein

MIA SEEGER STIFTUNG

THE MIA SEEGER FOUNDATION

IMPRESSUM / PUBLISHING DETAILS

HERAUSGEBER / PUBLISHED BY
Mia Seeger Stiftung

REDAKTION / EDITORS
Marion Ascherl, Schwäbisch Gmünd
Wolfgang Berger, Stuttgart

ÜBERSETZUNG / TRANSLATION
Alison Du Bovis, Jork

GRAFIKDESIGN / GRAPHIC DESIGN
stapelberg & fritz, Stuttgart

**AUSSTELLUNGSGESTALTUNG /
EXHIBITION DESIGN**
Thomas Simianer, Stuttgart

FOTOS / PHOTOS
Prize-winners, commended entrants,
Karl Fisch

**JURYVORBEREITUNG /
JUDGING ORGANISED BY**
Renate Seeger, Iris Steinmetz,
Marion Ascherl

**DIGITALE TECHNIK, VIDEO-KONFERENZEN /
DIGITAL TECHNOLOGY, VIDEO CONFERENCES**
Stefan Lippert, UP Designstudio

MIA SEEGER STIFTUNG
c/o Design Center
Baden-Württemberg
im Haus der Wirtschaft
Willi-Bleicher-Straße 19
D-70174 Stuttgart

T +49 711 123 2781
F +49 711 123 2771

E-Mail: design@rps.bwl.de
www.mia-seeger.de
instagram.com/miaseeger

Mia Seeger war die »Grande Dame« des Design. Mit der Weißenhofsiedlung 1927 in Stuttgart begann ihre Laufbahn. Bald war sie an weiteren Ausstellungen des Deutschen Werkbundes beteiligt. Die Bundesrepublik hat sie vielfach als Kommissarin zu Triennalen in Mailand entsandt und zur ersten Leiterin des Rat für Formgebung berufen, den sie zwölf Jahre lang führte. Sie war selbst keine Designerin, sondern Design-Vermittlerin und -Beraterin. 1986 rief sie die nach ihr benannte Stiftung ins Leben, deren Zweck die Bildung junger Gestalterinnen und Gestalter ist. Namhafte Sponsoren aus der Wirtschaft haben sich ihren Zielen angeschlossen.

Mit der Absicht, besonders den Nachwuchs im Design zu fördern und ihn dabei zur Auseinandersetzung mit sozialen Fragen aufzufordern, schreibt die Stiftung jährlich den Mia Seeger Preis unter dem Motto »was mehr als einem nützt« aus. Seit Jahren kann sie die Ergebnisse ihres Designwettbewerbs im Rahmen der Ausstellung »Focus Open – Internationaler Designpreis Baden-Württemberg« präsentieren. Dafür ist sie dem Design Center sehr dankbar, auch für die Vorbereitung und Organisation der Jurierung.

Darüber hinaus erfreut sich die Stiftung schon länger einer vertraglich vereinbarten Kooperation mit dem Rat für Formgebung. Er trägt auch dazu bei, das Wirken der Stiftung, insbesondere die Kontinuität des Mia Seeger Preises finanziell zu sichern. Auch andere Spender haben mit einmaligen Zuwendungen dazu beigetragen, 2016 Alexander Neumeister und im Jahr danach die Hans Schwörer Stiftung. Wer in dieser oder ähnlicher Weise die gemeinnützige Arbeit der Mia Seeger Stiftung unterstützen möchte, wendet sich am besten an die Geschäftsführerin der Stiftung, Marion Ascherl.

Mia Seeger was the »grande dame« of design. Her career began with the Weissenhof Estate in Stuttgart in 1927. She was soon involved with further exhibitions by the Deutscher Werkbund as well. The Federal Republic of Germany frequently sent her to the Triennial exhibitions in Milan as its commissioner and appointed her the first director of the German Design Council, which she headed for twelve years. She herself was not a designer but a design mediator and adviser. She established the foundation that bears her name in 1986 for the purpose of promoting young designers' education. Renowned sponsors from commerce and industry have joined the foundation in the pursuit of its goals.

With the specific aim of promoting young designers and challenging them to tackle social issues, the foundation invites entries for the annual Mia Seeger Prize under the motto »benefiting more than the individual«. For some years now, it has been able to present the results of its design competition within the context of the Focus Open – Baden-Württemberg International Design Award. The foundation is deeply obliged to the Design Center for its assistance, as well as for the preparation and organisation of the judging.

In addition, the foundation has had a cooperation agreement with the German Design Council for some time now. This contract helps ensure the financial security of the foundation's work, and in particular the continuity of the Mia Seeger Prize. Other benefactors have also provided valuable support in the form of one-off donations, including Alexander Neumeister in 2016 and the Hans Schwörer Foundation in the following year. Anybody who would like to support the Mia Seeger Foundation's non-profit work in this or a similar way should please contact the foundation's managing director Marion Ascherl.

Über ihre Arbeit informiert die Stiftung auf ihrer Internetseite: www.mia-seeger.de. Darüber hinaus gibt es News und Posts rund um Design mit sozialem Anspruch auf instagram.com/miaseeger.

Detailed information about the foundation's work is available on its website: www.mia-seeger.de. The foundation also publishes news and posts about design with a social slant at Instagram.com/miaseeger.

244
245

APPENDIX
A—Z

ADRESSEN / ADDRESSES

A

AMF – Andreas Maier GmbH & Co. KG
Waiblinger Str. 116
70734 Fellbach
T +49 711 5766 0
www.amf.de
S/P 21

AOK Baden-Württemberg
Hauptverwaltung
Presselstr. 19
70191 Stuttgart
T +49 711 12853 801
www.aok.de/pk/bw
S/P 182

Artenhaus
Gebelstr. 18
75446 Wiernsheim
T +49 157 504 370 27
www.lichtstahl.com
S/P 123

Artline
Zimmermühlenweg 14-18
61440 Oberursel
T +49 6171 632 02
www.artline.de
S/P 104

Atelier Brückner GmbH
Krefelder Str. 32
70376 Stuttgart
T +49 711 5000 77 0
www.atelier-brueckner.com
S/P 185

B

Belchengruppe GmbH
Hegenheimerstr. 105
CH-4055 Basel
T +41 61 511 211 2
www.belchengruppe.ch
S/P 122

BeSafe
Krøderen
NO-3535 Krøderen
T +47 3214 7550
www.besafe.com
S/P 152

Robert Bosch GmbH
Robert-Bosch-Platz 1
70839 Gerlingen
T +49 711 400 4099 0
www.bosch.com
S/P 203

Bosch Corporate Design Team und United Digital Group
Robert-Bosch-Platz 1
70839 Gerlingen
T +49 711 400 4099 0
www.bosch.com
S/P 203

Braake Design
Turnierstr. 3
50999 Stuttgart
T +49 711 459 9989 0
www.braake.com
S/P 35

Bullfrog Marketing & Design GmbH
Landwehrstr. 32
96247 Michelau
T + 49 9571 9479 60
www.bullfrog-design.de
S/P 106

Bunse05
Kinkelstr. 5
58097 Hagen
T +49 2331 348 6190
www.bunse05.de
S/P 38

Busch-Jaeger Elektro GmbH
Freisenbergstr. 2
58513 Lüdenscheid
T +49 2351 9561 1600
www.busch-jaeger.de
S/P 164, 167
Dörte Thinius
S/P 164, 167

C

Corporate Friends GmbH
Pulsnitzer Str. 46
01917 Kamenz
T +49 3578 7856 111
www.corporatefriends.de
S/P 133

D

Daikin Airconditioning Germany GmbH
Inselkammerstrasse 2
82008 Unterhaching
T +49 89 744 27 0
www.daikin.de
S/P 166

Daikin Europe N.V.
Zandvoordestraat 300
BE-8400 Ostende
T +32 2 529 61 11
www.daikin.eu
S/P 166

Diana Electronic-Systeme GmbH
Siemensstr. 2
71409 Schwaikheim
T +49 7195 97707 0
www.dianaelectronic.de
S/P 37
Martin Weller
S/P 37

DQBD GmbH
Schulstr. 15
73614 Schorndorf
T +49 7181 937 666 0
www.dqbd.de
S/P 51

E

Einfach Gut Spielen
Kapellhofstr. 1
99718 Trebra
T + 49 36379 409 44
www.einfach-gut-spielen.de
S/P 145
Silke Kegeler
S/P 145-147

Eis GmbH
Am Lenkwerk 3
33609 Bielefeld
T +49 800 445 0000
www.satisfyer.de
S/P 154

F

F209 GmbH
Zentstr. 4
69124 Heidelberg
T +49 151 2870 8226
www.f209.de
S/P 213

Fill GmbH
Fillstr. 1
A-4942 Gurten
+43 7757 701 0
www.fill.co.at
S/P 32

Fischerwerke GmbH & Co. KG
Klaus-Fischer-Str. 1
72178 Waldachtal
T +49 7443 12 0
www.fischer.de
S/P 34

Christophe de la Fontaine
Schloss Haggn 24
94362 Neukirchen
T +49 9961 9437 677
www.christophedelafontaine.com
S/P 139

Formagenda GmbH
Münchner Freiheit 24
80802 München
T +49 89 4142 4088 0
www.formagenda.com
S/P 139

Formquadrat GmbH
Brucknerstr. 3-5
A-4020 Linz
T +43 732 777 244
www.formquadrat.com
S/P 32

Fruitcore Robotics GmbH
Macairestr. 3
78467 Konstanz
T +49 7531 9459 920
www.fruitcore.de
S/P 33, 209
Christoph Keller
S/P 33

G

Gebrüder Martin GmbH & Co. KG
KLS Martin Platz 1
78532 Tuttlingen
T +49 7461 706 0
www.klsmartin.com
S/P 47

Geze GmbH
Reinhold-Vöster-Str. 21-29
71229 Leonberg
T +49 7152 203 0
www.geze.de
S/P 165

Grohe AG
Feldmühleplatz 15
40545 Düsseldorf
T +49 211 9130 3000
www.grohe.com
S/P 57, 61, 76

Grohe Deutschland Vertriebs GmbH
Zur Porta 9
32457 Porta Westfalica
T +49 571 3989333
www.grohe.de
S/P 57, 61, 76

H

Robert Herder GmbH und Co. KG
Ellerstr. 16
42697 Solingen
T +49 212 267 050
www.windmuehlenmesser.de
S/P 75
Tim Wieland
S/P 75

HomeBrace Germany UG
Birkenweg 12
73660 Urbach
T +49 7181 255 600
www.homebrace.com
S/P 51

I

Internationale Bauaustellung – IBA Basel 2020
Münsterplatz 11
CH-4001 Basel
T +41 61 385 80 80
www.iba-basel.net
S/P 187

Inwerk GmbH
Krefelder Str. 78-82
40670 Meerbusch
T +49 2159 69640 0
www.inwerk-bueromoebel.de
S/P 102
Karl Bell
S/P 102

J

Jangled Nerves GmbH
Hallstr. 25
70376 Stuttgart
T +49 711 550 375 0
www.jn.de
S/P 186

Marco Jouvenal
Gebelstr. 18
75446 Wiernsheim
T +49 157 504 370 27
www.lichtstahl.com
S/P 123

K

Silke Kegeler
Kapellhofstr. 1
99718 Trebra
T +49 36379 40944
S/P 145

KTM AG
Stallhofner Str. 3
A-5230 Mattighofen
T +43 7742 6000 0
www.ktmgroup.com
S/P 185

L

Lengsfeld Designkonzepte GmbH
Horburgstr. 22
CH-4057 Basel
T +41 61 683 39 71
www.lengsfeld.ch
S/P 187

Lignotrend Produktions GmbH
Landstr. 25
79809 Weilheim
T +49 7755 9200 0
www.lignotrend.com
S/P 221

Livable Cities GmbH
Hafenstr. 25
68159 Mannheim
T +49 621 150 28 570
www.citydecks.de
S/P 183

M

Peter Maly
Pfingstholzallee 2
21521 Aumühle
T +49 4104 695525
www.peter-maly.de
S/P 155

Maomi
Augartenstr. 68
68163 Mannheim
T +49 621 391 868 07
www.maomi.de
S/P 77

Micro Mobility Systems AG
Bahnhofstr. 10
CH-8700 Küsnacht
T +41 44 913 1850
www.micro-mobility.com
S/P 153

Micro Mobility Systems D GmbH
Fuhrmannstr. 7
72351 Geislingen-Binsdorf
T +49 7428 9418 300
www.microscooter-shop.de
S/P 153

Miele & Cie. KG
Carl-Miele-Str. 29
33332 Gütersloh
T +49 5241 89 0
www.miele.de
S/P 67, 81

Mono GmbH
Industriestr. 5
40822 Mettmann
T +49 2104 919 80
www.mono.de
S/P 74

N

Nimbus Group GmbH
Sieglestr. 41
70469 Stuttgart
T +49 711 63 30 14 0
www.nimbus-lighting.com
S/P 138

O

Object Carpet GmbH
Marie-Curie-Str. 3
73770 Denkendorf
T +49 711 3402 0
www.object-carpet.com
S/P 226

Ongo GmbH
Klopstockstr. 51
70193 Stuttgart
T +49 711 469 078 70
www.ongo.eu
S/P 103

P

Papero
Wiegenfeldring 4
85570 Markt Schwaben
T +49 8121 2508920
www.papero-bags.de
S/P 115

248
249

Kathrin Patel und Mark Patel
Am Dammacker 13b
28201 Bremen
T +49 177 7777690
www.kathrinpatel.de
S/P 226

Plus 10 GmbH
Werner-von-Siemens-Str. 6
86159 Augsburg
www.plus10.de
S/P 213

Pozsgai Möbelschreinerei
Schwarzwaldstr. 18
79423 Heitersheim
T +49 7634 79 81 67
www.pozsgai.de
S/P 105

Recaro Aircraft Seating GmbH & Co. KG
Daimlerstr. 21
74523 Schwäbisch Hall
T +49 791 503 7000
www.recaro-as.com
S/P 184

Recaro Gaming GmbH & Co. KG
Schloßstr. 70
70176 Stuttgart
T +49 711 504 376 44
www.recaro-gaming.com
S/P 107

Recaro Holding Inhouse Design
Jahnstr. 1
70597 Stuttgart
T +49 711 25277 0
www.recaro.com
S/P 107, 184

Ribler GmbH
Plieninger Str. 58
70567 Stuttgart
T +49 711 723045
www.ribler-gmbh.de
S/P 38

Rökona Textilwerke GmbH & Co. KG
Schaffhausenstr. 101
72072 Tübingen
T +49 7071 153 0
www.roekona.de
S/P 227

Rolf – Roland Wolf GmbH
Mühlbachweg 6
A-6671 Weißenbach a. Lech
T +43 5678 200 77
www.rolf-spectacles.com
S/P 124

Carl Sauter Pianofortemanufaktur GmbH & Co. KG
Max-Planck-Str. 20
78549 Spaichingen
T +49 7424 948 20
www.sauter-pianos.de
S/P 155

Schmiddem Design
Ansbacher Str. 71
10777 Berlin
T +49 30 614 016 24
www.schmiddem.com
S/P 104

Schreiber Innenausbau GmbH
Elterleiner Str. 62-64
09468 Geyer
T +49 201 17755071
www.schreiber-innenausbau.de
S/P 173

Solidfluid
Turmstr. 8
78467 Konstanz
T +49 7531 9450 230
www.solidfluid.de
S/P 209

Sprimag Spritzmaschinenbau GmbH & Co. KG
Henriettenstr. 90
73230 Kirchheim/Teck
T +49 7021 579 0
www.sprimag.de
S/P 35

Stadtnomaden GmbH
88377 Riedhausen
T +49 176 4947 1859
www.stadtnomaden.com
S/P 108
Linda Krapf, Oliver Krapf
S/P 108

StadtPalais Stuttgart – Museum für Stuttgart
Konrad-Adenauer-Str. 2
70173 Stuttgart
T +49 711 216 258 00
www.stadtpalais-stuttgart.de
S/P 186

Studiobeier GmbH
Ahornstr. 46
96247 Michelau
T +49 9571 947 9613
www.studiobeier.de
S/P 106
Kurt Beier
S/P 106
Kati Quinger
S/P 106

Supernova Design GmbH & Co. KG
Industriestr. 26
79194 Gundelfingen
T +49 761 600 629 0
www.supernova-lights.com
S/P 195

System 180 GmbH
Ernst-Augustin-Str. 3
12489 Berlin
T +49 30 7885841
www.system180.com
S/P 91

Typenraum GmbH & Co. KG
Herdweg 19
70174 Stuttgart
T +49 711 224 824 00
www.typenraum.com
S/P 182

UP Designstudio GmbH & Co. KG
Dornierstr. 17
70469 Stuttgart
T +49 711 3265460
www.updesignstudio.com
S/P 47, 103

Wahrmann Design
45549 Sprockhövel
T +49 2324 717 22
www.wahrmann-design.de
S/P 74

White ID GmbH & Co. KG
Nicolaus-Otto-Str. 8
73614 Schorndorf
T +49 7181 99198 0
www.white-id.com
S/P 152

Wiha Werkzeuge GmbH
Obertalstr. 3-7
78136 Schonach
T +49 7722 959 0
www.wiha.com
S/P 36

Yalla Yalla!
Hafenstr. 25
68159 Mannheim
T +49 621 391 81 723
www.yallayalla.studio
S/P 183

Yellow Design GmbH
Bissingerstr. 6
75172 Pforzheim
T +49 7231 457 640
www.yellowdesign.com
S/P 166

Zimmer + Rohde GmbH
Zimmersmühlenweg 14-18
61440 Oberursel
T +49 6171 632 02
www.zimmer-rohde.de
S/P 104

NAMENSREGISTER/
INDEX OF NAMES

A

AMF – Andreas Maier GmbH & Co. KG
S/P 21
AOK Baden-Württemberg
S/P 182
Artenhaus
S/P 123
Artline
S/P 104
Atelier Brückner GmbH
S/P 185

B

Belchengruppe GmbH
S/P 122
BeSafe
S/P 152
Beier, Kurt
S/P 106
Bell, Karl
S/P 102
Robert Bosch GmbH
S/P 203
Bosch Corporate Design Team und
United Digital Group
S/P 203
Braake Design
S/P 35
Bullfrog Marketing & Design GmbH
S/P 106
Bunse05
S/P 38
Busch-Jaeger Elektro GmbH
S/P 164, 167

C

Corporate Friends GmbH
S/P 133

D

Daikin Airconditioning Germany GmbH
S/P 166
Daikin Europe N.V.
S/P 166
Diana Electronic-Systeme GmbH
S/P 37
DQBD GmbH
S/P 51

E

Einfach Gut Spielen
S/P 145
Eis GmbH
S/P 154

F

F209 GmbH
S/P 213
Fill GmbH
S/P 32
Fischerwerke GmbH & Co. KG
S/P 34
Fontaine, Christophe de la
S/P 139
Formagenda GmbH
S/P 139
Formquadrat GmbH
S/P 32
Fruitcore Robotics GmbH
S/P 33, 209

G

Gebrüder Martin GmbH & Co. KG
S/P 47
Geze GmbH
S/P 165
Grohe AG
S/P 57, 61, 76
Grohe Deutschland Vertriebs GmbH
S/P 57, 61, 76

H

Robert Herder GmbH & Co. KG
S/P 75
HomeBrace Germany UG
S/P 51

I

Internationale Bauaustellung –
IBA Basel 2020
S/P 187
Inwerk GmbH
S/P 102

J

Jangled Nerves GmbH
S/P 186
Jouvenal, Marco
S/P 123

K

Keller, Christoph
S/P 33
Kegeler, Silke
S/P 145
Krapf, Linda
S/P 108
Krapf, Oliver
S/P 108
KTM AG
S/P 185

L

Lengsfeld Designkonzepte GmbH
S/P 187
Lignotrend Produktions GmbH
S/P 221
Livable Cities GmbH
S/P 183

M

Maly, Peter
S/P 155
Maomi
S/P 77
Micro Mobility Systems AG
S/P 153
Micro Mobility Systems D GmbH
S/P 153
Miele & Cie. KG
S/P 67, 81
Mono GmbH
S/P 74

N

Nimbus Group GmbH
S/P 138

O

Object Carpet GmbH
S/P 226
Ongo GmbH
S/P 103

P

Papero
S/P 115
Patel, Kathrin
S/P 226
Patel, Mark
S/P 226
Plus 10 GmbH
S/P 213
Pozsgai Möbelschreinerei
S/P 105

Q

Quinger, Kati
S/P 106

R

Recaro Aircraft
Seating GmbH & Co. KG
S/P 184
Recaro Gaming GmbH & Co. KG
S/P 107
Recaro Holding Inhouse Design
S/P 107, 184
Ribler GmbH
S/P 38
Rökona Textilwerke GmbH & Co. KG
S/P 227
Rolf – Roland Wolf GmbH
S/P 124

S

Carl Sauter Pianofortemanufaktur
GmbH & Co. KG
S/P 155
Schmiddem Design
S/P 104
Schreiber Innenausbau GmbH
S/P 173
Solidfluid
S/P 209
Sprimag Spritzmaschinenbau
GmbH & Co. KG
S/P 35
Stadtnomaden GmbH
S/P 108
StadtPalais Stuttgart – Museum für
Stuttgart
S/P 186
Studiobeier GmbH
S/P 106
Supernova Design GmbH & Co. KG
S/P 195
System 180 GmbH
S/P 91

T

Thinius, Dörte
S/P 164, 167
Typenraum GmbH & Co. KG
S/P 182

U

UP Designstudio GmbH & Co. KG
S/P 47, 103

W

Wahrmann Design
S/P 74
Weller, Martin
S/P 37
White ID GmbH & Co. KG
S/P 152
Wieland, Tim
S/P 75
Wiha Werkzeuge GmbH
S/P 36

Y

Yalla Yalla!
S/P 183
Yellow Design GmbH
S/P 166

Z

Zimmer + Rohde GmbH
S/P 104

LET'S THANK ...

GRAFIKDESIGN
GRAPHIC DESIGN
stapelberg&fritz gmbh
Julian Hölzer
Daniel Fritz

TEXT & REDAKTION
TEXT & EDITORIAL SUPERVISION
Armin Scharf

JURY
Bettina Baacke
Holm Gießler
Meike Harde
Tina Kammer
Reinhard Renner
Luciana Silvares

LEKTORAT
COPY-EDITING
Dr. Petra Kiedaisch
Gabriele Betz
Armin Scharf

ANMELDUNG
APPLICATION

AUSSCHREIBUNG
CALL FOR ENTRIES

TEAM FOCUS OPEN
Hildegard Hild
Michael Kern
Iris Steinmetz

JURIERUNG
JUDGING

JAHRBUCH
YEARBOOK

VERLAG & VERTRIEB
PUBLISHING & DISTRIBUTION
avedition
Dr. Petra Kiedaisch

ÜBERSETZUNG
TRANSLATION
Alison Du Bovis

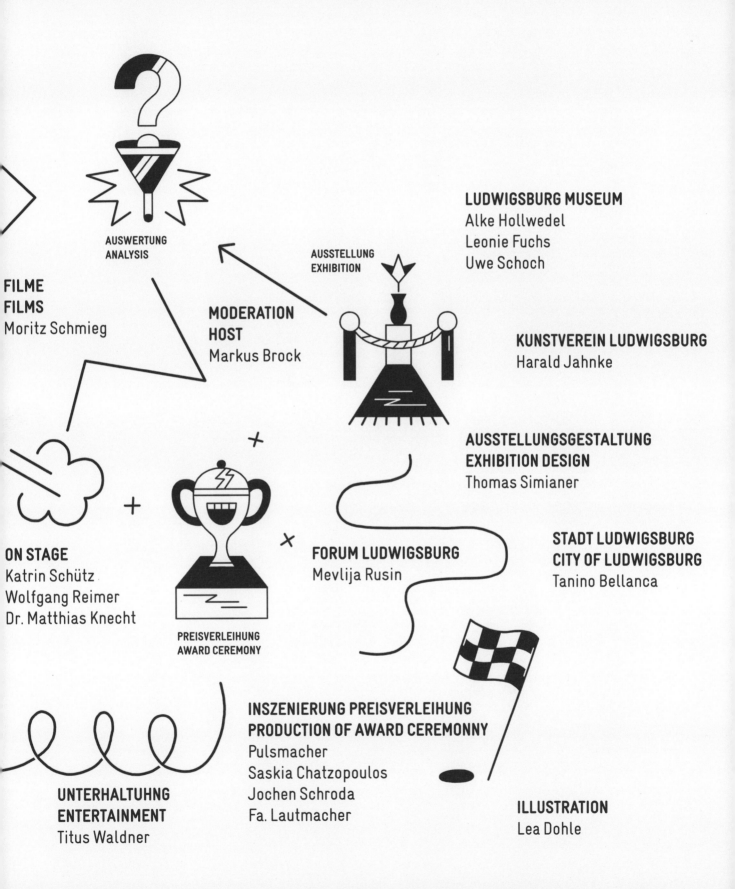

DESIGN IM DIALOG

Beratung, Fortbildung, Information und Präsentationen – das Design Center Baden-Württemberg ist eine nicht-kommerzielle Plattform für Design-Profis, Einsteiger und Unternehmer zugleich

DESIGN LESE
Vorträge, Medienpräsentationen und Diskussionsrunden zu aktuellen Themenbereichen aus Industrie, Design, Technik, Forschung und Wirtschaft.

DESIGN LESE LECTURES
Lectures, media presentations and panel discussions on up-to-the-minute topics from industry, design, technology, research and business.

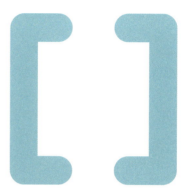

EINSICHTEN
Austauschplattform für Industrie, Designwirtschaft, Forschung und Ausbildung. Unternehmen, Designagenturen und auch Design-Ausbildungsstätten erhalten die Möglichkeit, sich im Haus der Wirtschaft in Stuttgart detailliert zu präsentieren.

EINSICHTEN PRESENTATION PLATFORM
A platform for industry, the design sector, research and education where companies, design agencies and design schools are given the opportunity to stage detailed presentations at the Haus der Wirtschaft in Stuttgart.

DESIGN1ST BERATUNG
Im Rahmen unserer kostenfreien Design1st Beratung erhalten Unternehmer*innen Auskunft zu allen Fragen rund um Designleistungen und zu direkten Kooperationsmöglichkeiten mit der Designwirtschaft.

DESIGN1ST ADVISORY SERVICE
Our free Design1st advisory service provides entrepreneurs with information about anything to do with design services and advises them on the possibilities for direct cooperation with the design sector.

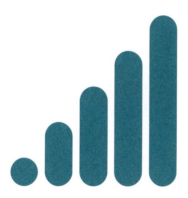

FIT FOR MARKET
Der richtige Schutz innovativer Produkte, die Anmeldung von Marken, die Honorierung kreativer Leistung oder die Vertragsgestaltung mit Designer*innen sind Themenfelder dieser Veranstaltungsreihe.

FIT FOR MAKET
This series of events covers topics like the right protection for innovative products, registering trademarks, appropriate payment for creative services and contractual arrangements with designers.

DESIGN IN DIALOGUE

Advice, training, information and presentations – the Design Center Baden-Württemberg is a non-commercial platform aimed not just at design professionals but at newcomers and entrepreneurs too.

254
255

DESIGN CENTER ROADSHOW
Veranstaltungen mit und bei unterschiedlichsten externen Kooperationspartnern, als Foren des Austauschs zwischen Industrie und Designwirtschaft.

DESIGN CENTER ROADSHOW
Events hosted by a wide range of external cooperation partners as forums where industry and the design sector can swap ideas and views.

DESIGN BIBLIOTHEK
Präsenzbibliothek für Designprofis und Designinteressierte, mit Online-Katalog und einem spezialisierten Publikationsbestand von rund 10.000 Büchern rund um das Thema Gestaltung.

DESIGN LIBRARY
A bricks-and-mortar library for design professionals and anyone interested in design, with an online catalogue and a specialised collection of around 10,000 publications on all aspects of design.

ENTDECKT
Die Präsentationsplattform für den Designnachwuchs! Vielversprechende Designtalente erhalten die Möglichkeit, sich samt ihrer aktuellen Projekte im Design Center der breiten Öffentlichkeit zu präsentieren.

ENTDECKT SHOWCASE
A presentation platform for up-and-coming designers that gives promising and talented newcomers the chance to introduce themselves and their latest projects to a broad public at the Design Center.

KONGRESSE & WORKSHOPS
Veranstaltungen zur Vermittlung von Know-how aus den unterschiedlichsten designrelevanten Disziplinen und Forschungsbereichen, aber auch aus dem weiten Feld des Marketings.

CONGRESSES & WORKSHOPS
Events that share know-how from all sorts of design-relevant disciplines and research areas, as well as from the broad field of marketing.

IMPRESSUM /
PUBLISHING DETAILS

HERAUSGEBER / PUBLISHER
Design Center Baden-Württemberg
Regierungspräsidium Stuttgart
Willi-Bleicher-Straße 19
70174 Stuttgart
T +49 711 123 26 84
design@rps.bwl.de
www.design-center.de

**TEXT UND REDAKTION /
TEXT AND EDITORIAL SUPERVISION**
Armin Scharf
Tübingen
www.bueroscharf.de

LEKTORAT / COPY-EDITING
Petra Kiedaisch
Armin Scharf
Gabriele Betz
Tübingen
www.gabriele-betz.de

ÜBERSETZUNG / TRANSLATION
Alison Du Bovis
Jork
www.dubovis.de

GRAFIKDESIGN / GRAPHIC DESIGN
stapelberg&fritz GmbH
Julian Hölzer
Daniel Fritz
Stuttgart
www.stapelbergundfritz.com

ILLUSTRATIONEN / ILLUSTRATIONS
Lea Dohle Illustration Stuttgart
www.leadohle.de
Instagram @leadohle

LITHOGRAFIE / LITHOGRAPHY
Corinna Rieber Prepress

DRUCK / PRINTING
Offizin Scheufele GmbH + Co. KG
Stuttgart
www.scheufele.de

PAPIER / PAPER
Juwel Offset,
PEFC-zertifiziert /
PEFC certified

**VERLAG UND VERTRIEB /
PUBLISHING AND DISTRIBUTION**
av edition GmbH
Senefelderstraße 109
70176 Stuttgart
T +49 711 / 2202279-0
kontakt@avedition.de
www.avedition.de

© 2020
av edition GmbH,
Design Center Baden-Württemberg
und die Autoren / and the authors

Alle Rechte vorbehalten. /
All rights reserved.

ISBN 978-3-89986-335-2
Printed in Germany

Die Publikation erscheint
anlässlich der Ausstellung
»Focus Open 2020 –
Internationaler Designpreis
Baden-Württemberg
und Mia Seeger Preis 2020«

10. Oktober
bis 22. November 2020

This catalogue is published to
accompany the exhibition
»Focus Open 2020 –
Baden-Württemberg International
Design Award and
Mia Seeger Prize 2020«

10 October
to 22 November 2020

VERANSTALTER / ORGANISER
Design Center Baden-Württemberg
Regierungspräsidium Stuttgart
Willi-Bleicher-Straße 19
70174 Stuttgart
T +49 711 123 26 84

**VERANTWORTUNG UND KONZEPTION /
RESPONSIBILITY AND CONCEPT**
Christiane Nicolaus

**PROJEKTLEITUNG /
PROJECT MANAGER**
Hildegard Hild

ORGANISATION / ADMINISTRATION
Michael Kern

**AUSSTELLUNGSGESTALTUNG /
EXHIBITION DESIGN**
Thomas Simianer

**INSZENIERUNG PREISVERLEIHUNG /
PRODUCTION OF AWARD CEREMONY**
pulsmacher
Ludwigsburg
www.pulsmacher.de